IMAGES
of Aviation

OREGON AIRFIELDS DURING WORLD WAR II

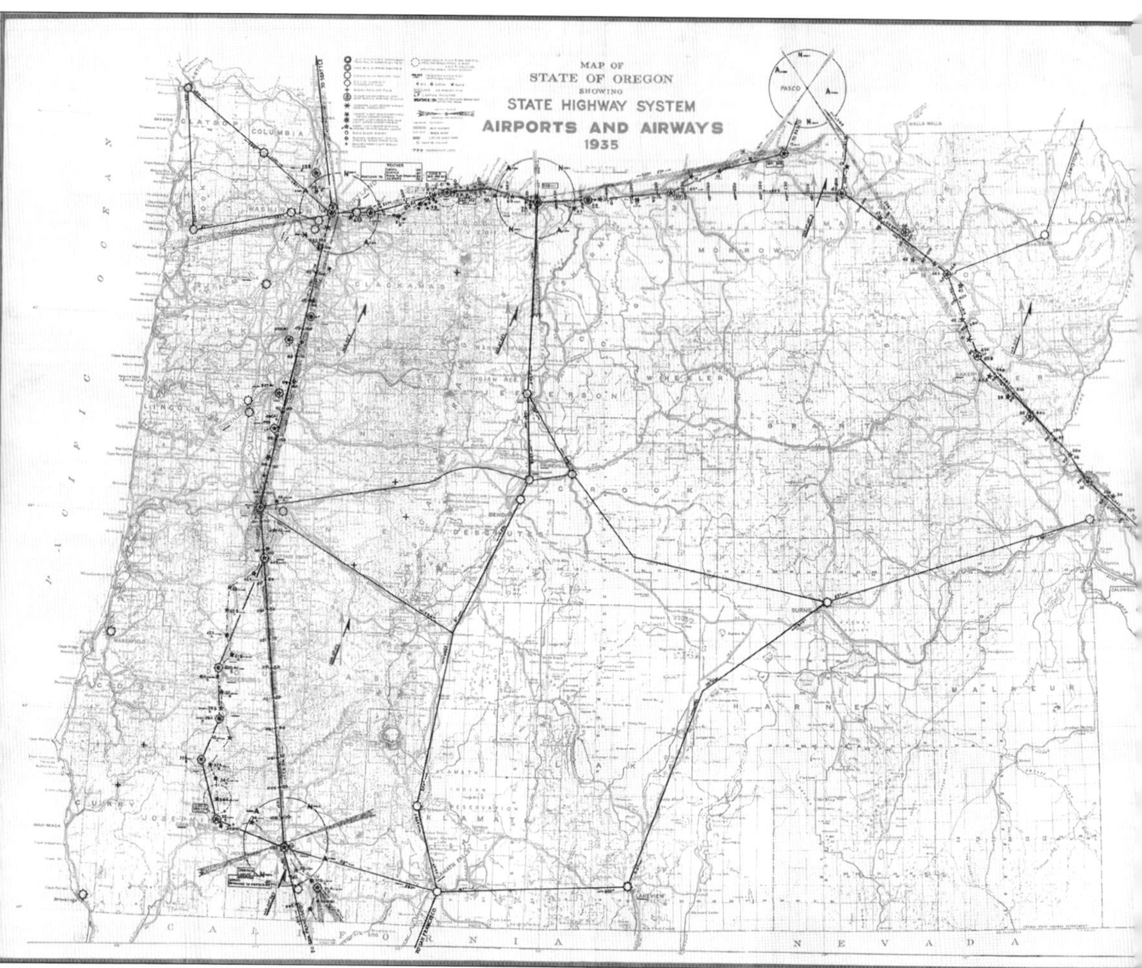

This 1935 map was created by the Oregon State Board of Aeronautics to capture the airpaths and airfields of Oregon. The lines correspond to frequently traveled civilian airpaths. The circles were known airports at the time, whether private or municipality-owned. The majority of the airports repurposed as US military airstrips during World War II already existed as commercial and/or recreational airfields. (Courtesy of the Oregon State Board of Aeronautics.)

On the Cover: In the 1920s and 1930s, commercial and recreational flight exploded in Oregon. Klamath Falls was no exception. To promote this ever-growing industry, the city began to host air shows, inviting pilots and their aircraft to land on the rough open field south of the city. Three men with pilot goggles stand near this early-20th-century biplane, letting the public get close to the aircraft. (Courtesy of the Klamath County Museum.)

IMAGES
of Aviation

OREGON AIRFIELDS DURING WORLD WAR II

Andretta Schellinger

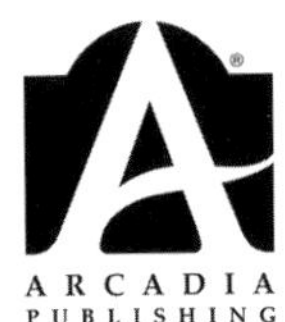

ISBN 978-1-4671-6240-1

Published by Arcadia Publishing
Charleston, South Carolina

Printed in the United States of America

Library of Congress Control Number: 2025937592

For all general information, please contact Arcadia Publishing:
Telephone 843-853-2070
Fax 843-853-0044
E-mail sales@arcadiapublishing.com

Visit us on the Internet at www.arcadiapublishing.com

To my husband for driving to museums around the state

Contents

Acknowledgments

In the nearly 80 years since the US military filled Oregon airfields with planes and personnel, there have been numerous organizations and individuals seeking to preserve the history of that time. Unfortunately, as years pass, documents and photographs are lost or pushed to the wayside for more current history. Without those who assisted in this project, this book would not have been possible.

Life, at times, can throw you curveballs, and a good editor keeps those distractions and pitfalls from causing an author to go astray. Since the initial contract was signed, I took on a full-time teaching job, which drastically decreased the amount of time I was able to dedicate to travel. My daughter also graduated high school, and we drove her across the country for college. Thankfully, Caitrin Cunningham, my Arcadia editor, has been through the entire process. Without her support, I may have lost the forest through the trees.

This book would not be a reality without the generous assistance from museums, historical societies, and archives around the state of Oregon. This list is only a partial one of those who assisted in my research but left such an impression that they deserved to be thanked individually. Marie Lee from Lake County Museum, who sat for hours just talking about Lake County, which allowed me to reconnect with that part of my personal history. Debbie Rasmussen graciously allowed me to take over the Pendleton Air Museum for a few hours. Patti Larkin searched and took the time to provide images in Benton County, which opened an entirely new avenue of research. Sire Pro with Coos County History Museum, Matt Voelkel at Klamath County Museum, Christian Gurling with Tillamook Air Museum, and Cheryl and Dale Carson from the Ontario Airport were instrumental in helping to acquire photographs and information needed for this book to become a reality.

No author writes alone, and this is specifically true for this book. Without the support and knowledge of my family, this book may not have passed the finish line. Thanks to my grandfather Charles Stolsig; my mom, Terry Journey; and last but not least, my husband, Jon, who sat next to me while I worked and made phone calls to museums around the state. He also accompanied me to museums and historical societies around the state. During this process, I acquired photographs from numerous locations; however, for certain airfields, the images all came from one or two sources.

Common source acronyms that are used in the book are as follows:

DHM	Deschutes Historical Museum
KCM	Klamath County Museum
LCM	Lake County Museum
OHS	Oregon Historical Society
PAM	Pendleton Air Museum
SOHS	Southern Oregon Historical Society
TAM	Tillamook Air Museum
USFS	United States Forest Service
WHC	Willamette Heritage Center

Common airfield acronyms that are used in this book are as follows:

AAB	Army Air Base
AAF	Army Airfield
AUX	Auxiliary
FS	Flight Strip
MCAAF	Marine Corps Auxiliary Air Facility
NAF	Naval Air Facility
NAS	Naval Air Station
OLF	Naval Outlying Landing Field

INTRODUCTION

When Orville and Wilbur Wright achieved flight on December 17, 1903, in Kitty Hawk, North Carolina, the United States was already enamored with flight and aircraft. Their flight just cemented the desire of thousands to be in the air with birds. Once it was confirmed that man could indeed fly, it was an all-out race to become the second, third, and fourth man or woman to fly. Individuals created as many different airframes as possible to compete with not only the Wrights but others. The craze was not contained to the United States. In the years from 1904 to the start of World War I, there were hundreds of different aircraft built, including gliders, airships, biplanes, and monoplanes.

It was not long before the US military saw aircraft for what they could become: a machine for transportation, combat, and surveillance. On August 2, 1909, the US Army accepted Airplane No. 1, which led to the creation of the US Army Air Corps and the beginning of what is now known as the US Air Force. Even though the US Army was the first military branch to accept the use of planes, the Navy was quick to accept planes as well. Glenn Curtiss flew the first US Navy seaplane on January 27, 1911. The United States may have been one of the first to accept planes, but it was the Italians who first used the planes in war. The Italians performed reconnaissance and photoreconnaissance and even bombing raids during the Italo-Turkish War of 1911.

Civilians, on the other hand, saw it as a novelty, something that only a few had, but thankfully, the owners would allow others to look at them. If they were really lucky, the owner might even take it up for a flight. This delighted young and old and created a fever where everyone wanted to be in on it. The original fields that owners and pilots used soon became too small and rutted. Instead of owners expanding their own, many cities volunteered to create an airfield to not only take off and land but also to store their aircraft in. Air shows became frequent happenings, and entire towns would converged on a single airfield to see the newest aircraft and speak to pilots. Some of these airfields even began training civilians for what they saw as a growing industry, and growing it was.

By the end of World War I, there were so many aircraft in the air, along with airfields in every available field, that accidents were becoming commonplace. States realized that regulations were required to ensure the safety of individuals and maintain some form of structure. Oregon was no exception. There was such an increase in small airfields following the end of World War I that Oregon felt it necessary to create regulations to keep the public safe. In 1921, the Oregon Legislative Assembly created the Oregon State Board of Aeronautics, which was the first government agency in the United States to regulate aircraft and pilots. This agency began to create a usable map of airfields around Oregon, which allowed pilots to know where they could land in the event of an emergency. Municipalities, realizing that flight was the new frontier, began to propose the creation of municipal airports. The tactic worked, and in 1935, there were roughly 49 airfields and auxiliary fields throughout the state of Oregon.

When World War II started, it was primarily in Europe, and so while aircraft were being used and military personnel were trained on the newest aircraft, the main bases were on the Eastern Seaboard and in the Midwest. However, when Japan attacked the United States, it was quickly realized that the numbers needed to effectively fight two conflicts required additional personnel and air bases. California, Oregon, and Washington were all selected for air bases by the US Army Air Corps, US Navy, and US Marine Corps due to proximity to the Pacific Ocean. This growth allowed for more service members to be trained concurrently and more aircraft to be stationed around the United States.

During the height of the war in the Pacific, Oregon was home to at least 22 airfields and thousands of military personnel. Some of the bases were small, merely auxiliary airfields for specific training. Others were larger, with training, support, and full-time residents helping the war effort. However, just as fast as the US military came in to set up the bases, they left as quickly. When the war was winding down, the military began to decommission the majority of the bases, leaving the local communities reeling from the loss of revenue, jobs, and population. For smaller communities, the military's moving on resulted in the area ceasing to exist or at least becoming mostly a ghost town.

Due to the geographical makeup of Oregon, it was easy to see why the US military wanted to use it. Oregon goes from coastal regions to mountains and valleys and ultimately ends in an elevated desert in less than 300 miles. This allows pilots and crews to train on varying geographical features without having to travel long distances. Another thing that is unique to the Pacific Northwest is the varying temperatures and precipitation. Western Oregon is typically categorized as having mild, wet winters and warmer, slightly drier summers compared to Eastern Oregon, which experiences cold, snowy winters and hot, dry summers with extreme temperature variation. For the purposes of this book, the state is broken into four geographical regions: coastal, valley, Cascades, and Eastern Oregon.

Nearly 80 years have passed since airfields in Oregon were filled with military planes and personnel. Due to that length of time, much of the history has been lost or misplaced. In some cases, the entire airfield ceases to exist due to a lack of need following the decommissioning by the military. This is especially true for records and photographs. In some cases, the communities themselves did not want to be reminded of their past and intentionally removed most of the history concerning the military. Along with others who actively work in the same field, it is the goal of this book to preserve the history of Oregon's World War II airfields, to keep it alive for future generations, and to provide a resource for those seeking to better understand how Oregon supported the war effort. If not remembered or written down, history is lost, and it is the goal of this book to keep that history alive.

One

The Coast

Oregon's coastal region is long, with 362 miles of coastline, but relatively narrow, ranging between 30 and 60 miles wide from the high tide mark to where the mountain range crests. In that span, the elevation goes from zero to over 4,000 feet at the crest. While some areas are rocky and ill-suited for testing or any military action other than observation, others are flatter and provide ample space for airfields to be built. The northern coast near the Washington border is known for being rainy, windy, and having choppy water. The southern Oregon coastline, while similar in temperature and precipitation, is windier than the northern coast.

Due to the relatively narrowness of the region and the coastal mountain range at elevations of over 3,000 feet, there are quickly changing weather patterns. Astoria, at the most northern part of the coast, has an average temperature fluctuation of 38 Fahrenheit in the winter to 67 Fahrenheit in the summer and an average of 86 inches of rain a year. This is compared to the southern Oregon coast of Brookings, near the California border, which has an average temperature ranging from 41 Fahrenheit in the winter to 68 Fahrenheit in the summer. It receives approximately 84 inches of rain a year.

The US military favored the coastal region for the airships as a deterrent to Japan. The airships were used specifically for observation, which allowed other aircraft and personnel to train for conditions similar to those in Japan. Oregon's coast was a good location for training, given the need for rapid altitude changes along with the quickly changing weather patterns. Access to the ocean and needing a quick response time was important if Japanese submarines or aircraft were seen. The northernmost bases provided controlled access from the Pacific Ocean to the interior via the Columbia River, which allowed for troop and aircraft movement. Airfields of the coast included Astoria NAS, Blacklock, Newport OLF, North Bend NAAF, Tongue Point NAS, and Tillamook NAS. Documentation suggests that there was a naval air station in Clatsop; however, no historical imagery was located.

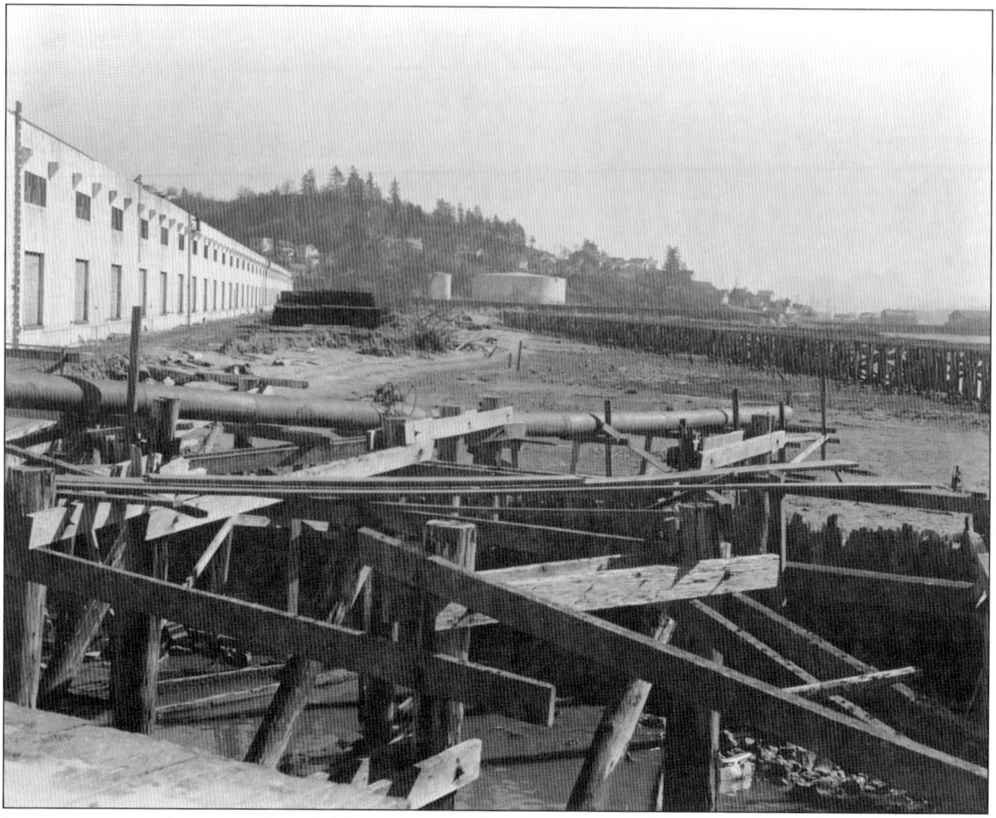

In preparation for a naval airfield, the Port of Astoria, along with the city and county, began to develop plans for infrastructure that was needed to accommodate not only the base but the additional population that a naval facility needed to be functional. The US Navy also supported the development by supplying needed materials, such as this pipe that was placed on a makeshift support structure. (Naval History and Heritage.)

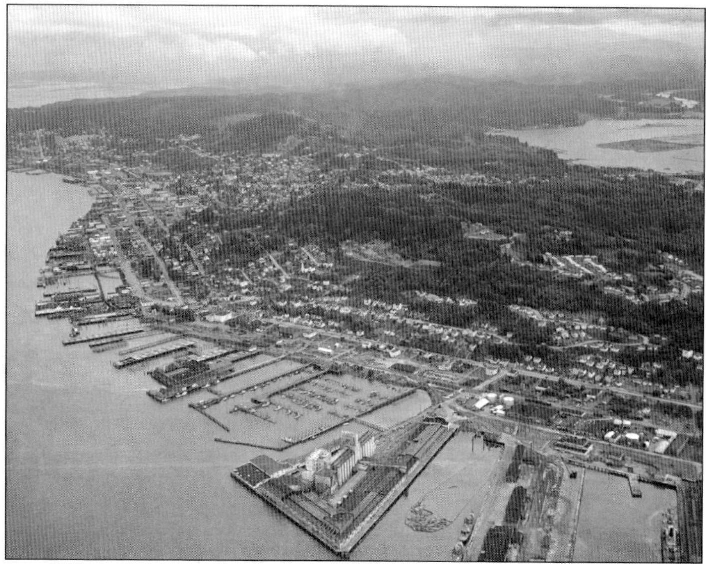

Astoria was already a thriving community when the military decided to build a base. To accommodate many of the newly arrived sailors and staff, housing needed to be built. Some of the naval officers were able to live at Fort Stevens and Tongue Point, but those who were not lived in Astoria. Having housing in the community allowed the military to integrate better than at other bases. (National Archives.)

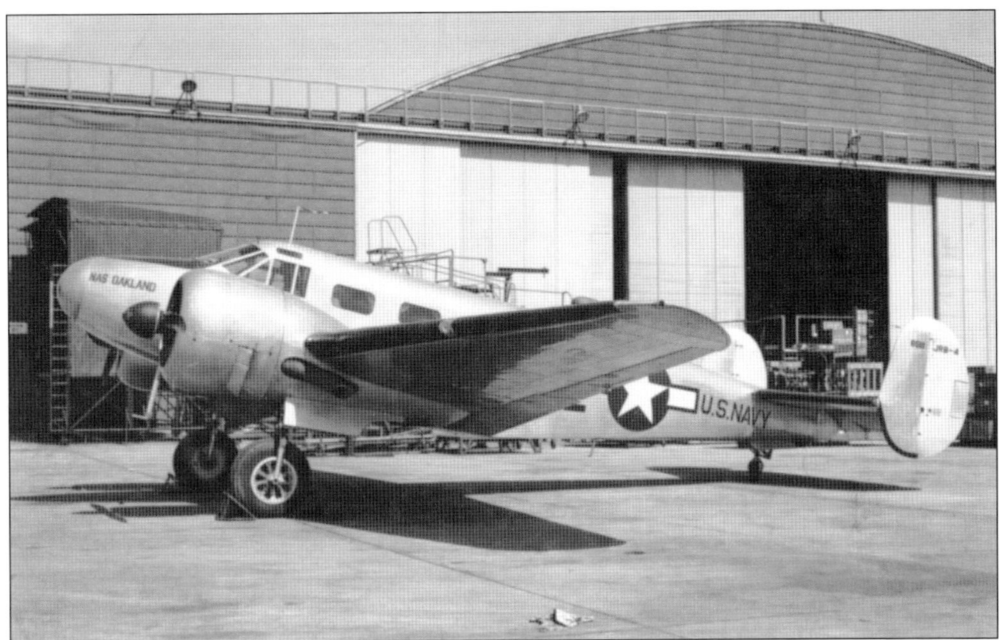

Astoria NAS, along with other neighboring air bases, served as a training facility for both active duty personnel and reservists. It was also a base that saw frequent visits due to its location. The JRB-4 Expeditor was commonly used for transport from one base to another. This specific JRB-4 was stationed at Oakland NAS before traveling to Astoria. After a stop in Astoria, it continued onto the Pacific theater to aid in the war effort. Following the war, this plane was transferred to the Japanese Maritime Self-Defense Force. (US Coast Guard.)

An SB2C Helldiver is seen flying over Astoria NAS. This was the first aerial photograph released by the US Navy of Astoria NAS. The primary focus of the Astoria NAS was to train pilots on newer combat aircraft for use on aircraft carriers. The SB2C, being a carrier-based dive bomber, was heavily trained on at Astoria NAS by the US Navy. (OHS Research Library, 007106.)

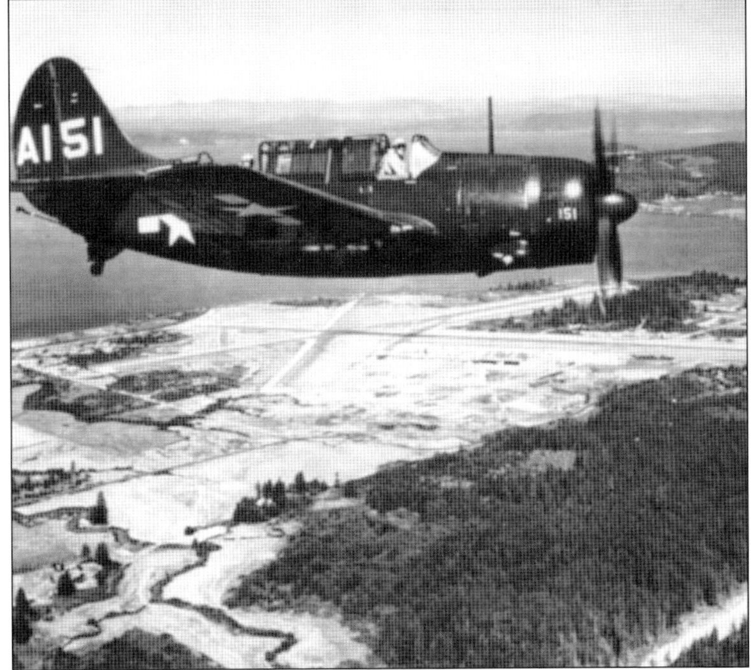

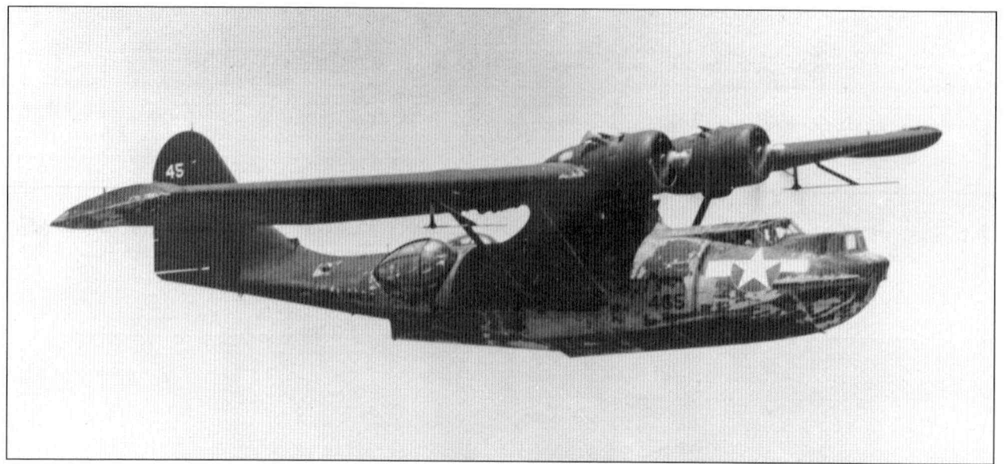

Taken by the US Navy in February 1943, this PBY Catalina was commonly seen above Astoria. The Navy used the PBY as a long-range patrol bomber with extended fuel tanks. These aircraft were able to land on water, making it perfect for many islands in the Pacific. This black cat was used for surveillance, as the radar can be seen under the wings. (Naval History and Heritage.)

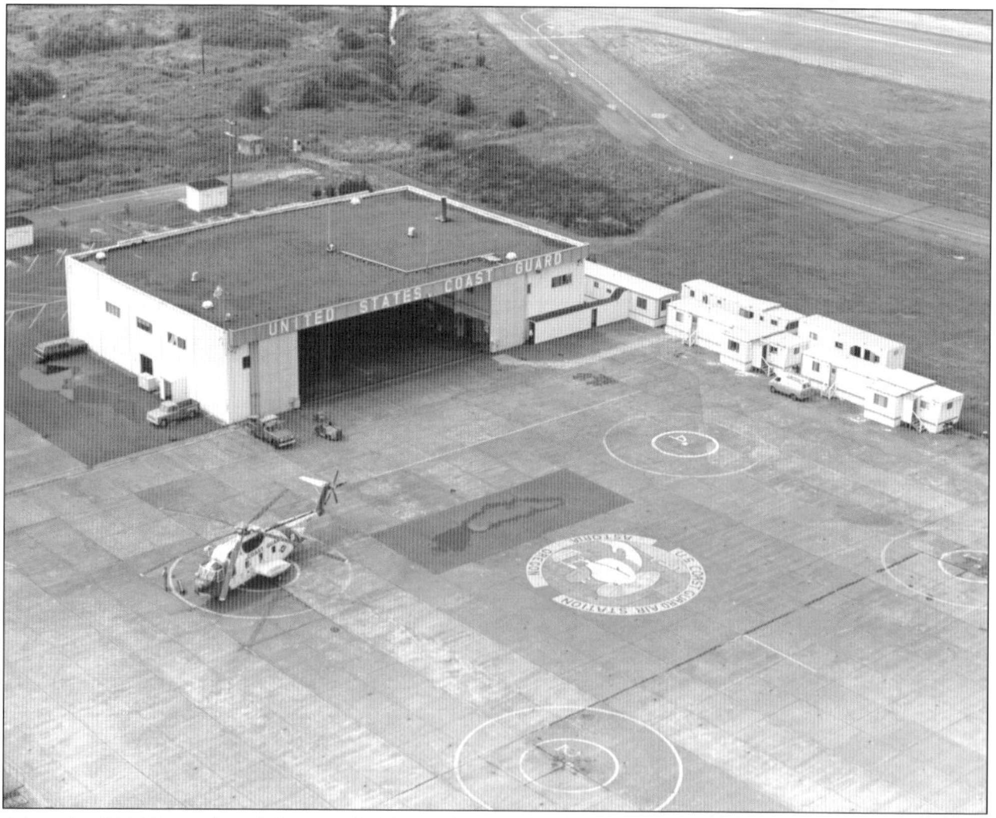

After the US Navy placed Astoria NAS on the surplus list, it was transferred back to the Port of Astoria. Its name was changed from Astoria NAS to Astoria Regional Airport and initially provided a runway and small terminal for commercial, cargo, and private aircraft. In 1964, two Coast Guard helicopters were stationed at Astoria Regional Airport before the Coast Guard moved most of its flight equipment in 1966 from Tongue Point. (US Coast Guard.)

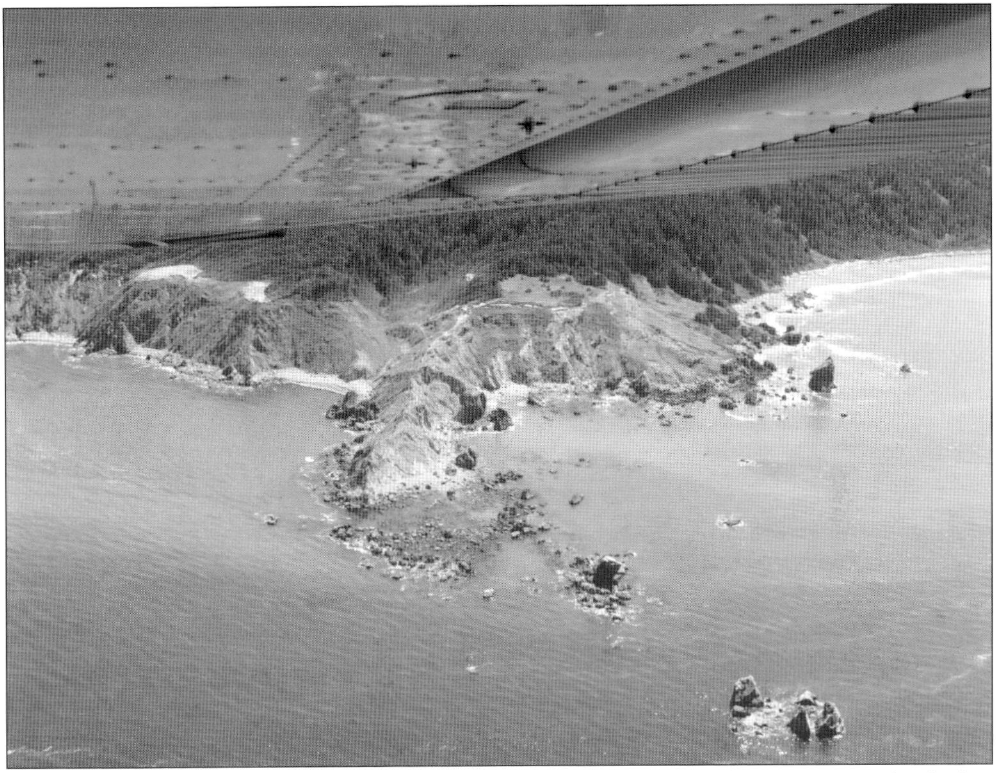

Blacklock Point was originally owned by the Blacklock brothers. After passing from individual to company and back to individual, the State of Oregon decided that it wanted to make a park out of the area. In 1936, the Blacklock Sandstone Company received a letter wanting to purchase the property, but at the time, the price suggested by the company was too high for the state. (Bandon Historical Society Museum.)

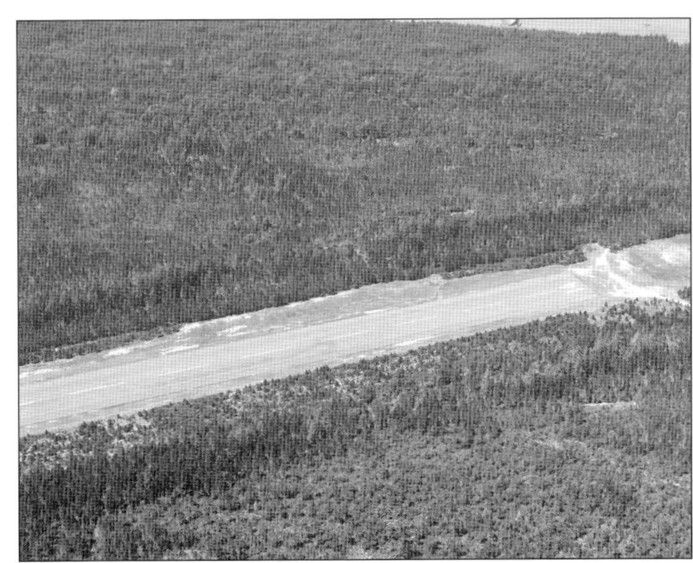

The state finally acquired the property on February 26, 1943. The next day, the US Army, along with Curry County and the Civil Aeronautics Administration (CAA), appeared to request that the state allow Curry County ownership. While the state refused, it did agree to allow Curry County a lease allowing the Navy to build on the property. The CAA, along with the Navy, spent $1 million to build an airport. (Bandon Historical Society Museum.)

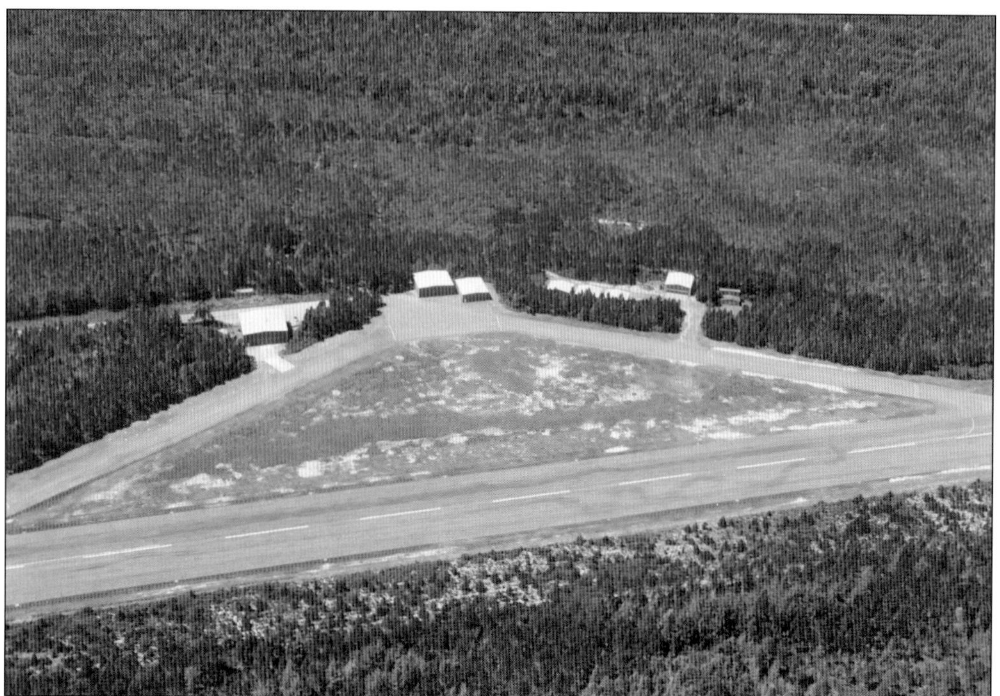

The airport at Blacklock is still present, having been renovated and maintained. When the state took over the property, it was renamed Cape Blanco State Park, with the airstrip being renamed Cape Blanco State Airport. The Oregon Department of Aviation owns the airport, and it is available for public use. Recently, the state put $4 million into renovating the property to ensure continued access by aircraft. (Bandon Historical Museum.)

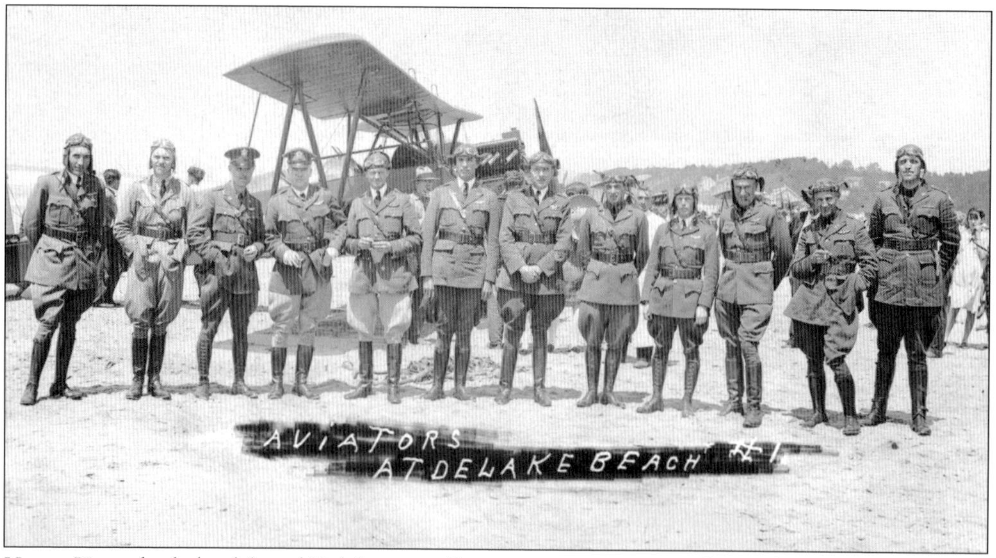

Henry Hostetler helped found Delake, a small community now part of Lincoln City. Being a pilot, he needed a place where he could land his aircraft. Being near the ocean, a makeshift landing strip on Delake beach became popular with aviators. In 1934, citizens of Delake agreed to build an airport. The beach was used by the military for emergency landings and beach training until the end of the war. (OHS Research Library, 0028P190.)

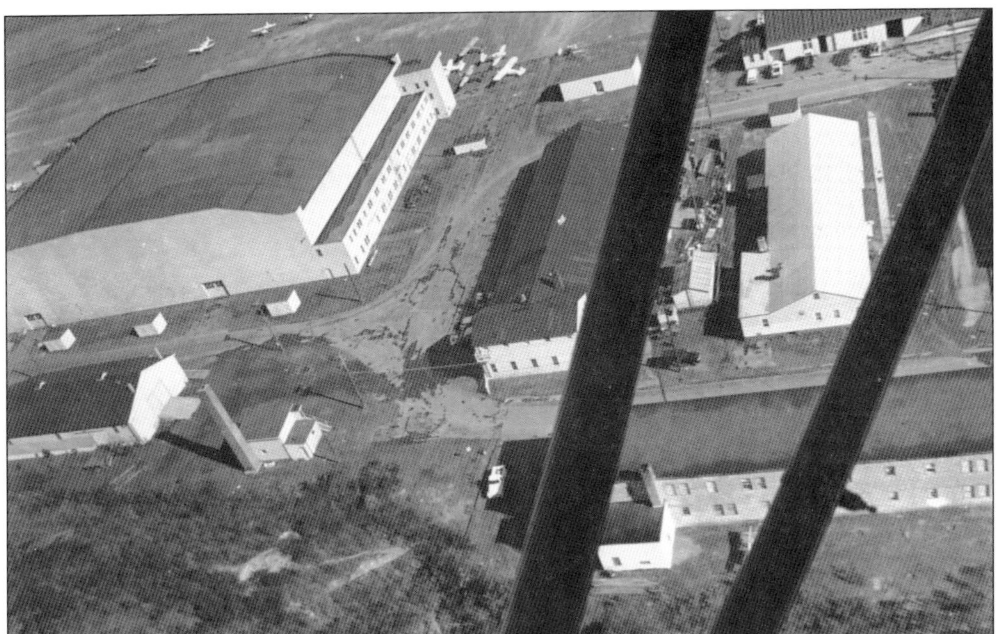

The cities of North Bend and Coos Bay realized that they needed to be involved with the ever-growing aircraft industry, and so in 1932, they opened the North Bend/Coos Bay Airport. The Navy, already having naval bases in the area, leased the land and began to construct necessary buildings in 1936. It was not until May 10, 1943, that the airfield was fully commissioned as the North Bend Naval Auxiliary Airfield. (Coos History Museum, CHM 009.16.21022.)

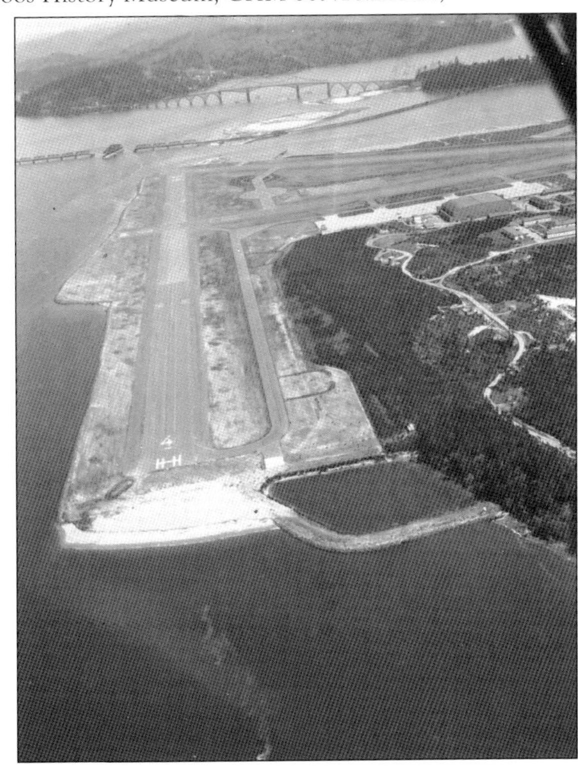

As North Bend NAAF was an auxiliary field for Astoria NAS, it was a base for overfill as well as a backup in case something happened to Astoria NAS due to a Japanese attack. The runways were useful for training, as they ended abruptly in the water. These trained pilots were deployed to mostly Pacific theater bases with similar runway attributes. (Coos History Museum, CHM 014.37.51.)

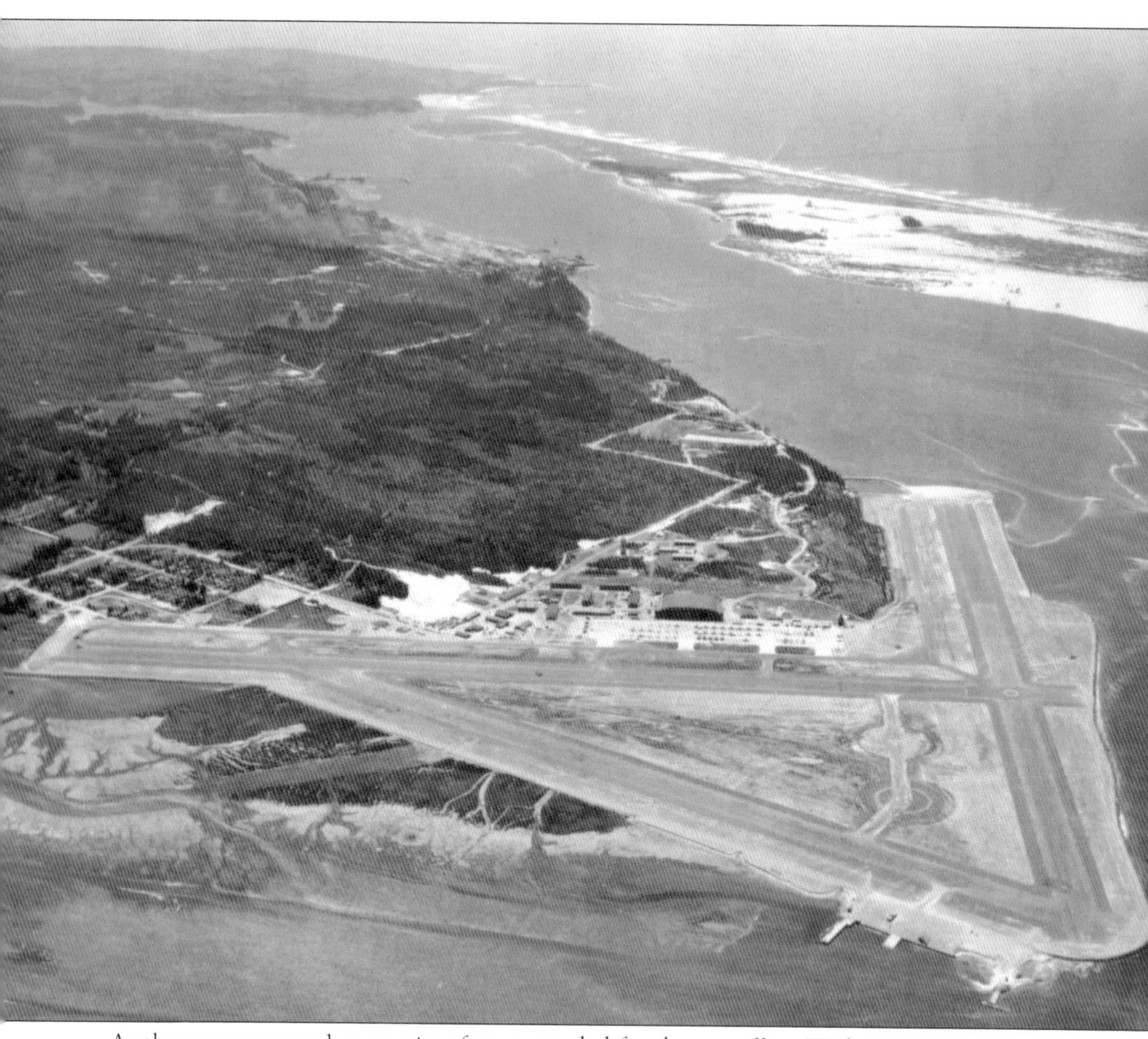

As the war progressed, more aircraft were needed for the war effort. With Astoria near capacity, more aircraft needed to be stationed at North Bend NAAF. Due to this increase, improvements were needed both to the buildings and the runways. Over the course of construction, the runways were lengthened slightly and rounded on the ends, giving a slight buffer between the runway and the water. This buffer allowed those being trained to learn how to be precise without risking damaging the aircraft or injuring themselves. Bases in some areas of the Pacific theater did not have the luxury of having buffers, and so the pilots had to learn how to quickly take off and land. This aerial view shows how much fill was needed to accomplish not only the runways but also the small extensions done to the three necessary runways. At the end of one of the runways is housing, showing how close the base was to the public. (Coos History Museum, CHM 981.267.2.)

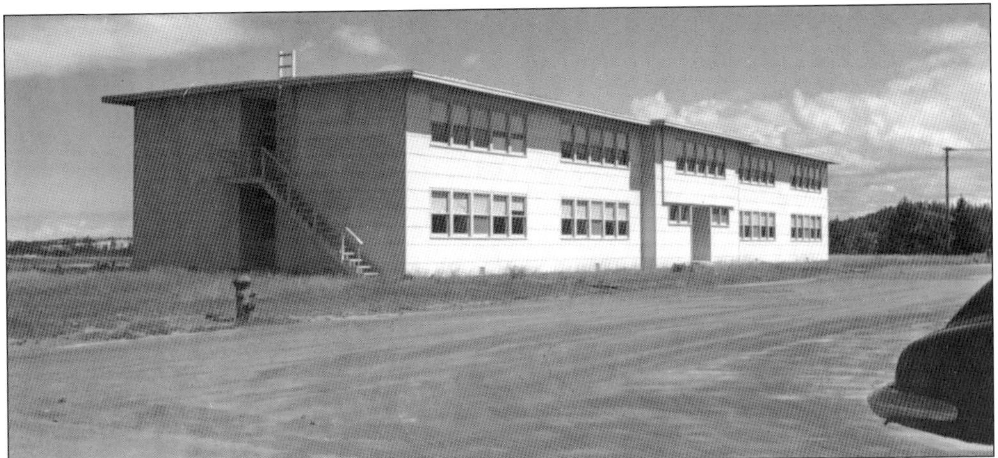

With so many naval individuals traveling to and from North Bend AAF, the base constructed a hotel for sailors' use while training. This building was used for many in lieu of barracks due to the short duration that many individuals stayed at the base. Housing for individuals who were stationed there was available, but some stayed in the community with their families. (Coos History Museum, CHM 992.N2.)

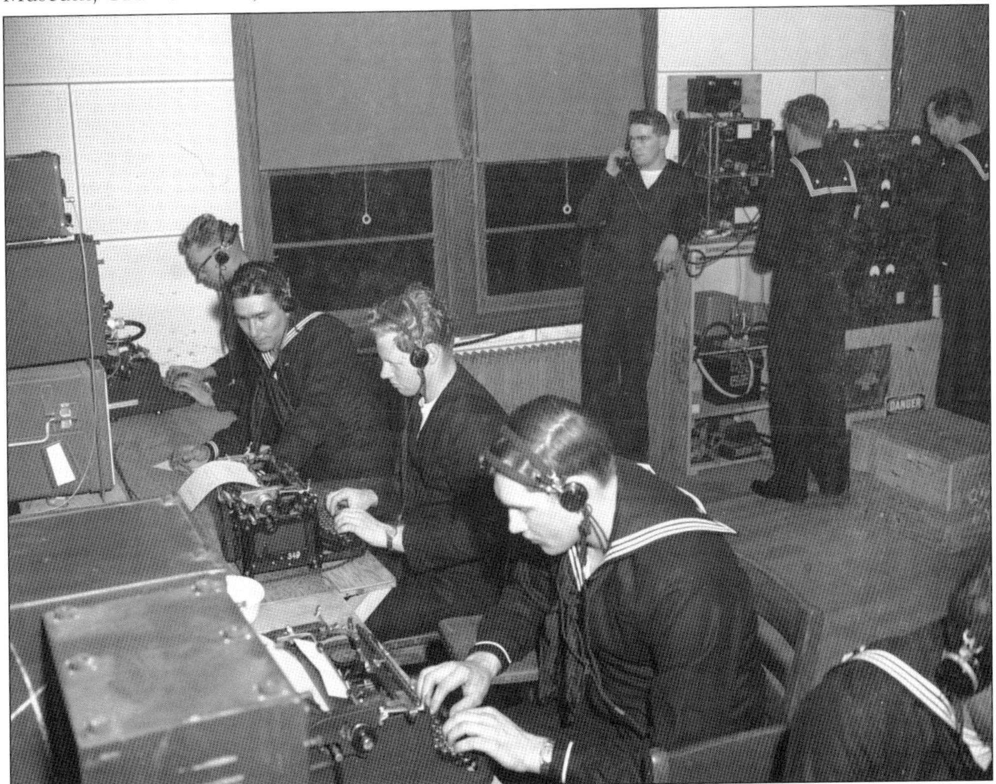

North Bend NAAF was used by the active duty Navy as well as the naval reserves for training during the war. The Navy used the base for training pilots, flight crews, and administration, while the naval reserves were also trained in naval code. These individuals were trained on how to send, receive, and translate codes that were used during the war by the US Navy. (Coos History Museum, CHM 995.1.5493.)

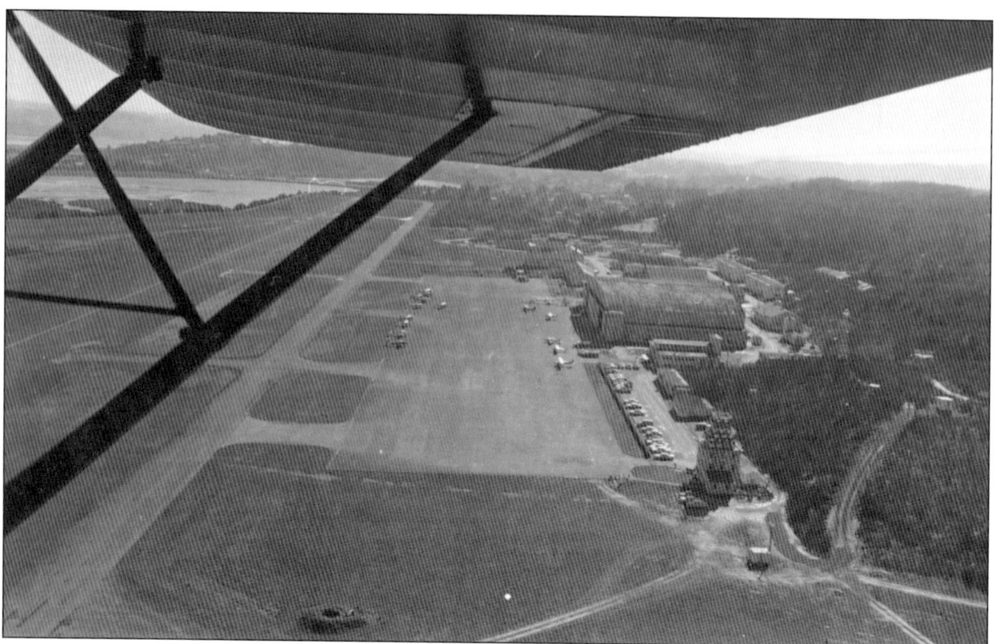

Following the war, the property was transferred to the City of North Bend in 1947 after the military considered it surplus property. The City of North Bend began to allow private aircraft owners access to the property while maintaining the land. The buildings that were not actively being used were leased if possible. West Coast with the DC-3 was the first commercial company to come in 1947. (Coos History Museum, CHM 009.16.21023.)

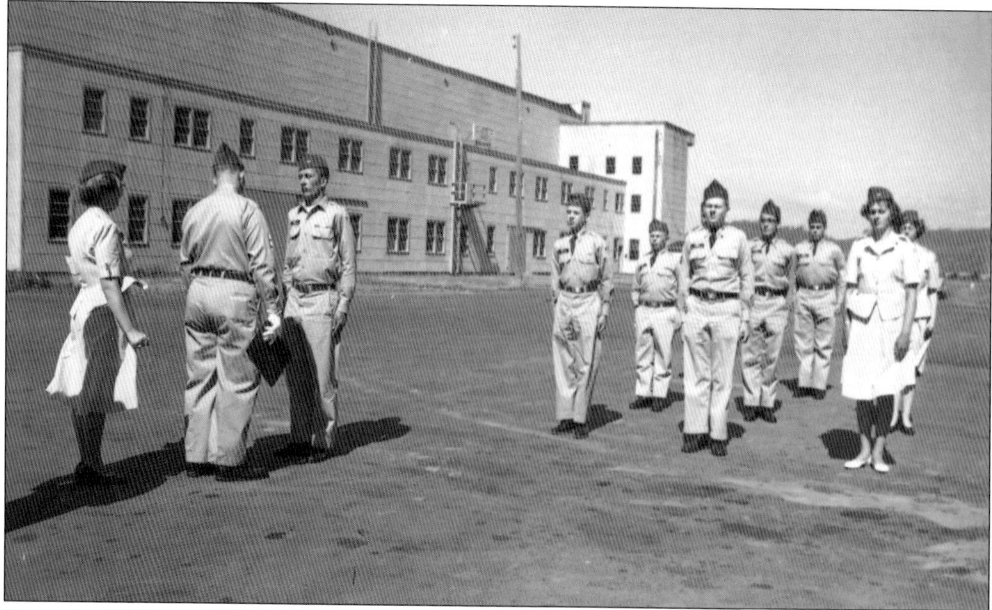

From the 1940s until the 1970s, the North Bend property was used by the Civilian Air Patrol as a training facility. In 1974, the US Coast Guard established the Coast Guard Air Station North Bend, utilizing the barracks and hotel for assigned personnel. Now called the Southwest Oregon Regional Airport, it is the only airport on the Oregon coast with passenger service. It is currently a joint Coast Guard-civilian airport. (Coos History Museum, CHM 009.16.22882.)

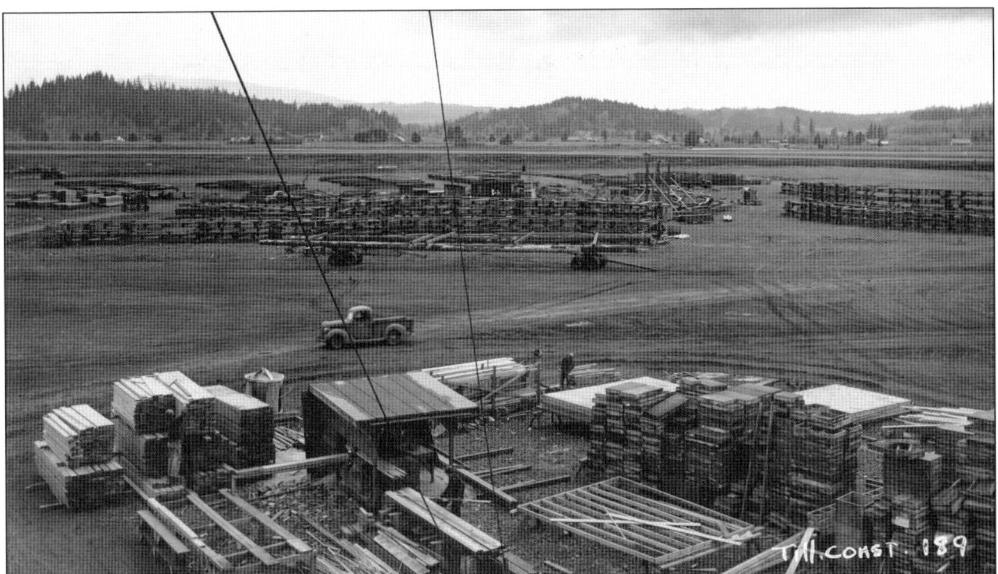

The construction for such a large base as Tillamook NAS took a lot of materials, which at the time were in short supply, but Oregon wood was readily available. Numerous contracts were signed with local logging companies and sawmills to ensure that there would be enough wood to build everything needed. The pieces in the back of this Tillamook lumberyard became the rafters for one of the two large hangars. (TAM.)

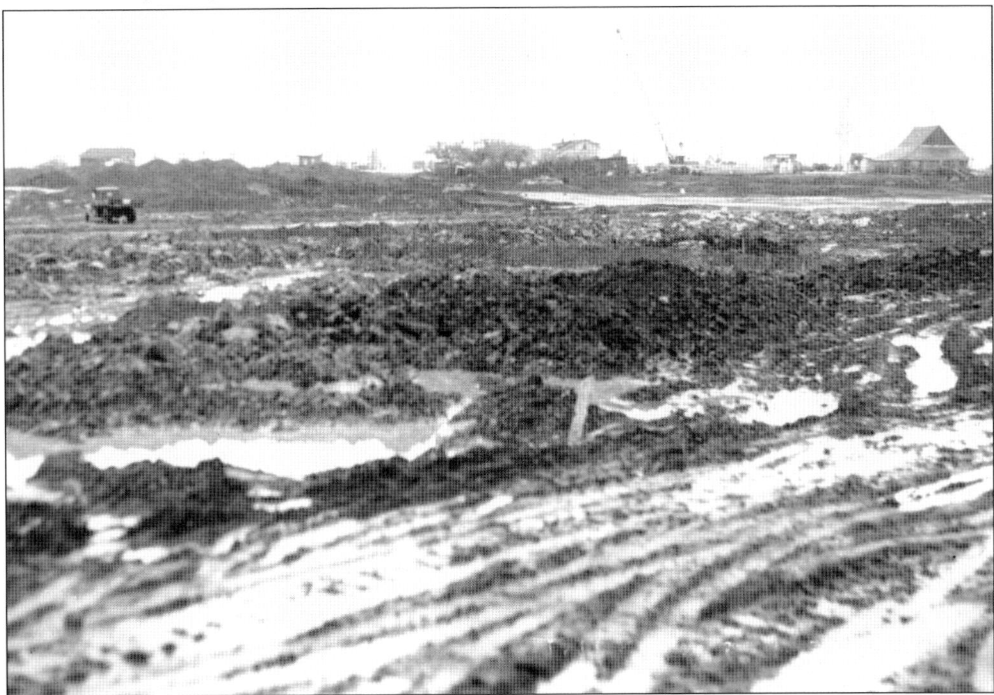

Construction was initially slow in 1941 because the land had not been developed. As construction began, it quickly turned into mud, requiring larger equipment and some earth filling. The military did not have the time to wait for the ground to dry out and so used what they learned in Tongue Point and Astoria to aid in construction. (TAM.)

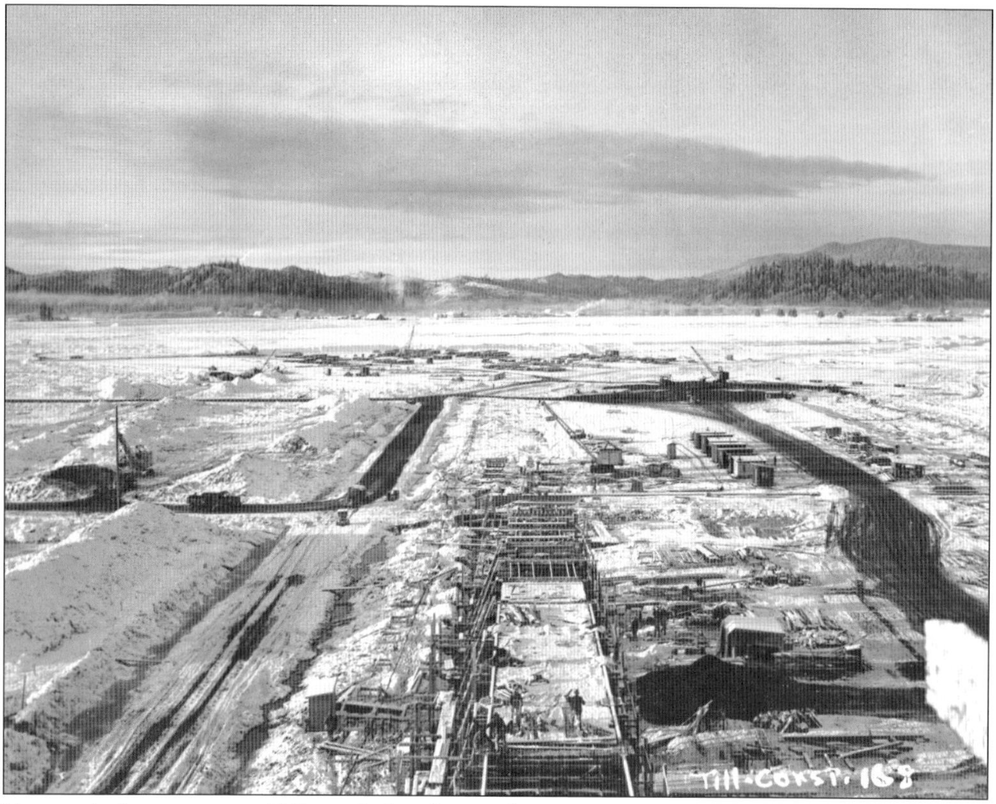

Very rarely does it snow in Tillamook, but during the construction of the administration building, it snowed enough to ensure the ground was white. This did not hinder the construction of the buildings, as the crew had already been working through the mud and rain. This was early in the construction, as the small huts were for workers to stay in to keep the progress steady. (TAM.)

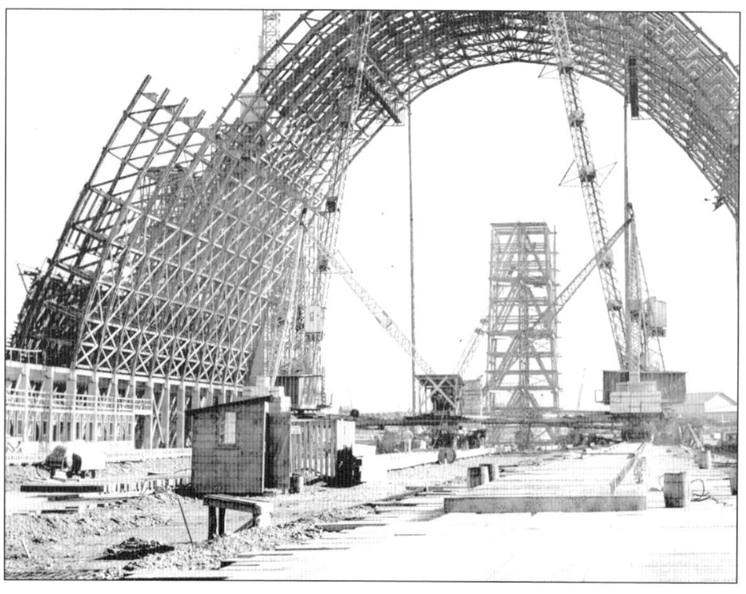

Each hangar required two million board feet of lumber to build completely, as steel was needed in the construction of ships. Hangar B was finished in 1943 and was the longer build. Hangar A, similar in size and scope to Hangar B, was built in just 27 days. The Navy needed the airships in Tillamook, and it wasted no time in building the hangars. (TAM.)

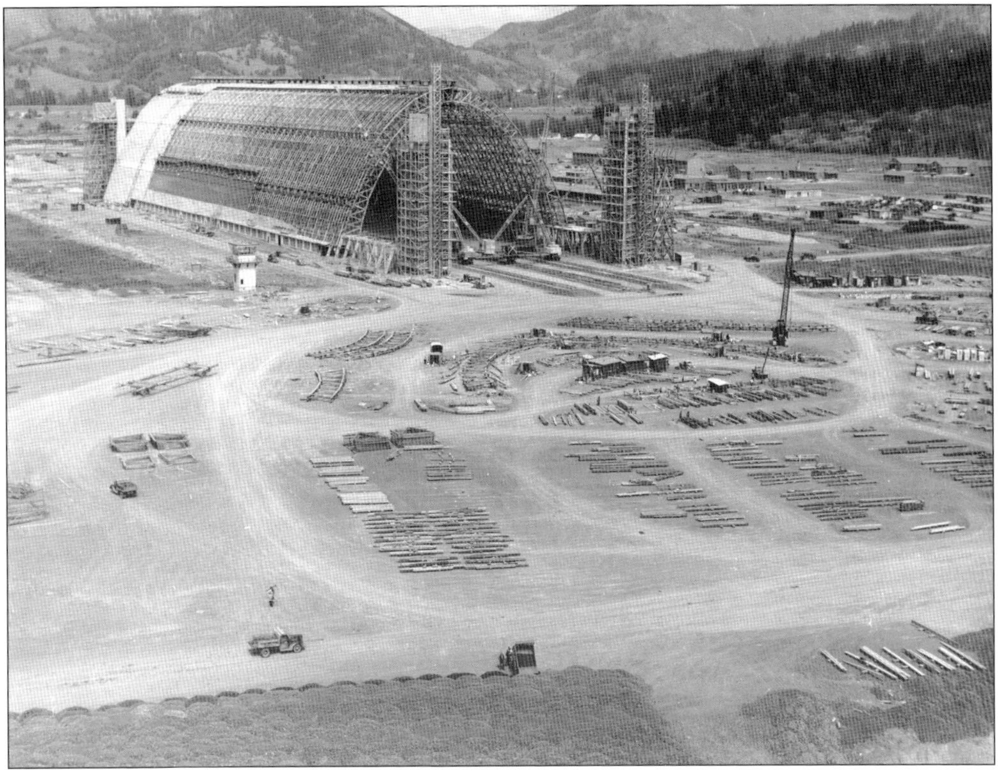

Unfortunately, even though the hangars at Tillamook were built quickly, an airship arrived in February 1943, and due to no hangars being complete, it was lost to a storm on March 27 that same year. The hangars were not constructed to accommodate airships until the entire building was complete. Due to the size, the US Navy placed cranes on tracks so they could be moved from one side to another. (TAM.)

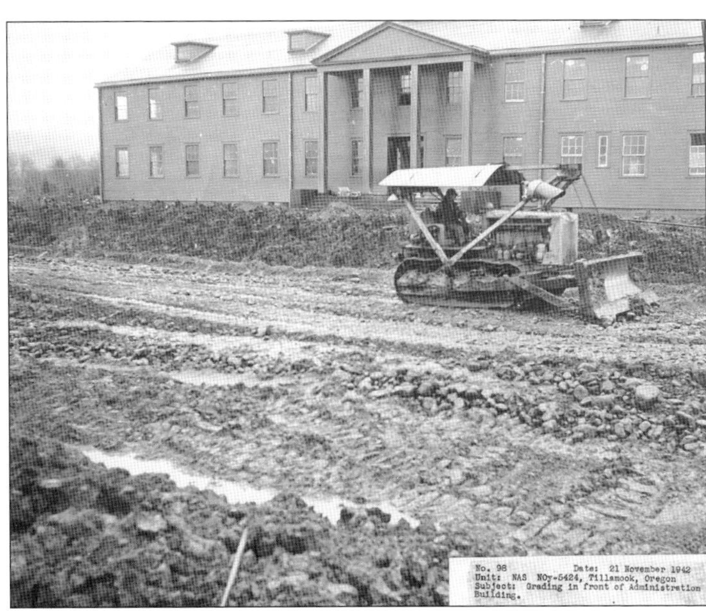

Once the base construction began, it was rapid. The administration building's shell went up before the front driveway was completed, as this individual is grading the area in front of the administration building to increase accessibility for individuals coming to work or reporting for duty. Tillamook receives an average of 88 inches of rain a year, so most of the construction occurred when the ground was wet. (TAM.)

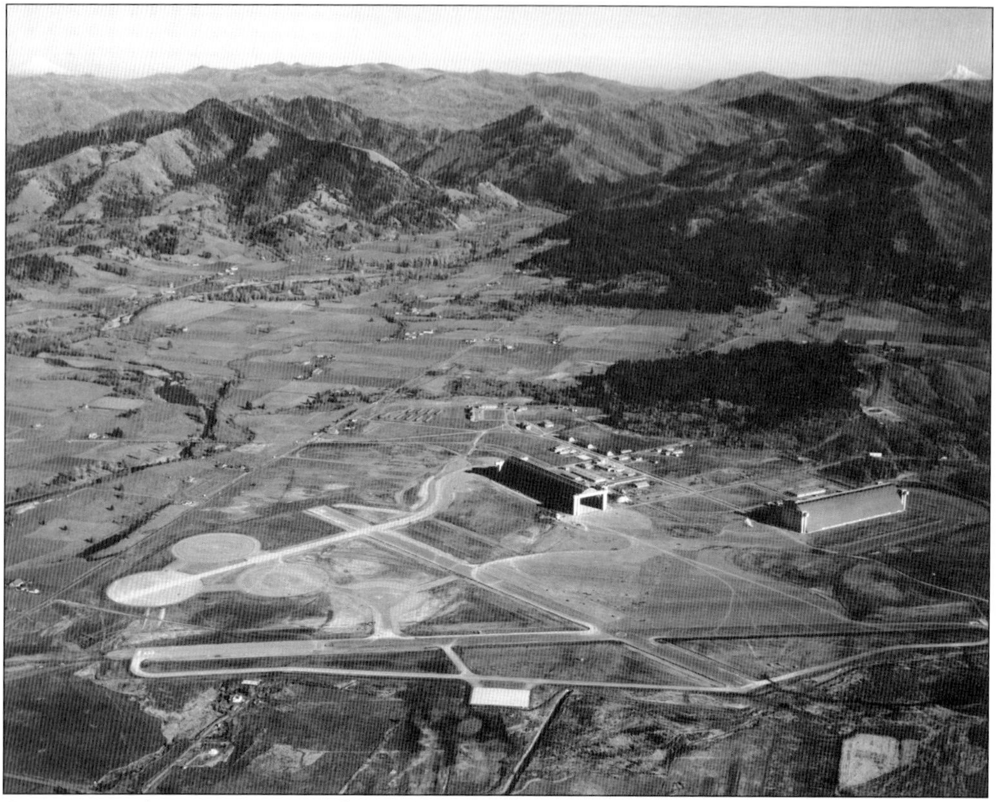

Construction began in 1942 at Tillamook, but it was not until 1943 that all buildings and hangars were completed. The 360-acre base had an advantage that other airship fields did not, as there were mountains directly to the west. This allowed for excellent training for pilots of both aircraft and airships in how to navigate drastic elevation changes, especially with a helium-based lift system that is affected by elevation. (TAM.)

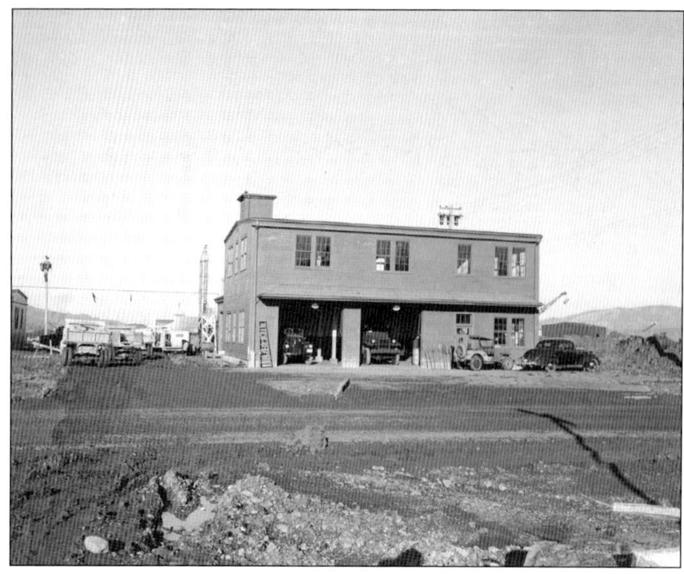

With any airfield, especially one designed with large airships and millions of cubic feet of helium, fire stations were some of the first buildings constructed after administration, housing, and a mess hall. Unfortunately, with the nature of airships, there were accidents that resulted in the need for firefighters. In the background, construction was occurring at a feverish pace to ensure that when it was finally commissioned, the base was ready. (TAM.)

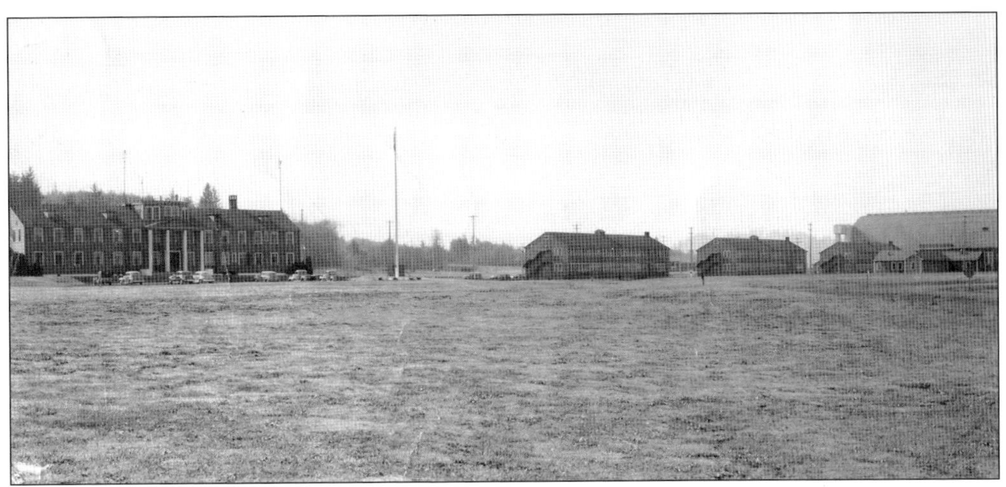

With final touches on the paint for the administration building, it matches the housing units that are next to it. With the lack of metal and other components for building, all the structures at Tillamook, including some of the plumbing, were created using wood from one of the many mills in the area. By having the buildings close, it decreased the amount of time for shift changes and emergencies. (TAM.)

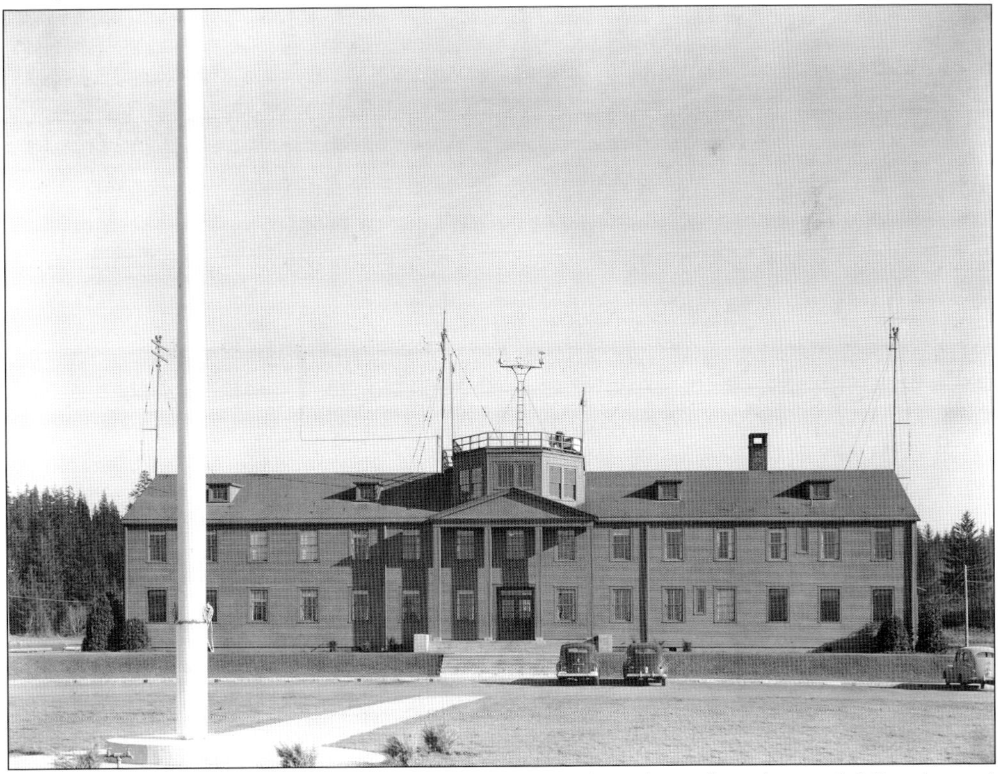

The administration building is seen completed with a flagpole, parking lot, and full radio and radar capabilities. By the time the base was commissioned in late 1942, all the buildings were either occupied or could be occupied, so military activities were able to start immediately. This was extremely important as the first submarine sighting was in September 1942, prompting the construction of this base. (TAM.)

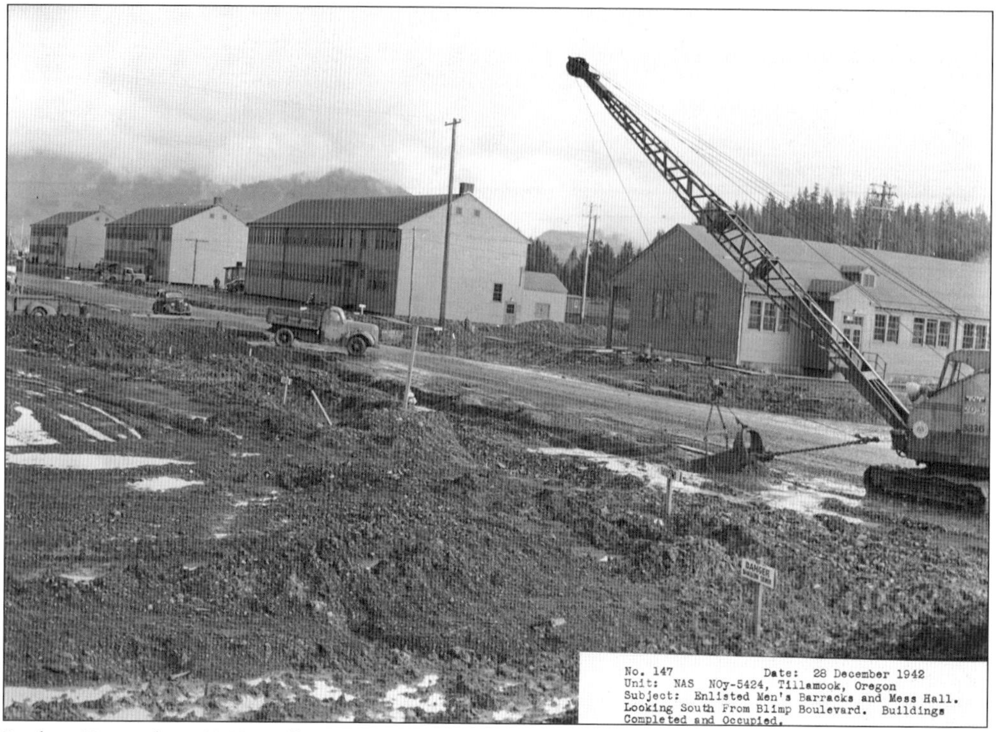

By late December 1942, Tillamook NAS was operational enough to bring soldiers in. Blimp Boulevard, one of the main streets on base, was still dirt, with the men's barracks and mess hall in the background. With submarine sightings, it was imperative that the base be constructed and filled as fast as possible. This resulted in some things being held off until later, like hardening the muddy roads seen in the photograph. (TAM.)

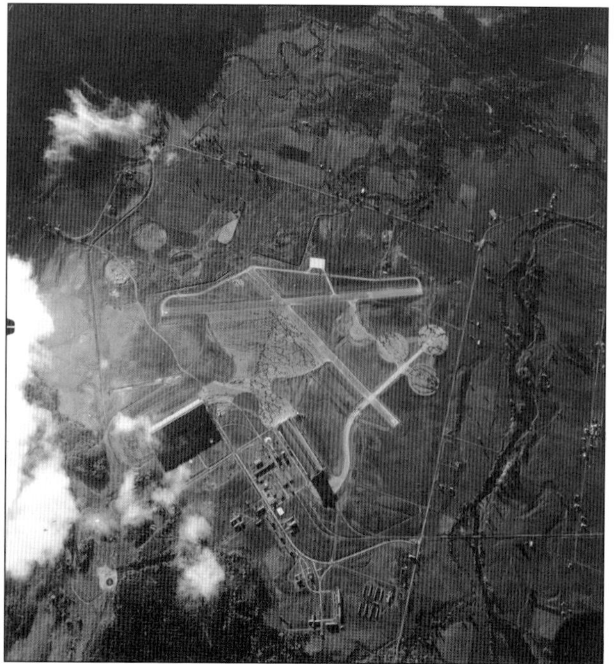

Due to the size of the airships and the need for a large base, Tillamook NAS was one of the larger bases in Oregon. Equipped with both runways and blimp pads, many different types of aircraft could land if needed. Tillamook NAS was the primary location for airships, with their patrol route from Washington to California. This image shows the entirety of the base from an aerial perspective. (TAM.)

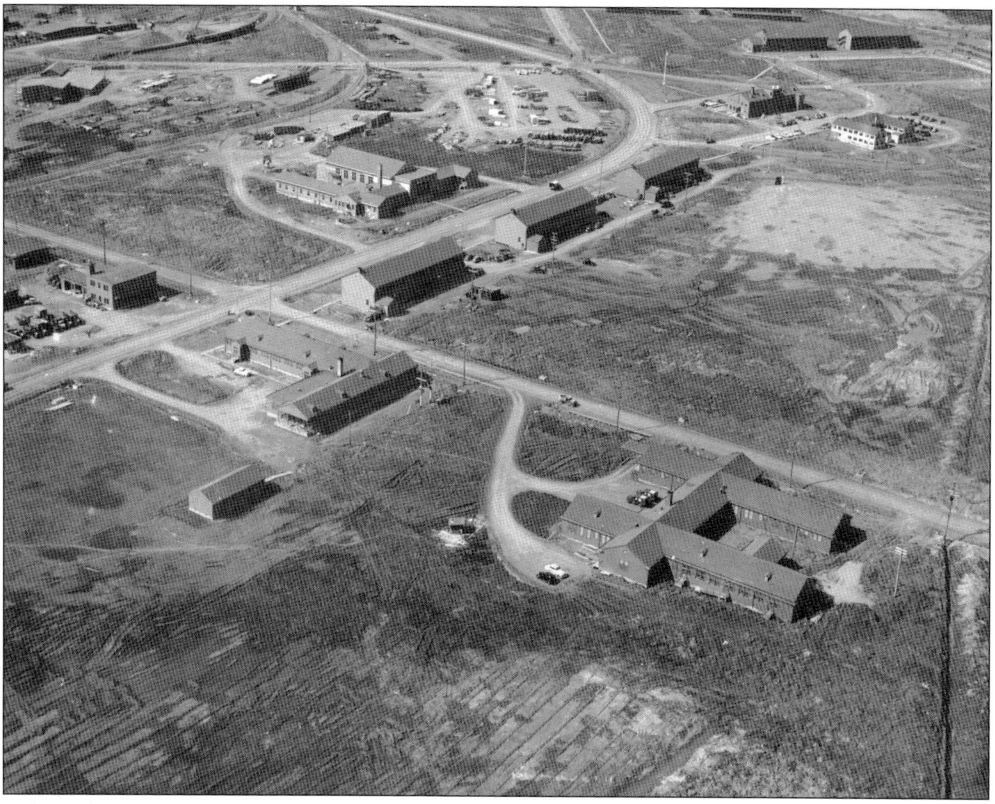

Military bases are full communities, especially large ones such as Tillamook. This image, taken May 18, 1943, shows the hospital, dispensary, barracks, and recreational facilities. In the background is the ordnance storage, which is where the munitions for both the airships and aircraft were kept. It was usually created at a distance to ensure that if something were to happen, most of the base would not be impacted. (TAM.)

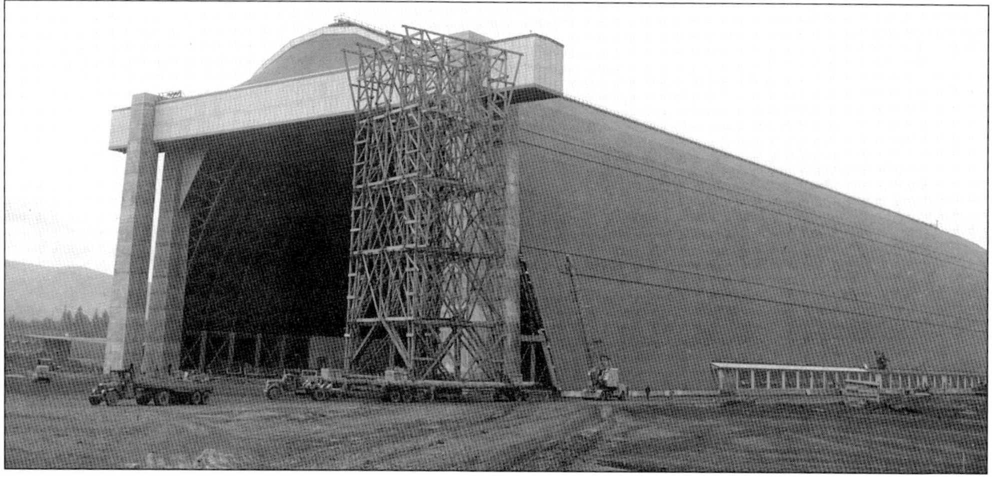

As part of the US military's goal of using airships for patrol, the US Navy began building 17 hangars around the United States. Two of these hangars, A and B, were slated to be built at Tillamook NAS. Hangar B was 1,072 feet long, 296 feet wide, and 15 stories tall. It could hold six airships comfortably, even though it almost never did. (TAM.)

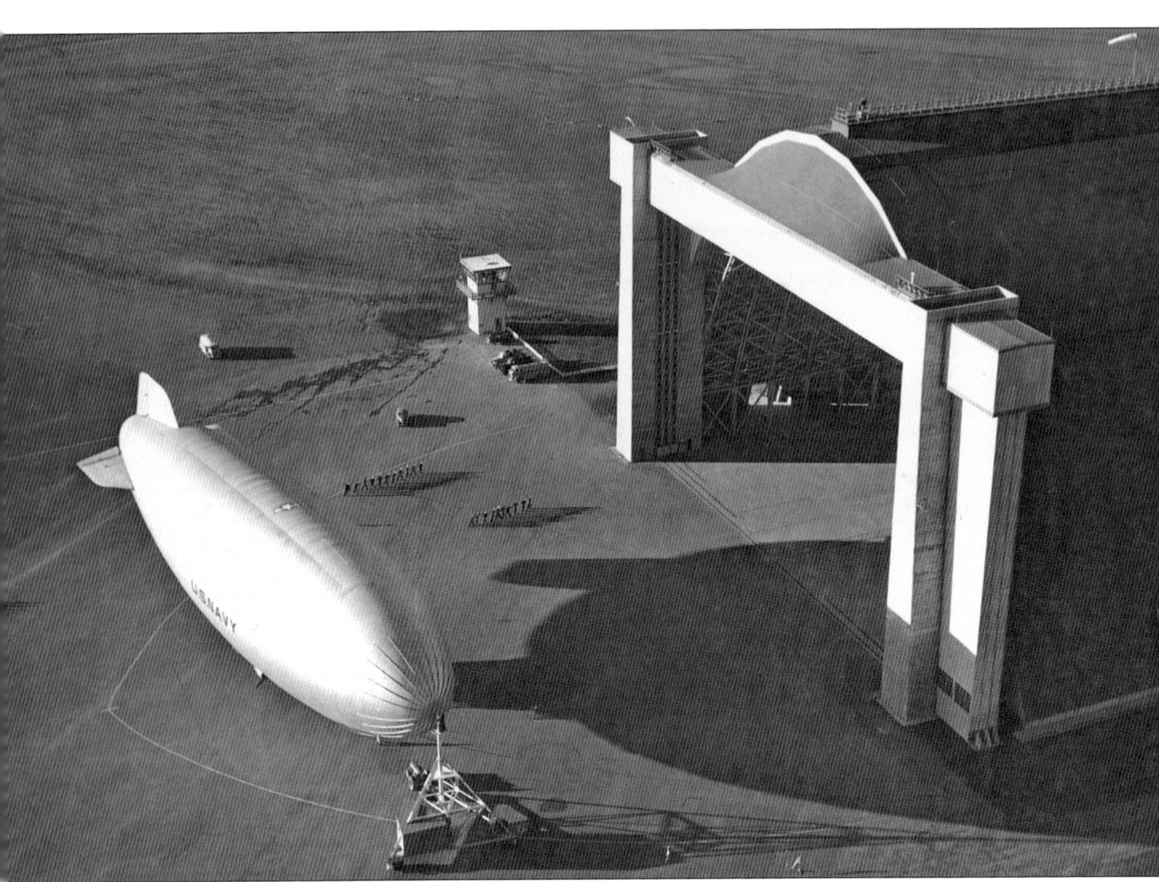

Pictured is an aerial view of an airship next to one of the two hangars. The immense size of the airship is the same as 17 average cars lined up front to back. In the background is a control tower and six vehicles. Even though three of the vehicles are large fire trucks, they are still very small compared to the airship. Two sets of men are holding on to the ropes to turn the airship around to place it in the hangar. A total of 21 men were needed specifically on the two ropes, while there are additional men below near the gondola, also helping to move the airship. The mobile mooring mast was used to allow the airship to freely move in the wind while still being tethered to the ground. If there were high winds projected, the airships would be taken inside the hangars. A tractor was required to move the mooring masts when needed. (TAM.)

Hangars A and B were so large that each one could fit officially six airships; it is apparent, though, that all eight airships that were permanently stationed at Tillamook NAS could fit in one hangar. Each airship is moored to a mooring mast as well as being tied down to the ground. The method in which the hangars were built meant that there was little that could damage the airships once inside. (TAM.)

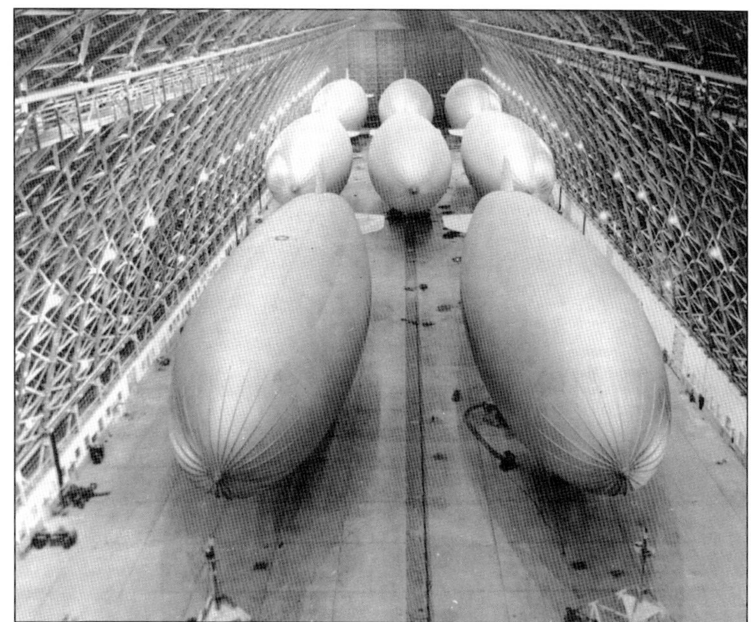

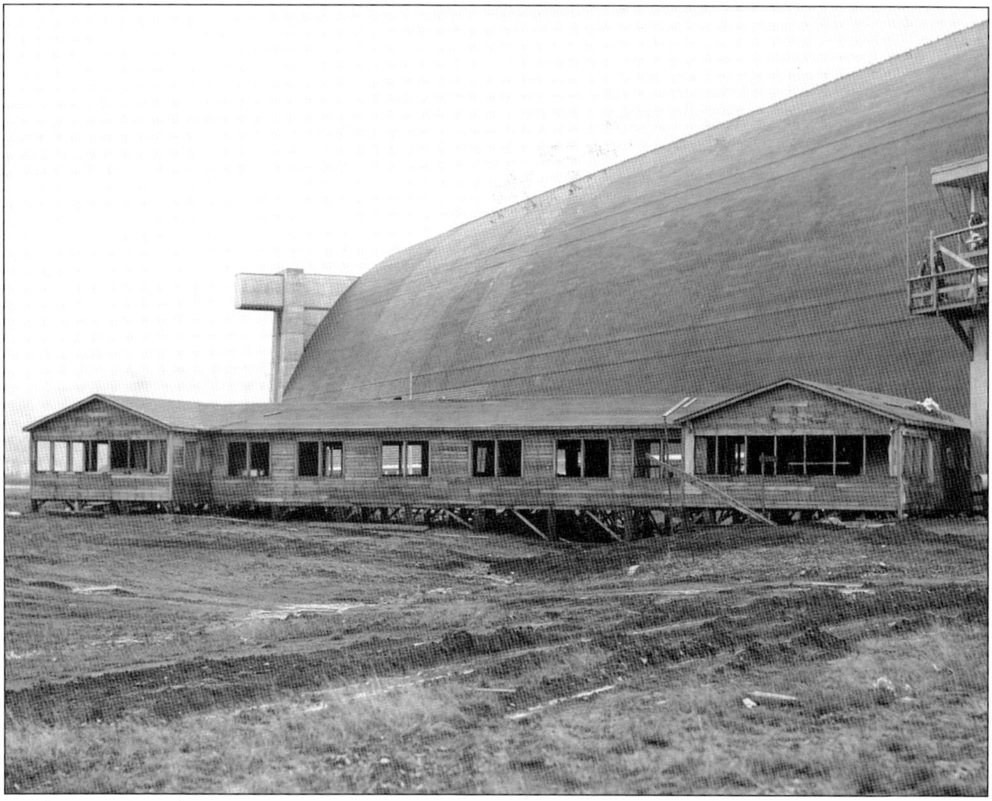

With aircraft and airships, two buildings must accompany the hangar. These are operations and the control tower. These two buildings were second to the hangar because the Navy had to get the airships protected and in the air. In normal situations, air traffic control towers are larger than hangars, but when the hangar is 15 stories tall, it makes the tower look small next to it. (TAM.)

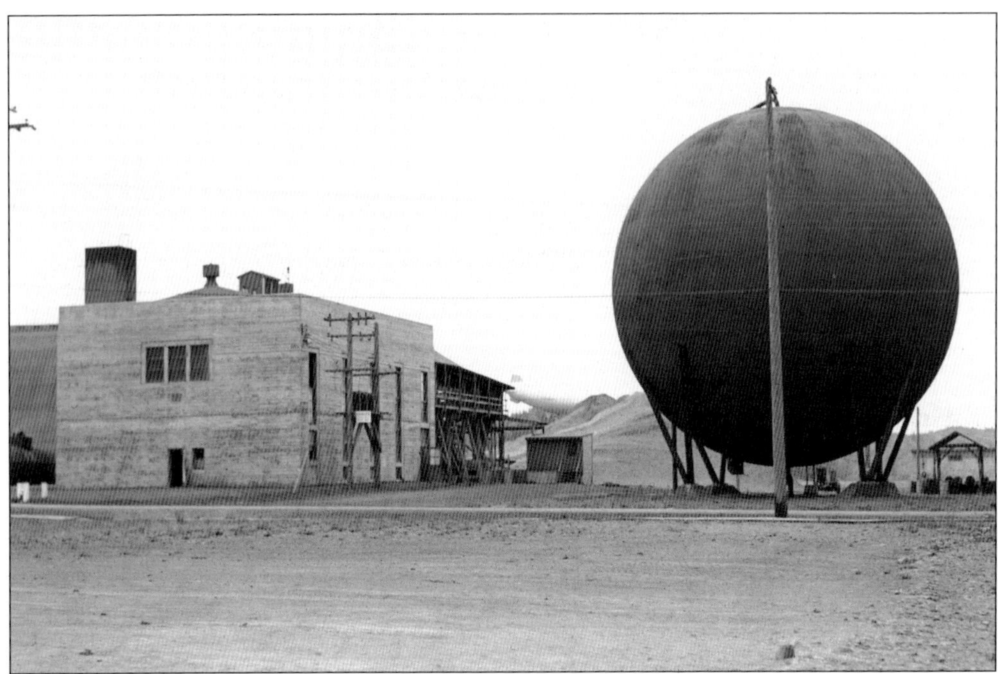

This large balloon-looking shape could be another reconnaissance aircraft, but it is not. The building to the left of the balloon is the heating plant for the entire base, while the balloon is the low-pressure helium tank used in the airships to keep them afloat. In the rear of the photograph, an airship is just passing behind the hills to the east of the base. (TAM.)

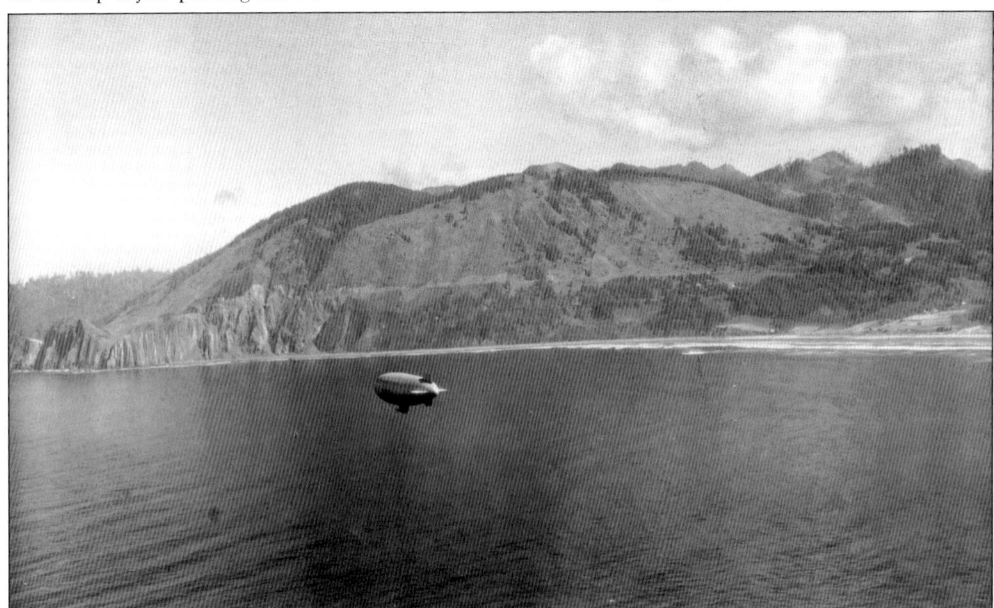

The US Navy used the airships for anti-submarine patrols and convoy escorts. Due to the windows of the gondola being 365 degrees, it allowed the crew to constantly watch for danger. There was danger to be found, with Japan having at least two submarines, I-25, and I-26, both with seaplanes that could be deployed to travel inland. The submarines traveled a course from Alaska to California. (TAM.)

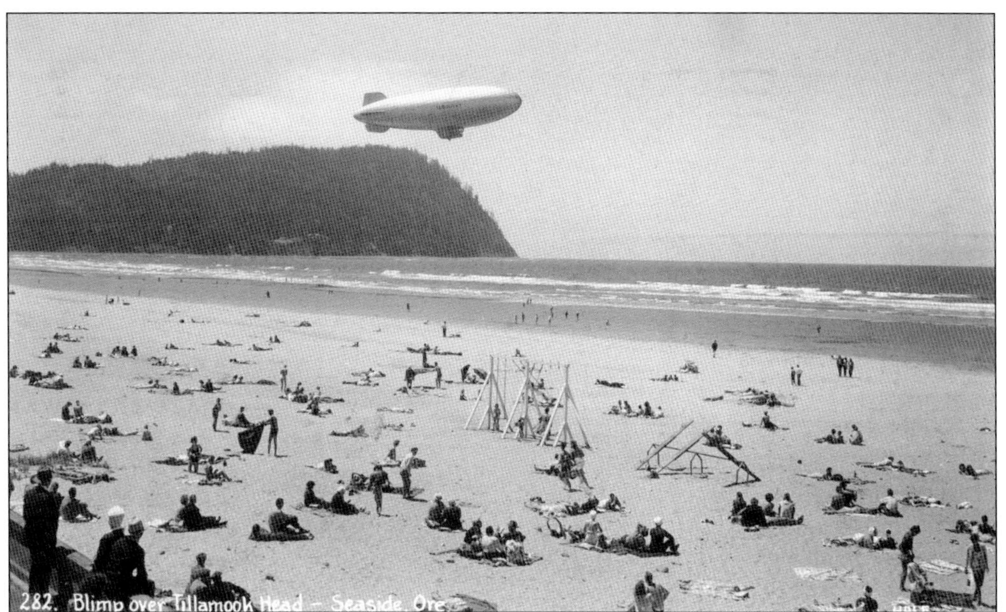

While on patrol, the airship could hold up to 425,000 cubic feet of helium with a lift capacity of 7,700 pounds. This capacity was necessary to ensure the power plant, crew, and any equipment could be carried without incident. This image shows an airship close to the beach patrolling after a submarine sighting. In some locations, airships were used at night, but Tillamook used them the entire day and night. (TAM.)

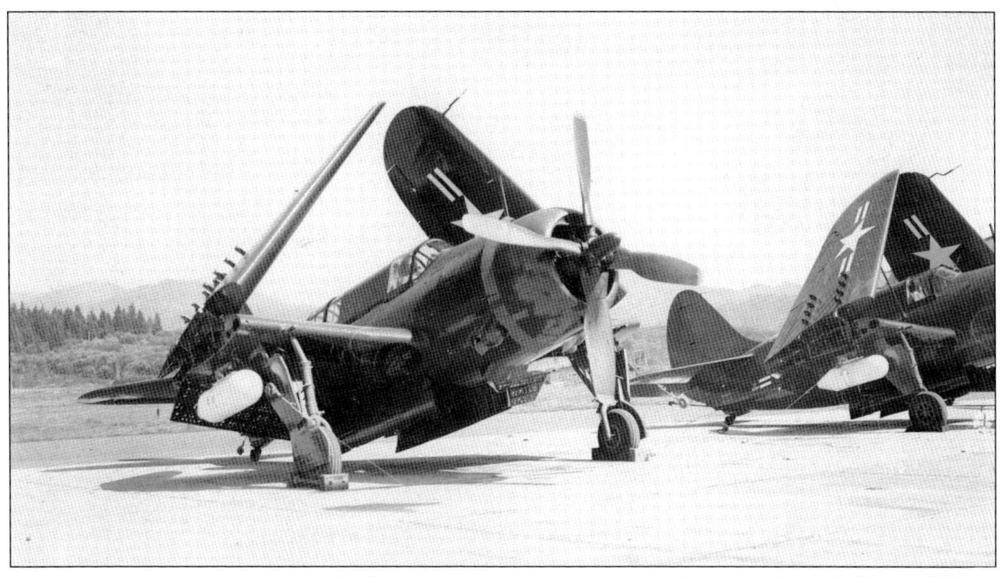

Airships were not the only aircraft that were stationed or landed at Tillamook NAS. These SB2Cs, used for training on other bases in Oregon, took a short trip to Tillamook for some coastal training before being sent to the Pacific theater. These aircraft with their foldable wings fit easily on an aircraft carrier and were used for dive bombing the enemy. (TAM.)

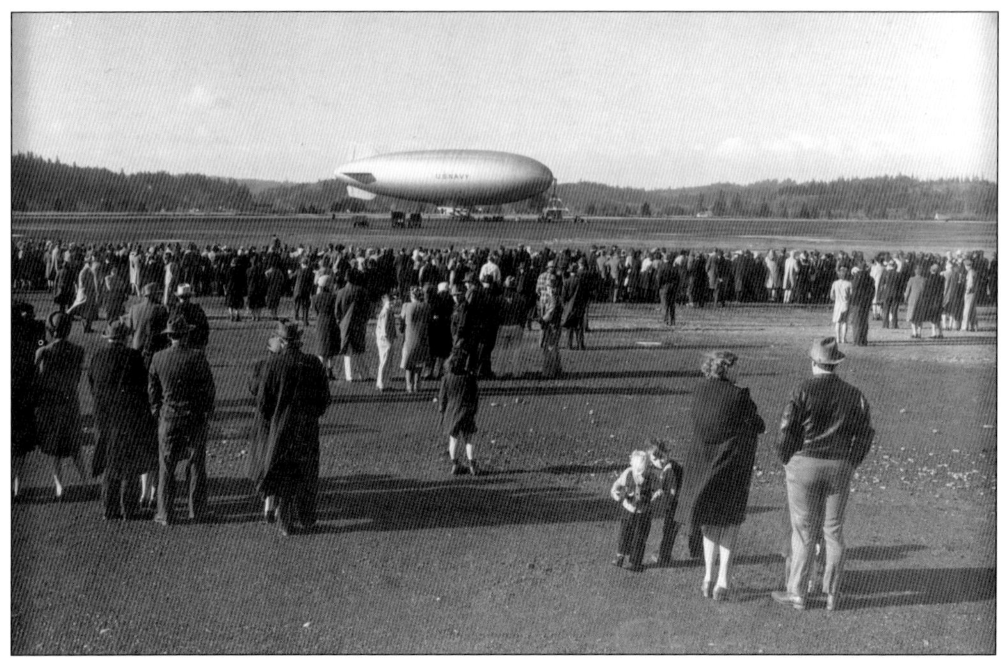

When the US Navy began to move the large airships, also known as blimps, into Tillamook, it knew that the public would want to see them. Tillamook NAS opened its fields to allow the citizens to come and admire the airships. Even with the distance, the airships loomed over the people as it is moored on the blimp pad. (TAM.)

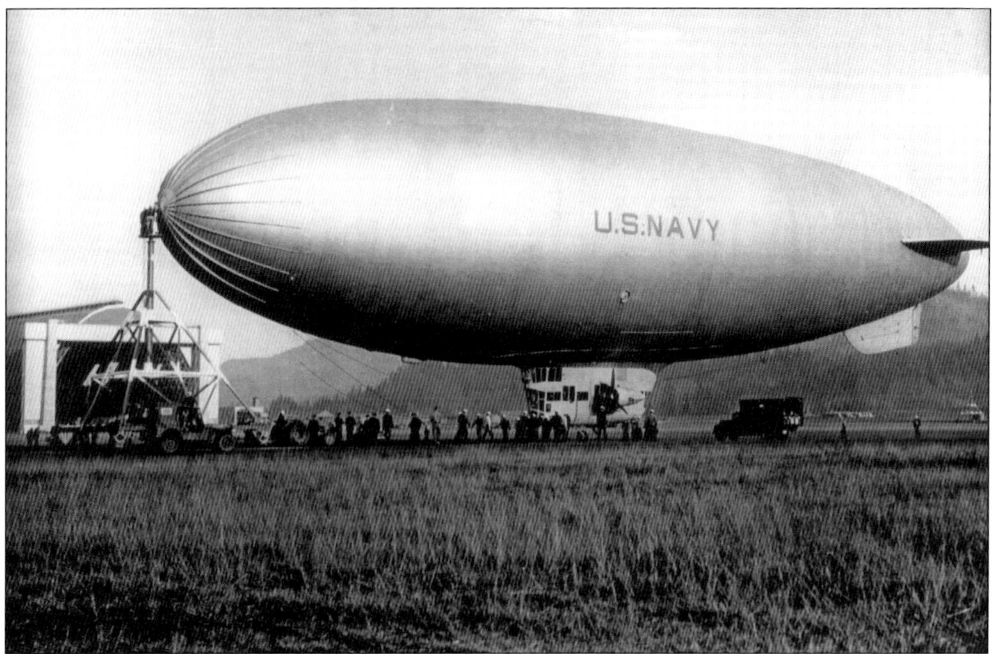

The US Navy airships were 252 feet long and staffed by only five to seven people on board in the small, enclosed gondola below the larger envelope or balloon-looking part of the airship. The main issue was that 40 to 50 individuals were needed on the ground to ensure the airship did not move once it was hooked to the mooring mast. (TAM.)

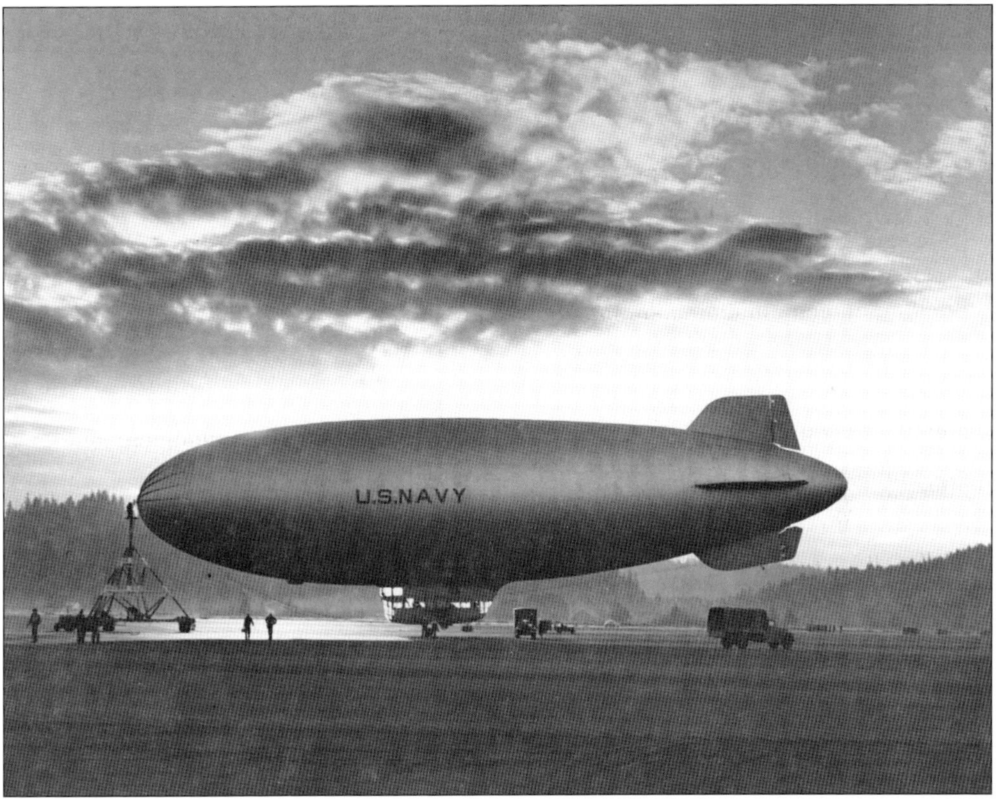

The two hangars created for the airships could only hold six each officially, and so if additional airships were brought in during transfers or needed to stop for refueling or crew change, the airship could remain outside attached to the mooring mast as well as tethered with a rope. This was only possible when the weather was favorable due to the wind being able to blow an unattended airship around. (TAM.)

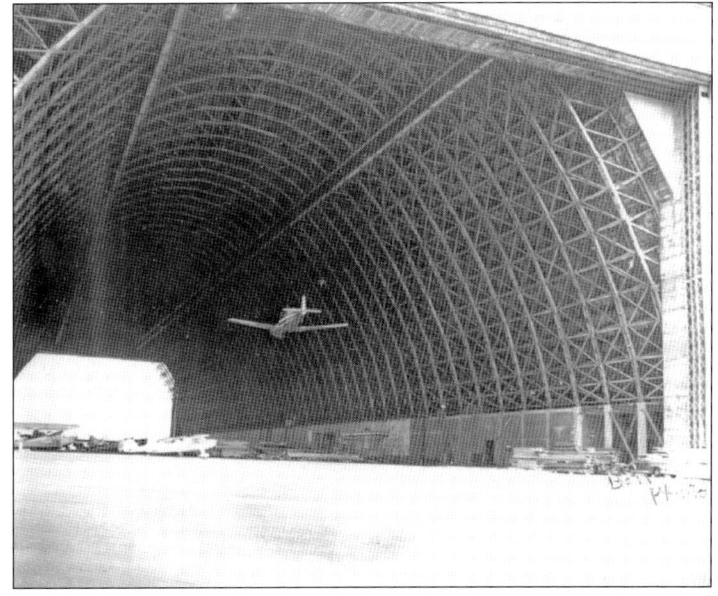

Hangar B was so large that, in comparison, this normal-sized aircraft looks small. Where only six airships could be stored in the hanger at one time, more than 30 smaller aircraft could be kept there if needed. As the Japanese surrendered, the airships were quickly transferred to other bases, leaving the hangars empty. First used by logging companies, soon private aircraft took residence in the hangers. (TAM.)

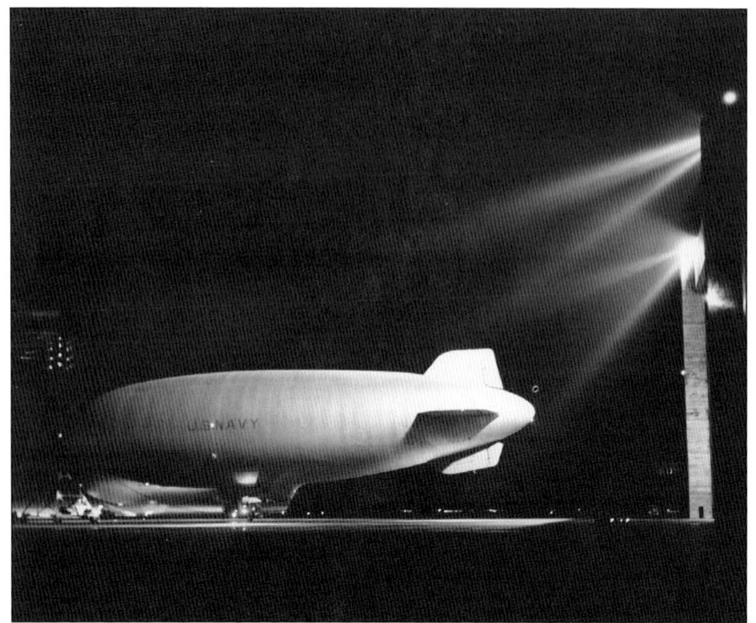

Even with knowing how large the hangars were, this image shows the comparison between the hangar and the airships. Patrolling was not limited to daytime, and so it was common for an airship to be pulled out by the mooring mast at night to do a routine patrol or, if a submarine was spotted, to do an emergency patrol. Airships could reach 78 miles per hour if needed. (TAM.)

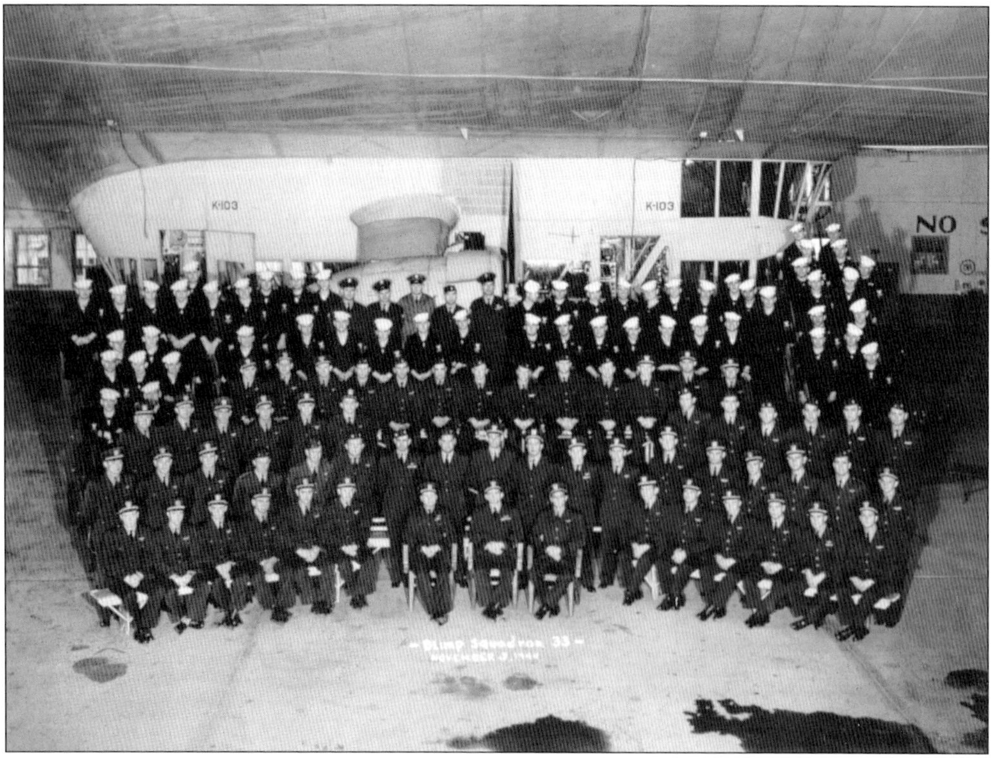

Airships needed large crews; each one needed at least 37, if not more, with the crew in the airship to work the controls as well as crew on the ground to maneuver the airship into place. This image from November 3, 1944, shows one blimp squadron posing in front of a gondola. Each squadron was made up of officers and enlisted personnel in a variety of positions, including administrative, radio, radar, and navigator. (TAM.)

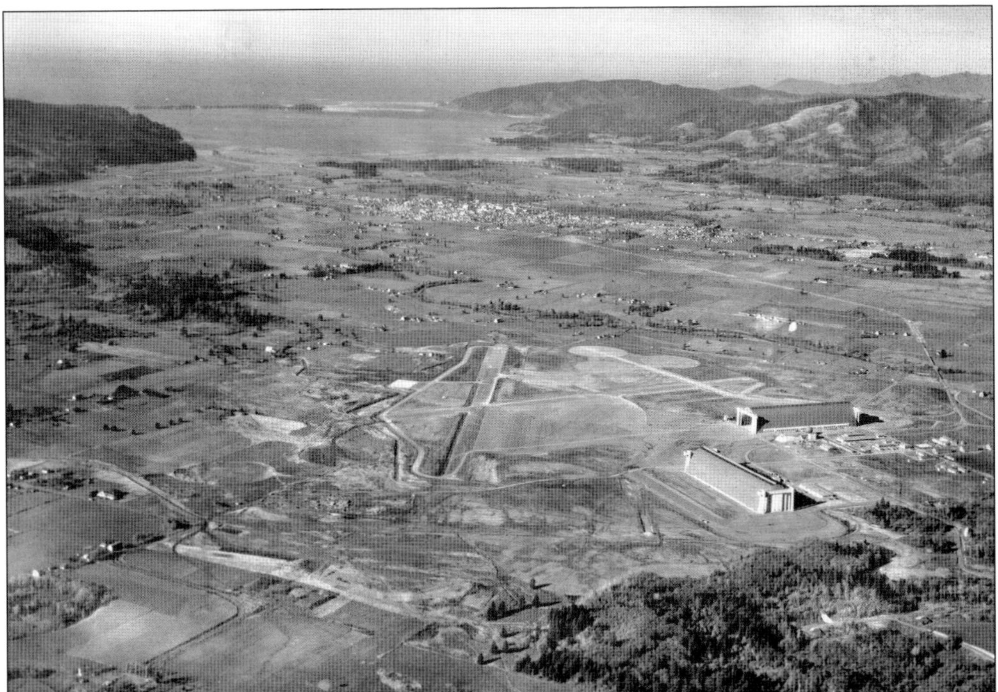

Pictured is another aerial view of the air base from the western mountains. Tillamook sits in a basin, allowing the airships to go out to the coastline and then patrol north and south. Any dangers coming over the mountains would be seen by patrolling aircraft or radar equipment. In October 1945, the last two airships left for California, leaving the base functional but empty until 1948, when the US Navy decommissioned it. (TAM.)

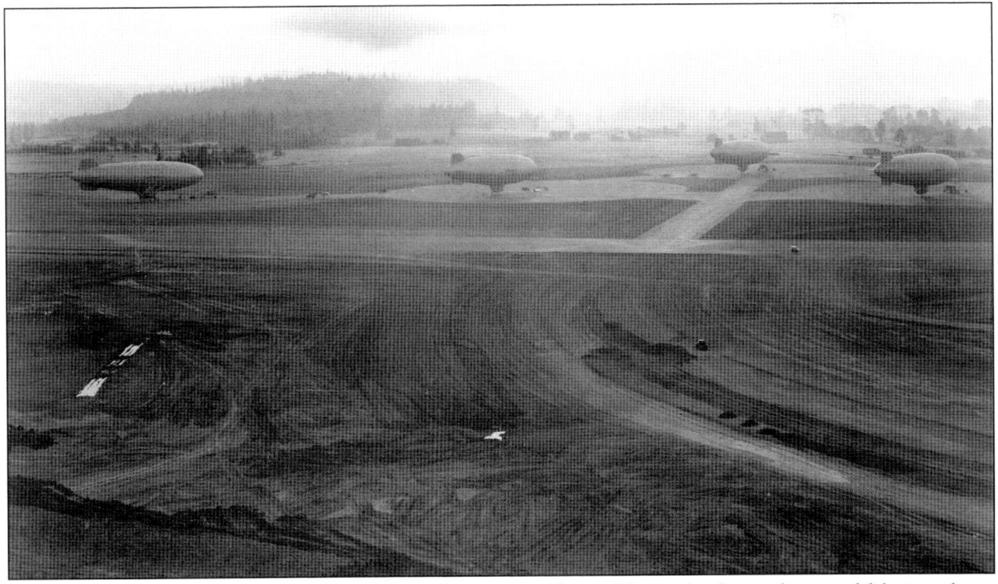

Hazy conditions did not stop the airships from patrolling. The only thing that could bring them down was high winds. That is also why the airships were equipped with two engines attached to the gondola. When the winds slightly pushed the airship off course, the engines could correct it. These four airships are tethered to the blimp pads, ready to take flight. (TAM.)

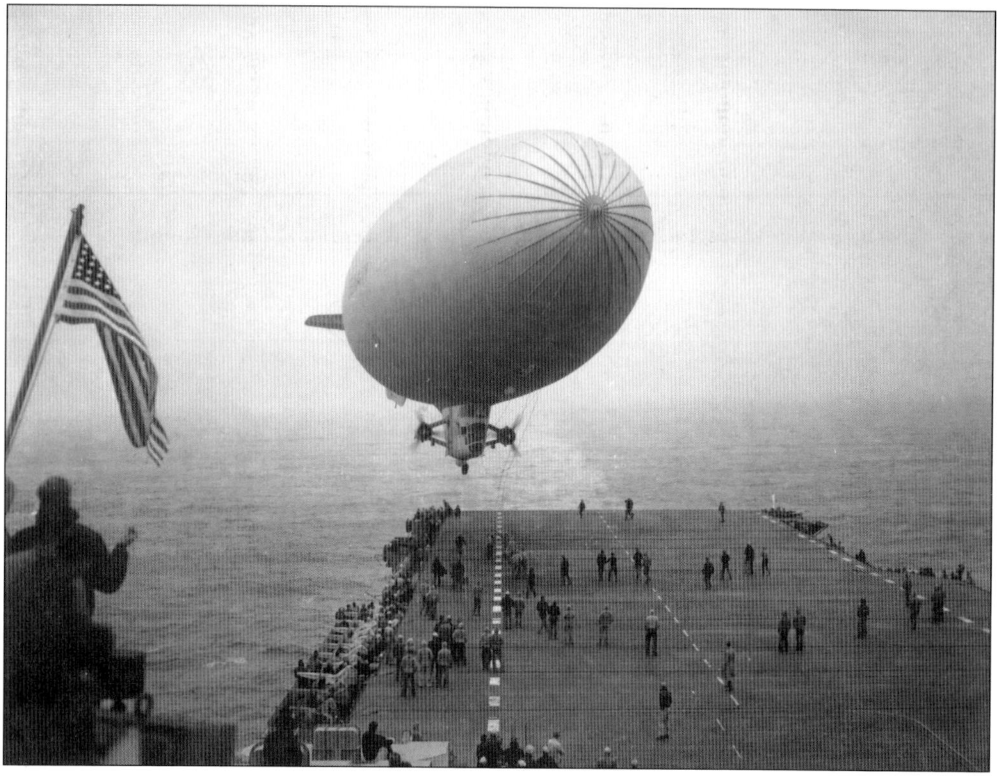

To transfer an airship overseas, it needed to go on an aircraft carrier. This airship is arriving from Tillamook NAS to assist in submarine detection during a convoy mission. With a range of 2,205 miles and the ability to stay afloat for over 38 hours, airships were extremely useful in areas with known submarine sightings. It allowed patrol aircraft to be used for other things. (TAM.)

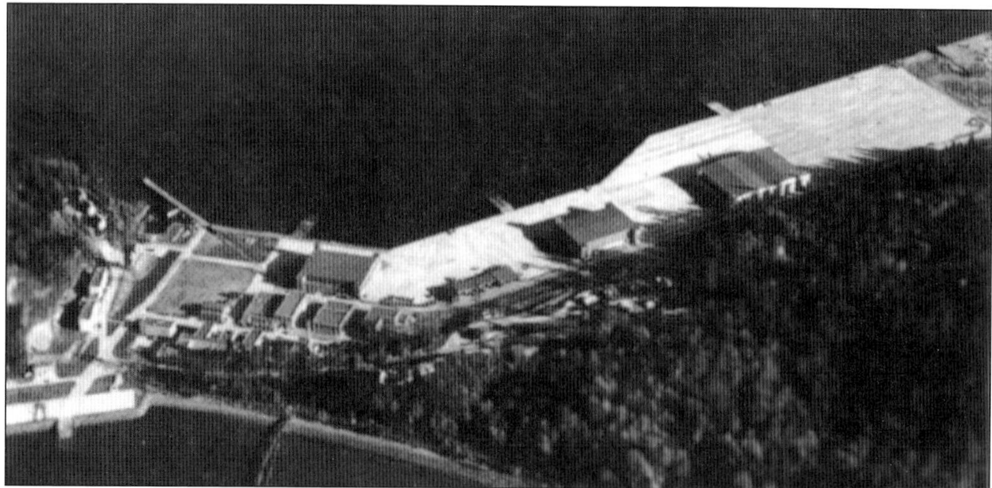

In January 1921, a total of 395 acres of property along the Columbia River were deeded to Clatsop County. The county immediately placed the property under the control of the US Navy. From 1924 until 1939, the location was used primarily for submarines and destroyers due to the geographical makeup of the land. In 1939, the Navy began to dredge and fill the land, allowing the entire subtidal area to be filled. (Naval History and Heritage.)

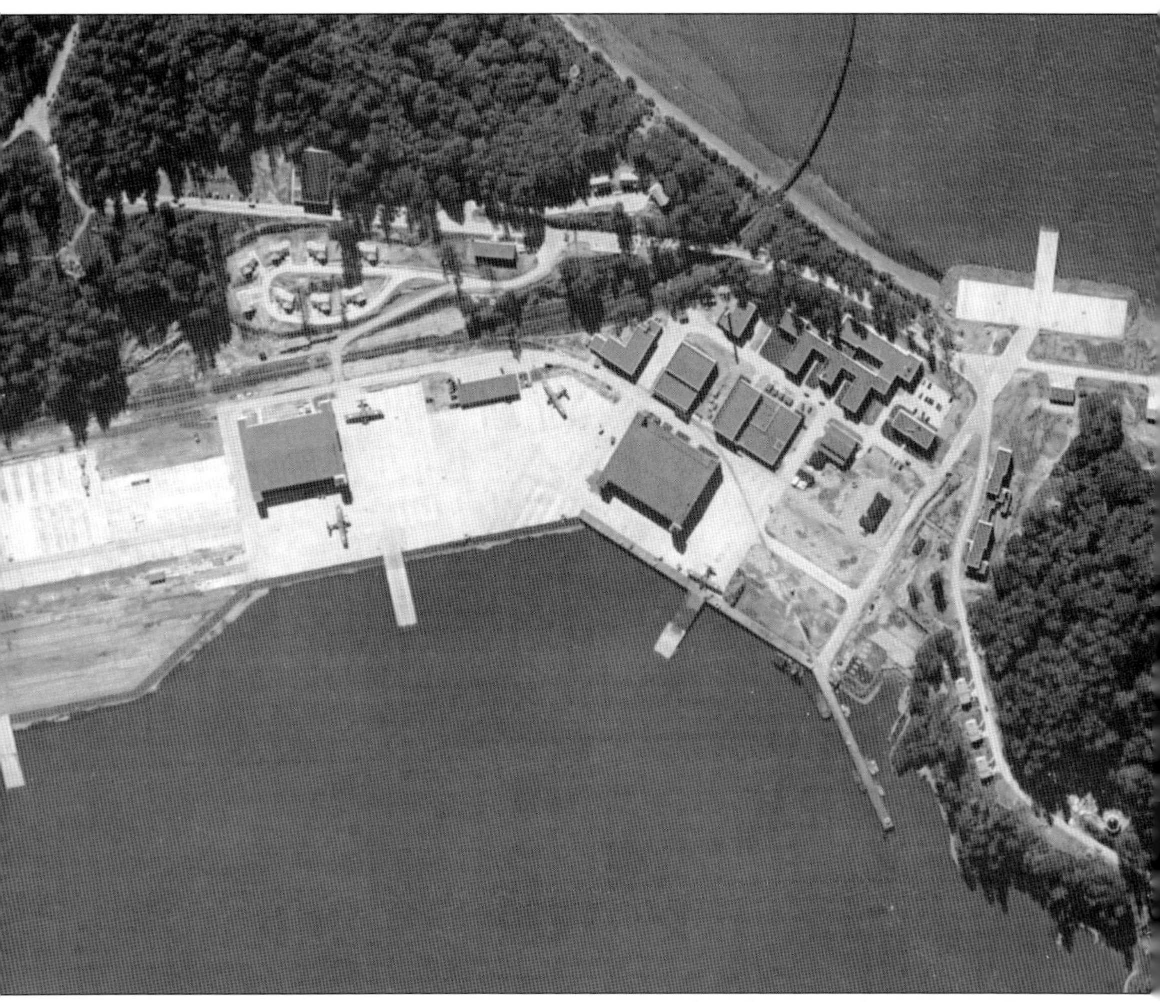

In 1941, the US Navy began to use Tongue Point as a seaplane base. New hangars, refueling stations, and additional facilities were constructed on land that was dredged and filled previously. Three large concrete ramps were built to allow the seaplanes access to the river, as can be seen on the water in the image. Three large aircraft sit on what could be considered an apron, although it is different than a traditional air base. This difference is due to having seaplanes versus more traditional aircraft. By early 1943, the Consolidated PBY Catalina, a patrol bomber, anti-submarine patrol, and a night attack and interdiction aircraft began to arrive at Tongue Point. The Catalina, known as a flying boat due to its unique use of its hull as the main floatation device, was used frequently in the Philippines during World War II. This aircraft was usually crewed by seven to nine individuals and could transport cargo if needed. (US Still Pictures.)

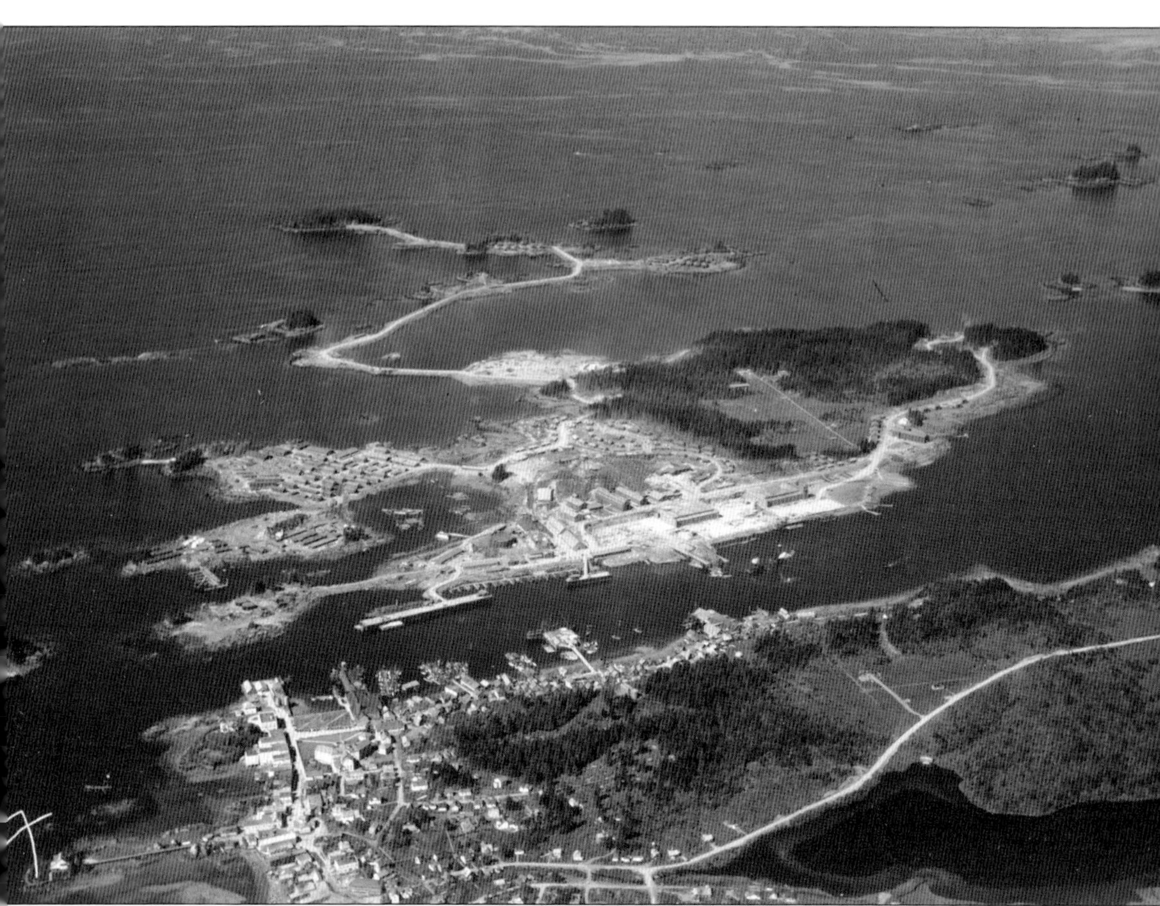

In 1946, the active duty operations ceased, and the base was transferred to the US Navy Pacific Reserve Fleet. To accommodate the increase in aircraft and ships, the base was further expanded to allow for increased training. Many of the sailors who trained on Tongue Point served in Korea on the PBY. Following 1962, the property was transferred to the US Coast Guard and Job Corps. The property is still used for Coast Guard ships on one side. The other side, along with many of the original buildings, including the housing used by the US Navy, is still present and used by Job Corps for young adults 16–24 to learn valuable skills that can translate to lifelong careers. Each Job Corps facility focuses on specific professions, with Tongue Point mostly construction-based training, such as construction, masonry, and electrical. (Naval History and Heritage.)

Two

THE VALLEYS

The valley portion of Oregon consists of two separate valley regions. The Willamette Valley spans from Portland in the north to the Calapooya Mountains south of Eugene. The Willamette Valley is 150 miles long and ranges from 20 to 40 miles wide. This region was called the promised land of milk and honey due to its rich soils and consists of the majority of Oregon's population. It is a region known for its vineyards.

The second valley that encompasses this portion is the Rogue Valley. It starts at the Calapooya Mountains in the north and ends at the Oregon-California border. It sits between the Oregon Coast Mountains to the west and the Cascade Mountains to the east. Originally a fur- and gold-producing region, it is now known for its vineyards and its long agricultural seasons.

This region's defining features are its moderate temperatures, which range from 40 Fahrenheit in the winter to 80 Fahrenheit in the summer. The Rogue Valley does see slightly more extreme temperature variations with fluctuations from 30 Fahrenheit in the winter to 90 Fahrenheit in the summer. Both valleys see rainfall with minimal snowfall. Combined, the valleys range from .3 inches monthly in the summer to 7.5 inches in the winter. The majority of the valley region is at a low elevation of between zero feet and 500 feet above sea level, with the highest elevation at 1,200 feet above sea level.

The military saw potential to train at various locations that were easily accessible to rivers. If the Japanese did decide to attack the mainland in full force, the bases in the valleys would be the first line of defense if the coastal bases were destroyed. These pilots and aircraft were able to train in conditions that were similar to those in parts of the Pacific while also being able to travel to different climates that afforded them broader knowledge. Airfields in the valley region include Albany, Bradwood, Corvallis AAF/NAS, Medford AAF, Portland AAB, Portland AAF Auxiliary, Sand Island AAF, and Salem AAF. Documentation states that bases at Hillsboro AAF and Aurora FS existed; however, no historical imagery was found.

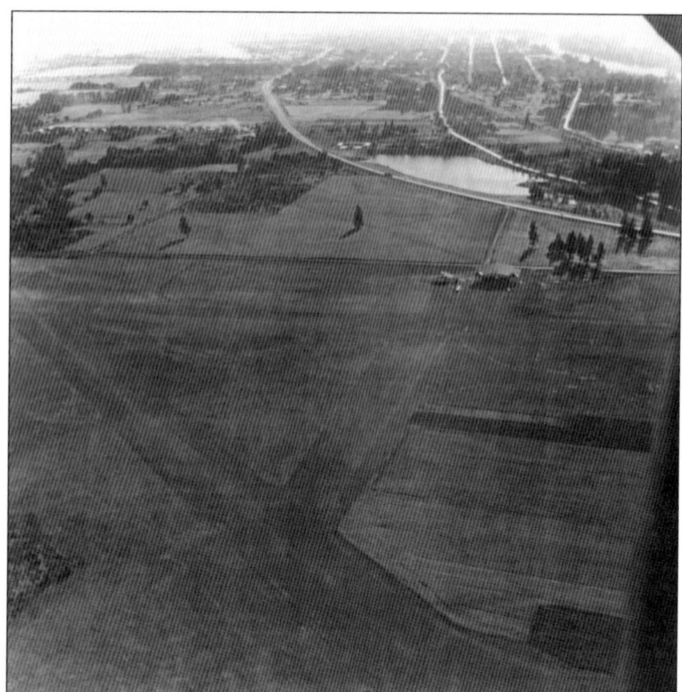

Albany Airport was built in 1929 by private owners who wanted to increase aircraft flights in the region. Less than two years later, the City of Albany realized how profitable an airport could be and bought the land and buildings. The runways in 1941 were flattened earth with three main runways. There was a large hangar as well as a smaller one for short-term storage. (Linn County Historical Society.)

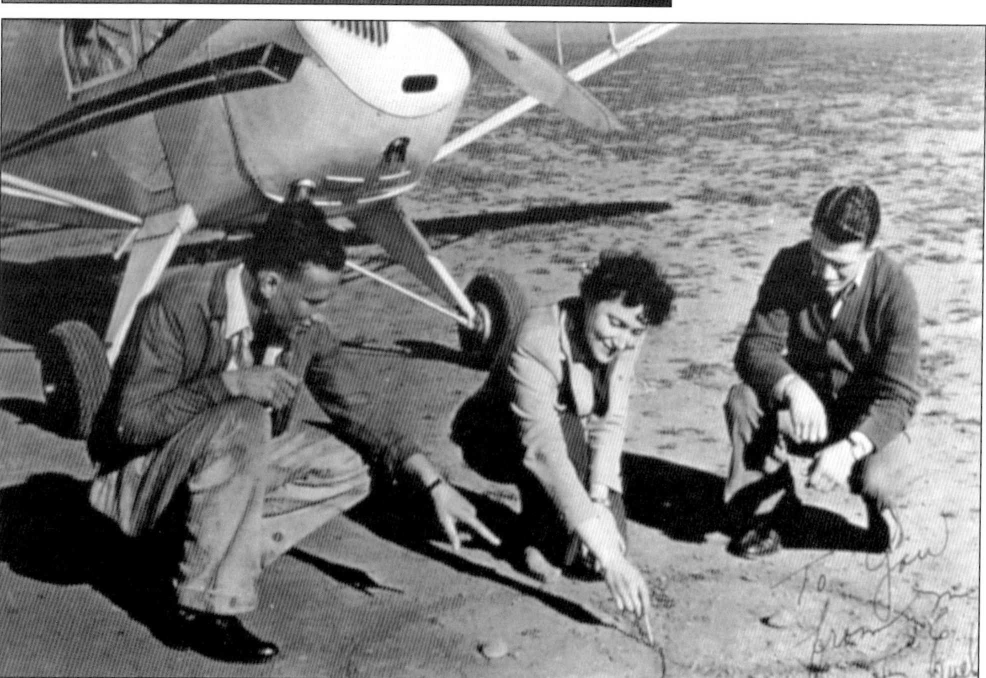

Howard Burleson (left) was an instructor at the Lincoln flying school before meeting his wife, Evelyn (center). Following their marriage, they traveled to North Dakota, where they managed a flying service out of Jamestown Municipal Airport from 1931 until 1937. Wanting to go farther west, they settled in Albany, managing the Albany Airport from 1937 until 1941. He maintained the airport while he and Evelyn trained both men and women students. (Linn County Historical Society.)

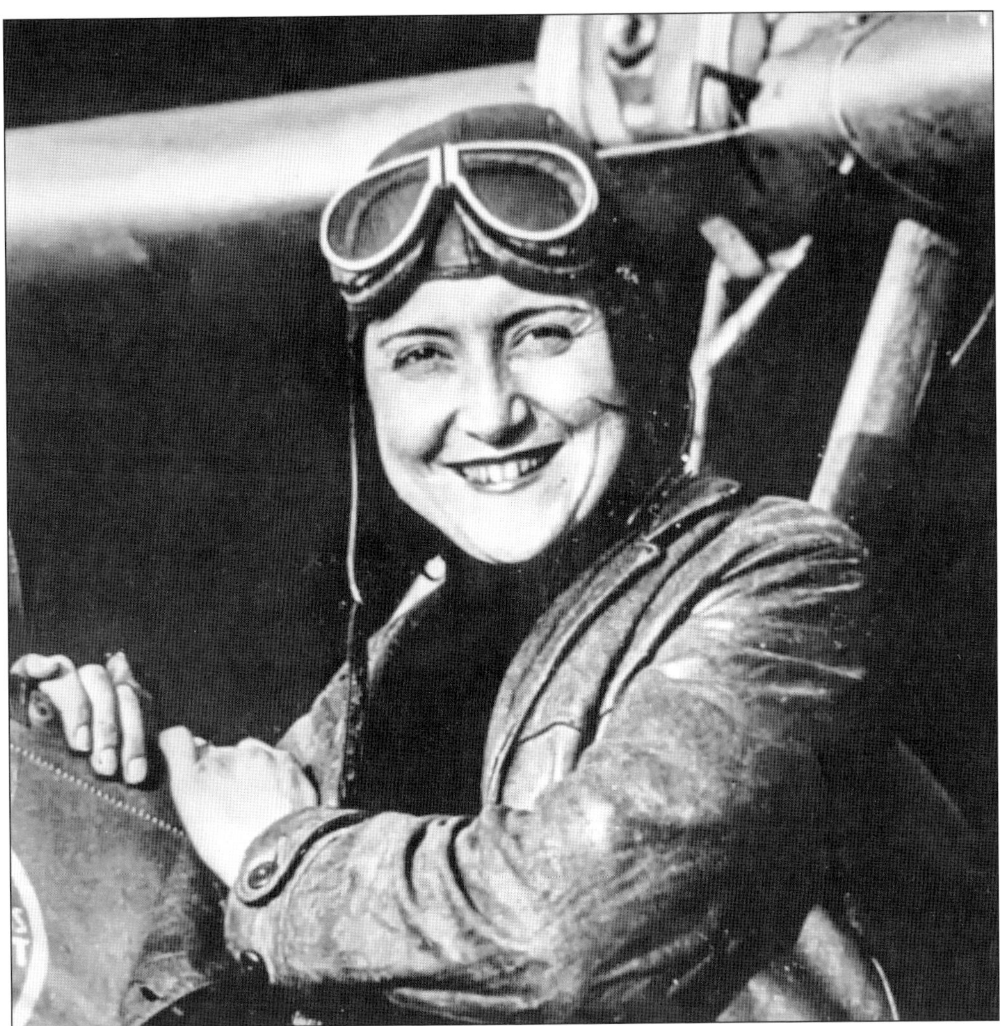

Evelyn Nicholas first saw an aircraft in 1926 and immediately wanted to be in the air. Her parents, worrying about the danger, would not let her, but in 1928, her mother allowed her to begin training even though they felt her desire would fade. It did not, and Evelyn became the first Nebraskan woman to obtain a pilot's license. After marrying her flight instructor, Howard Burleson, they moved to North Dakota, where she became the first licensed woman pilot there. After moving from North Dakota to Oregon in 1937, Howard and Evelyn managed the Albany Airport. It was not until Albany gained access to run a training program that Evelyn found her calling, becoming the second woman in the United States to receive a pilot instructor's license. Her enthusiasm for flying was apparent, and frequently, her classes were full. In 1941, Evelyn set the women's world record for speed and distance by flying nonstop from Vancouver, British Columbia, to Tijuana, Mexico. Although she was recruited by the British during World War II, she instead trained US Army cadets to fly in Alturas, California. (Oregon Aviation Historical Society & Museum.)

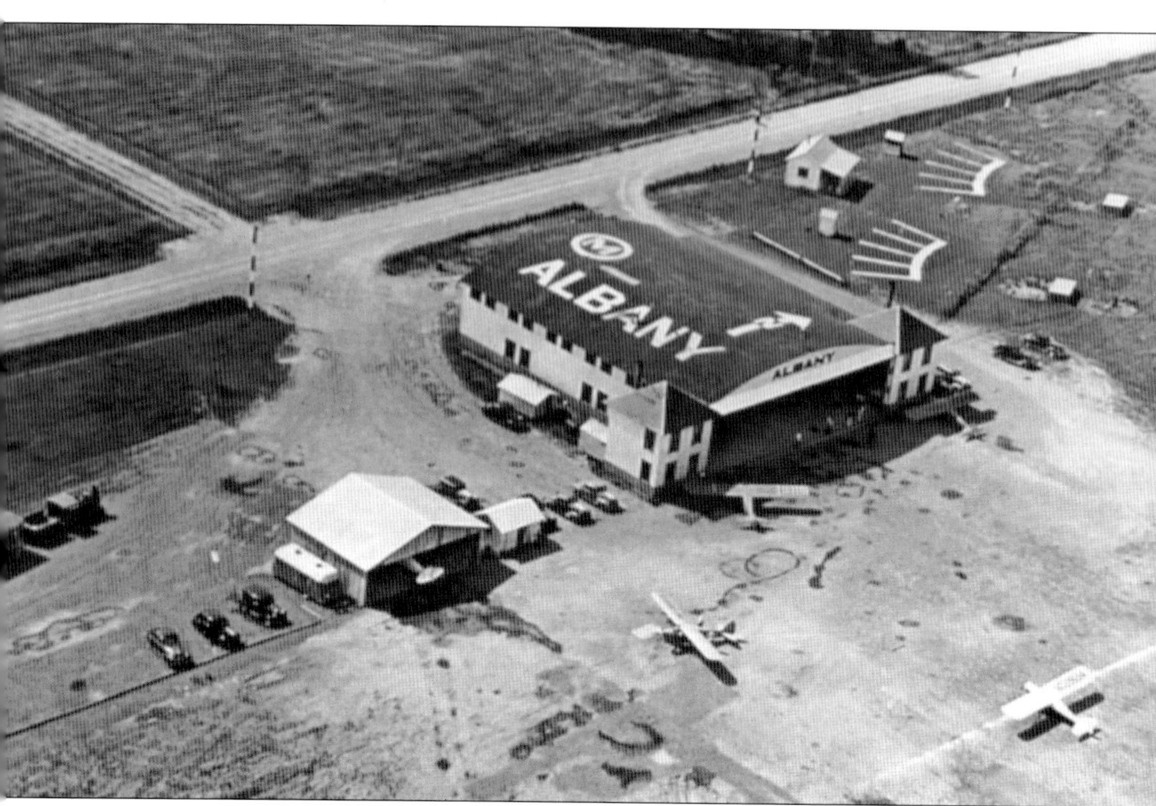

In 1939, with the war efforts expanding quickly into Oregon, the Albany Airport continued to train pilots. Before the military's expansion, it was used for private aircraft and pilot training. Seeing a need for military-qualified pilots, the airport switched from strictly private training to civilian air patrol training. This allowed the pilots, once licensed, to aid in the war effort as well. The hangar that already existed, as seen in the image, was large enough for the aircraft that the military may need to land on the field. Following the military no longer needing Albany Airport as a landing field, the city was returned to complete civilian control, and training continued to happen. The smaller hangar was used for a single aircraft that needed basic maintenance. The larger hangar was used primarily for storage and larger repairs that were needed for the aircraft. (Linn County Historical Society.)

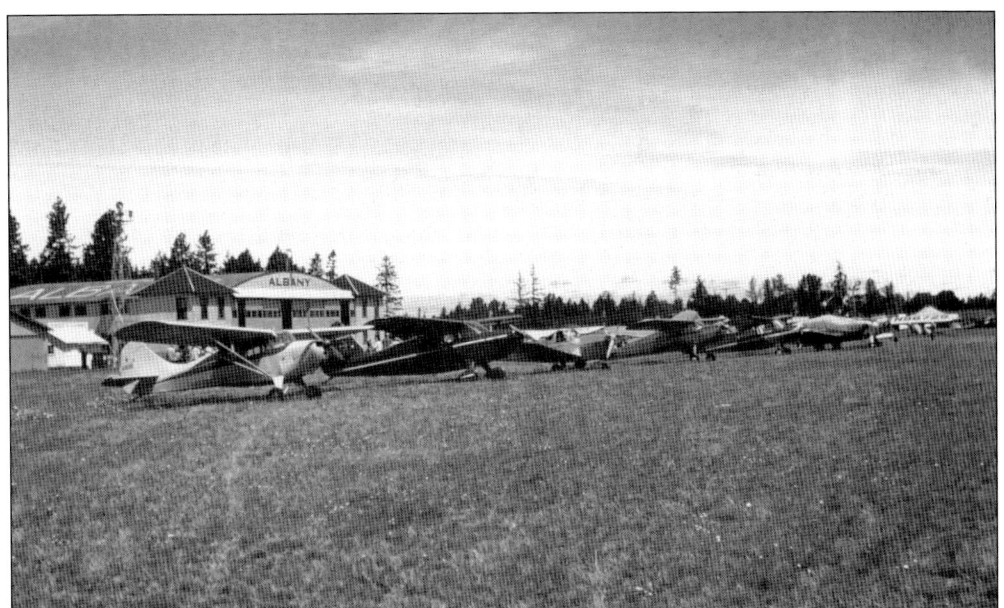

In 1954, the Albany Airport's lease was transferred from Howard Burleson to Harry Macfarlane. Macfarlane was already an established pilot at the airport, using the facilities for crop dusting. Burleson continued to instruct students until 1954 when the lease was transferred, at which point he retired. The airport frequently has fly-ins and other events that allow small aircraft operators the chance to socialize. (Linn County Historical Society.)

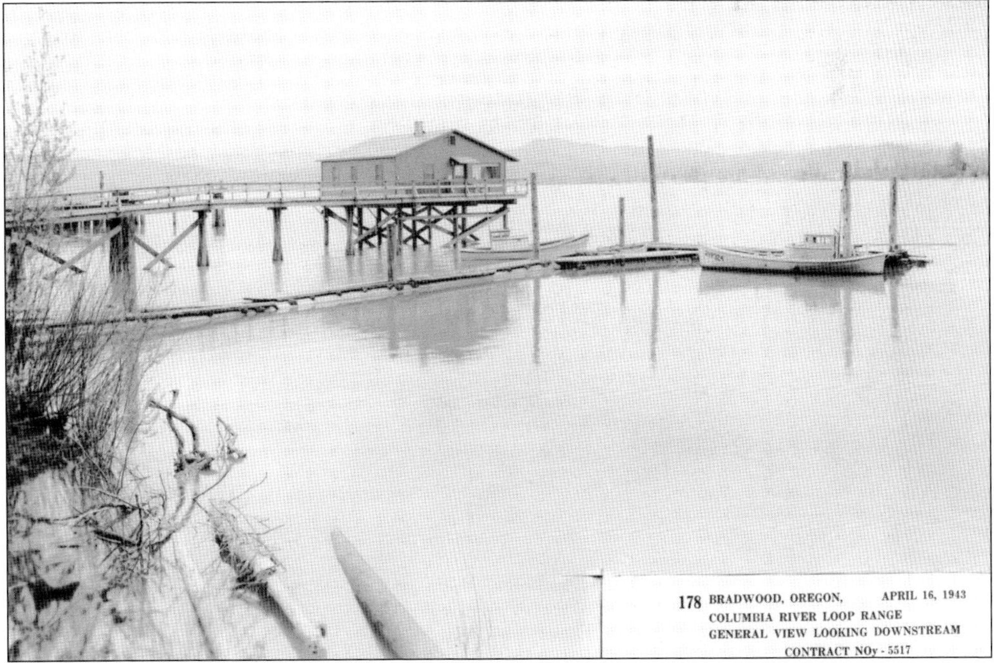

If a float aircraft needed to make an emergency landing, a Navy sub-post was created in the small town of Bradford on the Columbia River. The post was in an area that was calm and had enough room for small- to medium-sized float aircraft. The post consisted of a rudimentary dock along with a building that held naval equipment. The property is now privately owned. (US Still Pictures.)

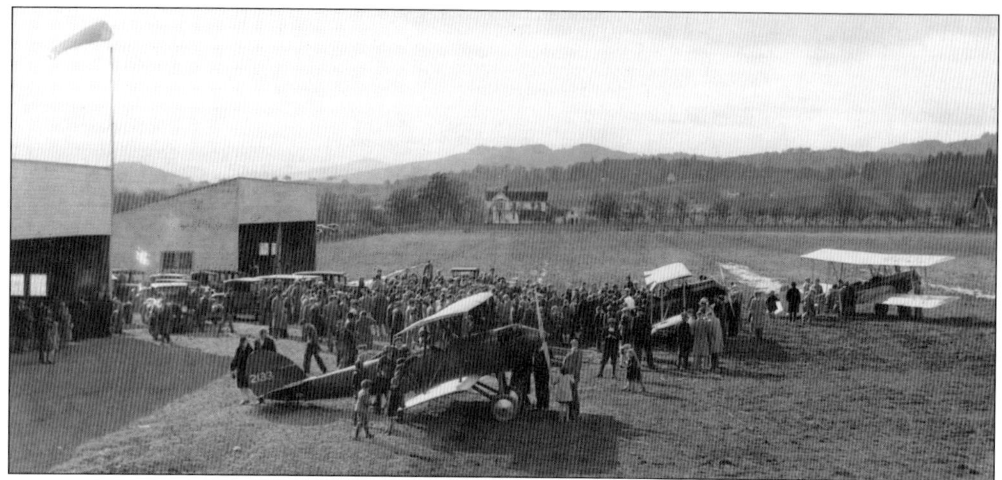

Dick Lyndon and his partner, Albert Parmenter, built this airport starting in the late 1920s. The first was the original Corvallis Airport, where Northwest Highland Avenue is now located. It was shortly abandoned when Parmenter moved to Eugene. Lyndon moved on to build additional airports. The aircraft above are, from left to right, a 1925 WACO Nine, a 1929 American Eagle, and a 1929 Swallow, all locally owned. (Corvallis Historical Images, Special Collections, Oregon State University.)

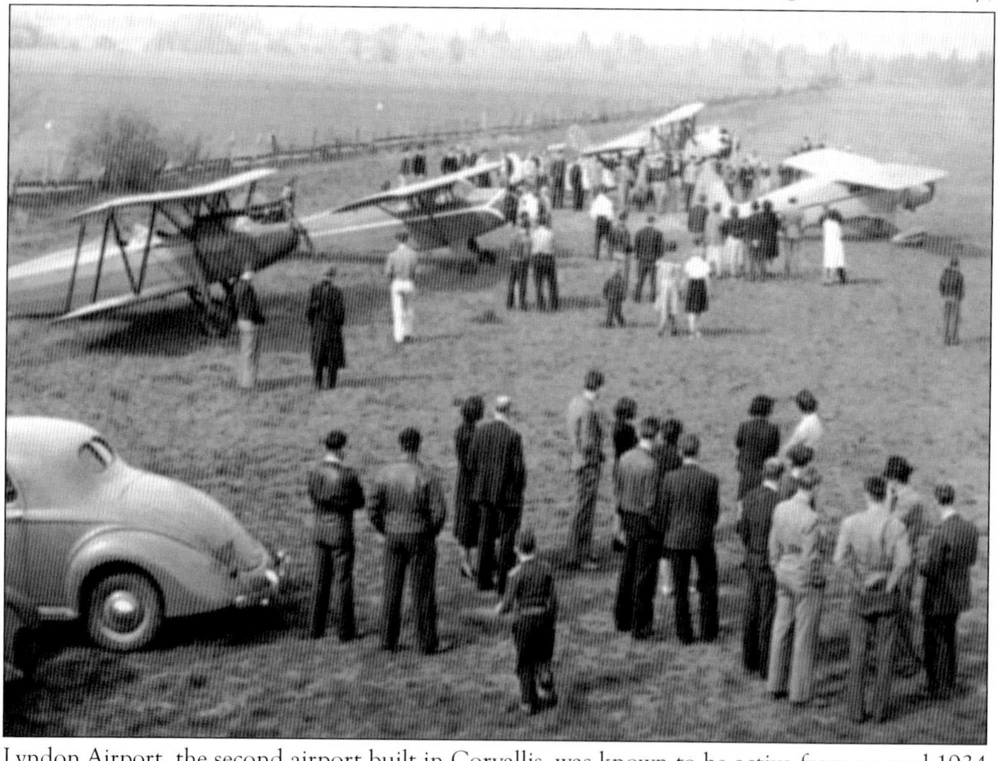

Lyndon Airport, the second airport built in Corvallis, was known to be active from around 1934 until it was abandoned in 1942. Built where Goodnight Avenue now exists, it was similar in size to the original Corvallis Airport and operated by Lyndon Airways. The aircraft above are, from left to right, unidentified, a Rearwing Sportster, a Fairchild 24, a 1936 Alexander Eaglerock, and unidentified. The aircraft were there for a regularly scheduled meetup and fly. (Corvallis Historical Images, Special Collections, Oregon State University.)

The land on which Corvallis AAF was built was originally farmland. While being built, the ground was cleared, and the first thing laid down was the apron. This aerial view of the airfield shows just the runways and a few necessary buildings. The buildings present were off the runway far enough that, in the event of an accident, they would not be affected. (USAF Museum.)

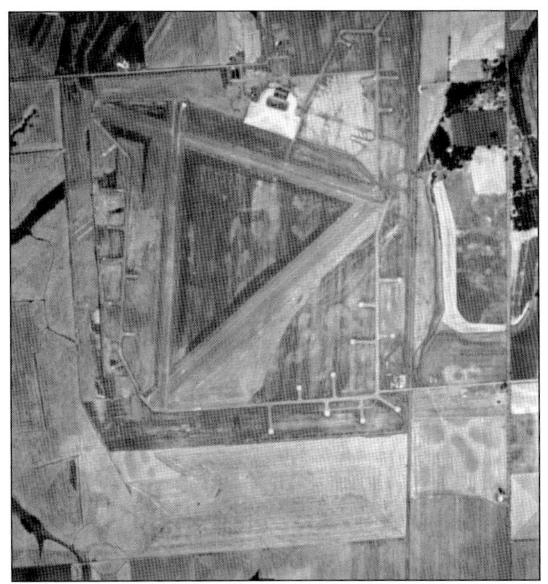

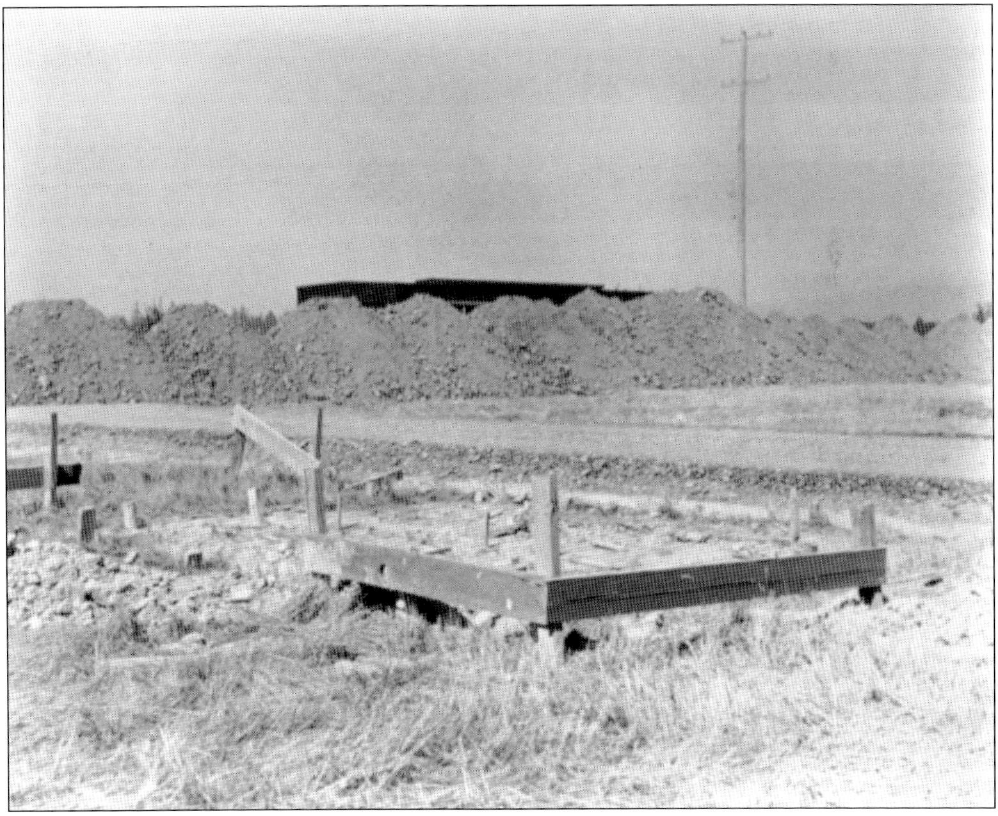

With the land uneven, it was usually necessary to bring in fill material, which is what these large piles of earth are. Behind it is construction housing and a work building. This building was usually on wheels and could be moved when needed to another jobsite or part of an airport. This decreased the need for some contractors to leave the property, which brought security as well as efficiency. (Benton County Museum, 2012-022.0014.)

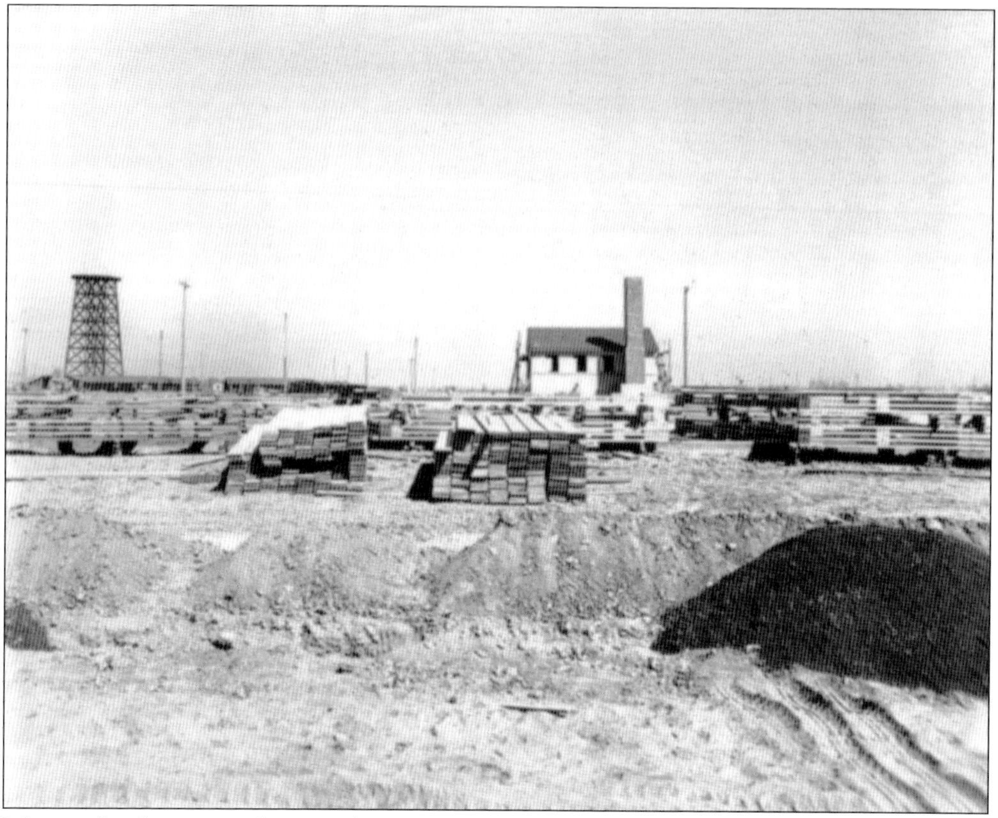

Like at other bases, metal was in short supply, and so much of the construction was made with wood. In the background, one can see the start of the water tower and the Building, Engineering, and Inspection structure. Inspectors and project managers worked in the building. Pallets of wood and other construction materials sat waiting for contractors to use them. Unseen is a dirt road between the woods and the foreground. (Benton County Museum, 2012-022.0023.)

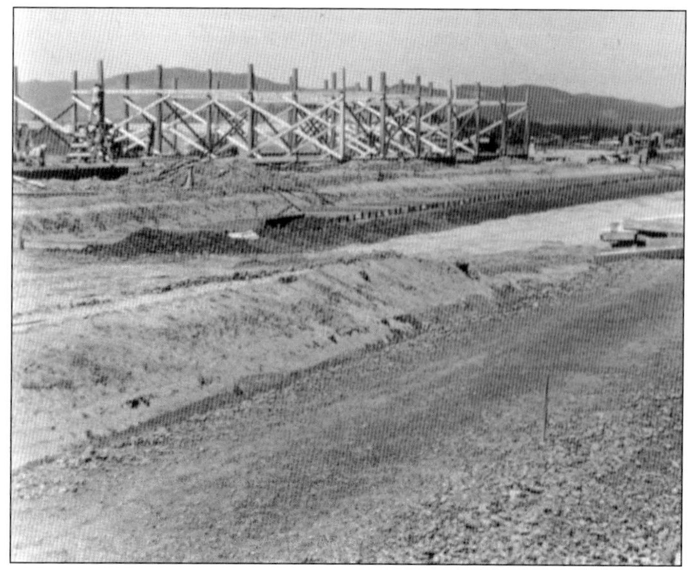

Because of the rudimentary runways and facilities at Corvallis Airport before the US Army came in, there was a lot of construction required. This construction at the end of the switch can be seen in its initial stages. Eventually, this would be a runway along with a building. At times, the military hired local contractors, and at others, they would send out their own engineers to build an airport. (Benton County Museum, 2012-022.0024.)

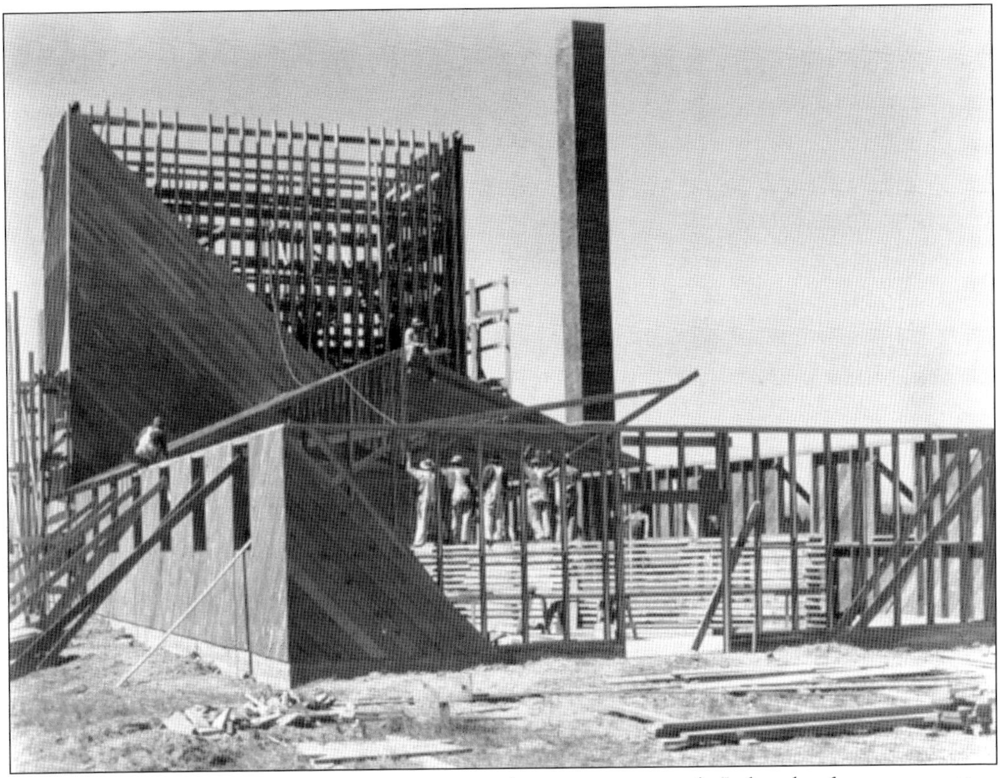

Initially, the air base was not going to accommodate paratroopers, but shortly after construction was finalized, the Army transferred the base to the Marine Corps. A parachute loft was required, and so construction began on that near the mechanic shop. Parachute lofts are used by paratroopers, airborne, smoke jumpers, and hobby skydivers as a location large enough to check the parachutes for damage; repair, clean, and dry them; and then repack them. (Benton County Museum, 2012-022.0025.)

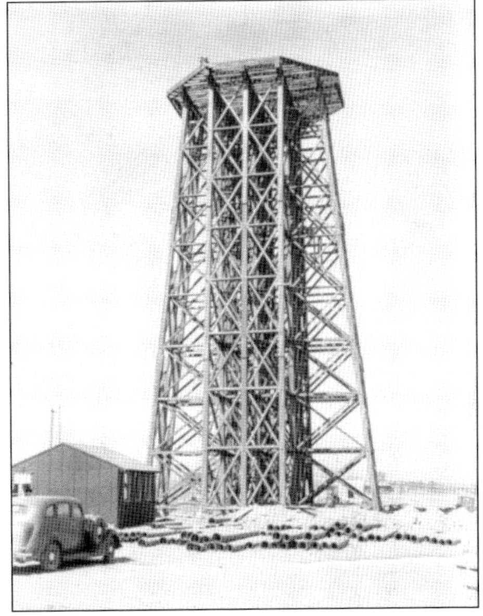

The construction of the Corvallis water tower began shortly after the US Army selected Corvallis as a base location. The water tower supplied water to the base when needed. Construction began in August 1942, and by the winter, all the buildings necessary for flight and operations were completed. The water tower was one of the last things built during construction. (Benton County Museum, 2012-022.0043.)

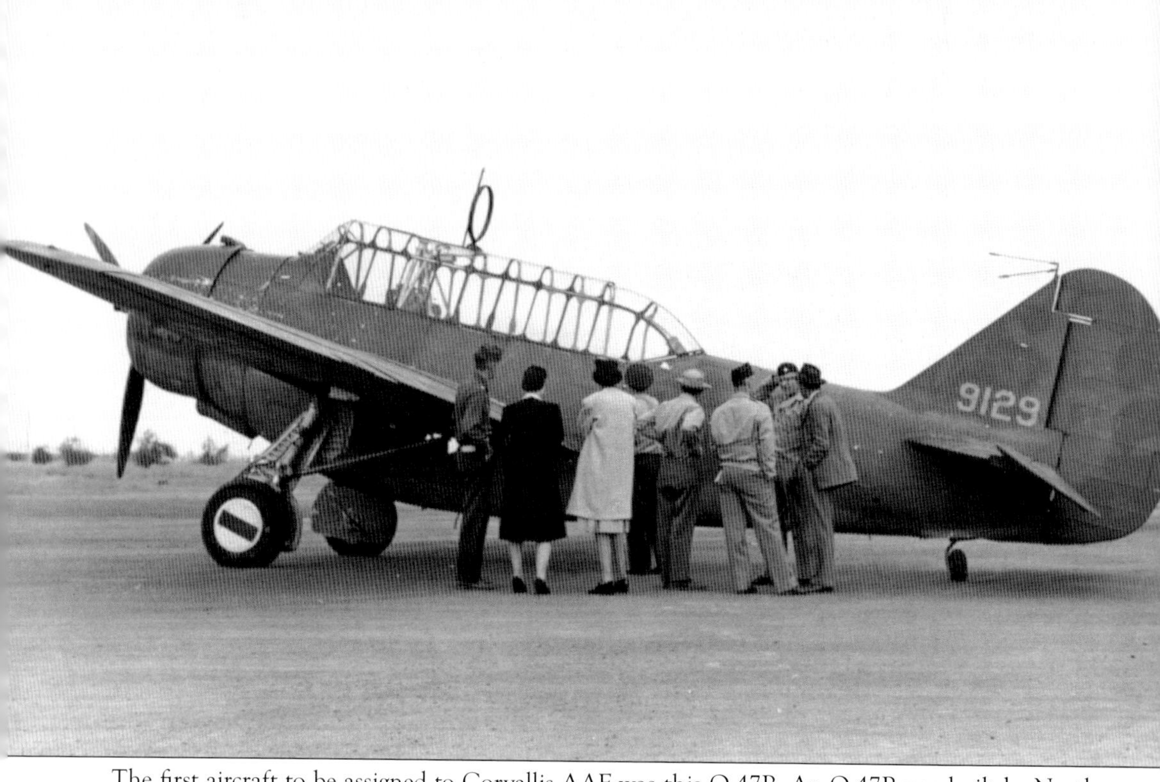

The first aircraft to be assigned to Corvallis AAF was this O-47B. An O-47B was built by North American as a fixed-wing observation aircraft. This aircraft was larger and heavier than previous versions and held three crew in tandem, allowing for someone dedicated to observing, so the pilot can focus on flying. A total of 239 of these aircraft were built specifically for the US Army Air Corps. One unique feature about early observation aircraft was the multiple long-range antennas seen on the cockpit glass. These aircraft were also built with large windows on the cockpit, providing for 360-degree visibility. This specific O-47B was used for training observers who would later be sent overseas. Anti-submarine patrol of the Oregon coast, in conjunction with bases along the coast, helped to give valuable training. The last thing this base was used for was target towing, when a plane tows a target for gun or missile training. (Benton County Museum, 2010-074.0001.01.)

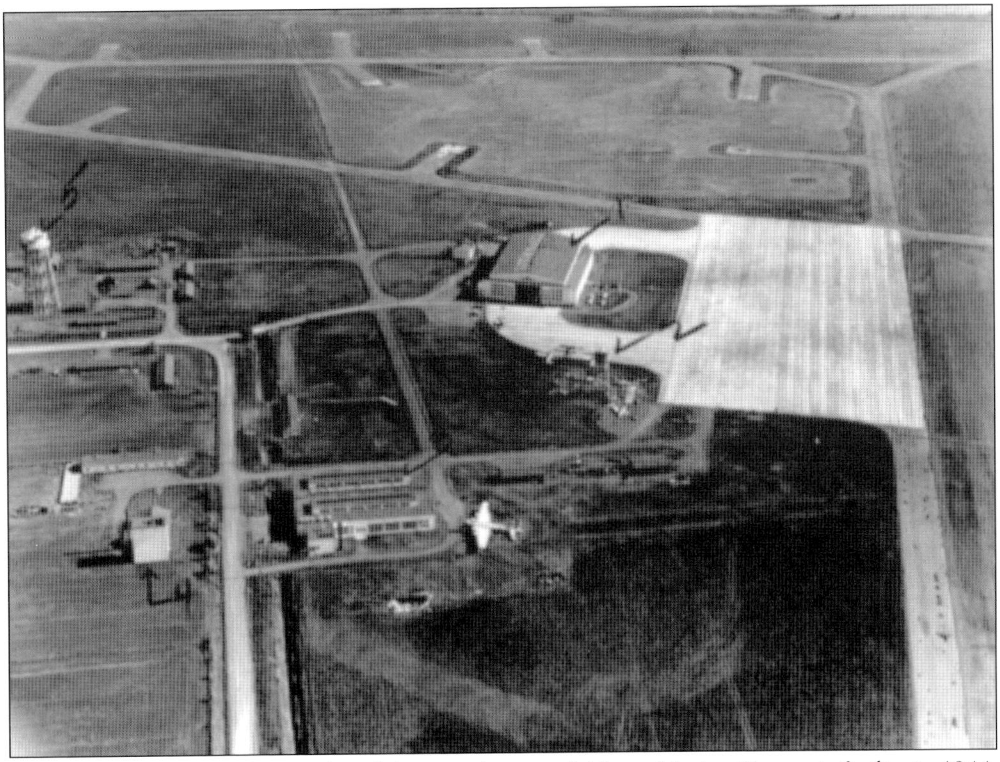

The base was temporarily transferred from an Army airfield to a Marine Corps air facility in 1944. During that time, Marine Aircraft Group 35 was stationed there as part of the Home Defense Network. Corvallis MCAAF's runways were large enough to station big C-46s for use in transport and to deliver paratroopers to hard-to-reach locations due to concerns of fires and balloon bombs. (Benton County Museum, 1985-062.0019C.)

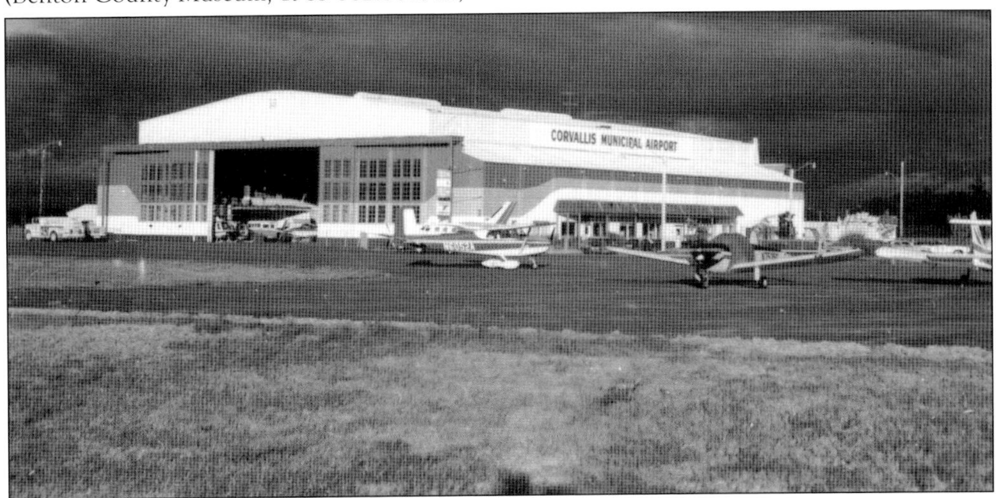

Following the military placing the airfield on surplus, the City of Corvallis regained ownership and changed the name to the Corvallis Municipal Airport. The hangar in the image is the original one used by the Army and Marine Corps during World War II. Civilian airline flights began in 1947. By early 2006, the airport had 154 aircraft based in Corvallis, with mostly private or commercial cargo flights arriving and departing. (Benton County Museum, 1980-002.0313.)

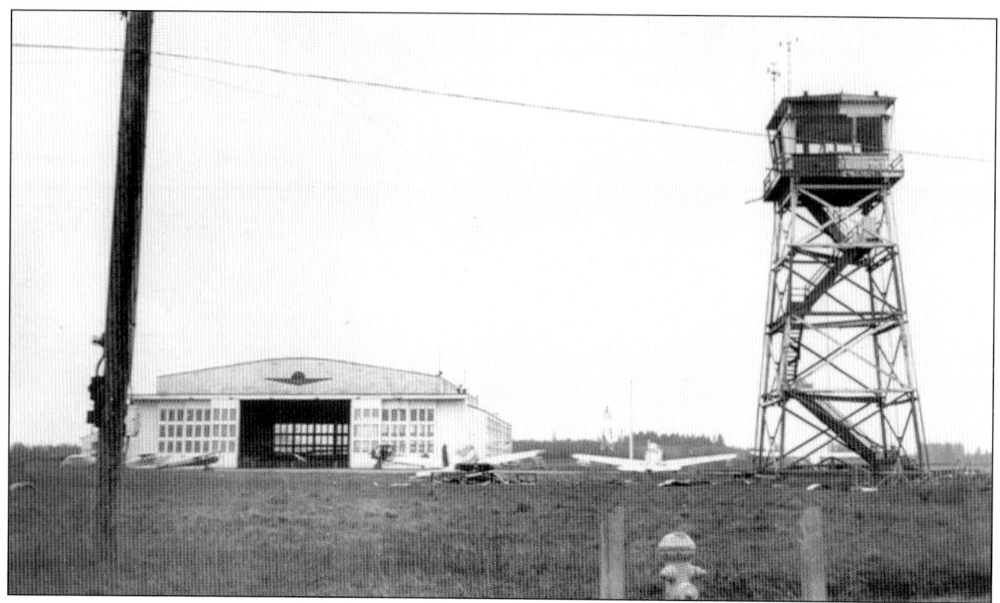

Depending on the location and needs of the military, when a base is considered surplus, many of the buildings and infrastructure stay with the land unless it has classified or sensitive information in it. When the military left Corvallis, the City of Corvallis not only got a newer airport, but the hangar and control tower were still usable and in good shape. (Benton County Museum, 185-062.0019E.)

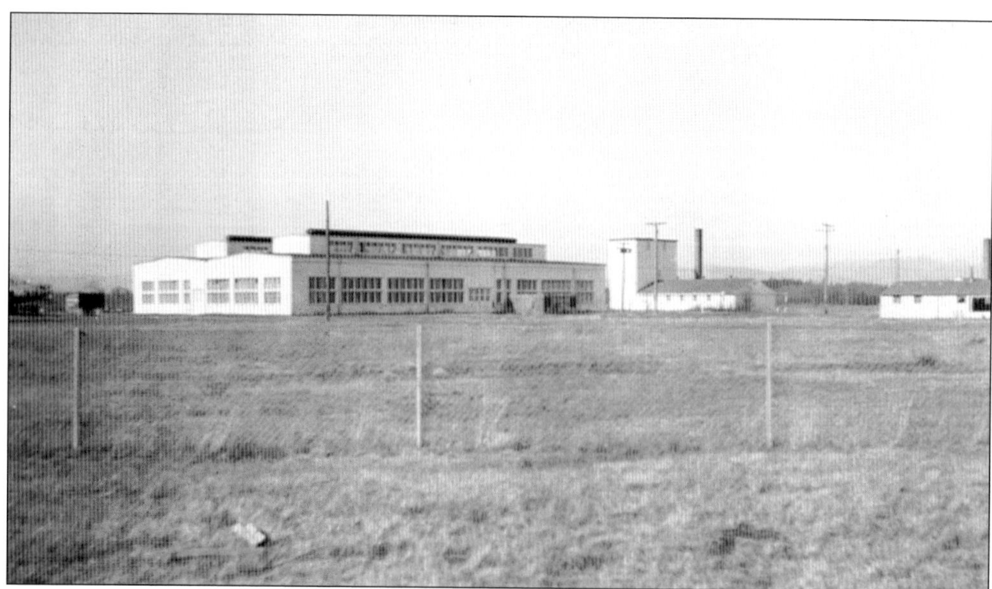

Another set of buildings accessible and usable were the machine shop and parachute loft. Since the Marines stationed there participated in home defense, it was required that they be able to jump into remote areas of Oregon. After jumping, the parachute loft was used to repair, dry, and repack parachutes so they could be used again. After leaving, the loft was used by local private companies. (Benton County Museum, 1985-062.0019G.)

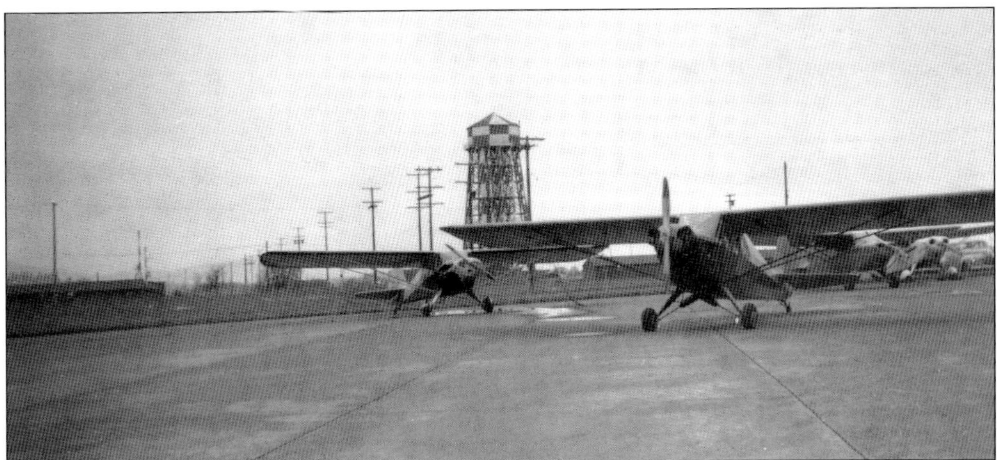

With established buildings and a runway, the first private and commercial aircraft moved in to Corvallis shortly. In 1947, there were already numerous small private aircraft, and West Coast moved in as well. These Piper aircraft are on the apron with the power lines and water tower in the background. The hangar is directly behind the photographer. For those with aircraft living near Corvallis, it was convenient to land and be able to drive home. (Benton County Museum, 1983-001.0031P.)

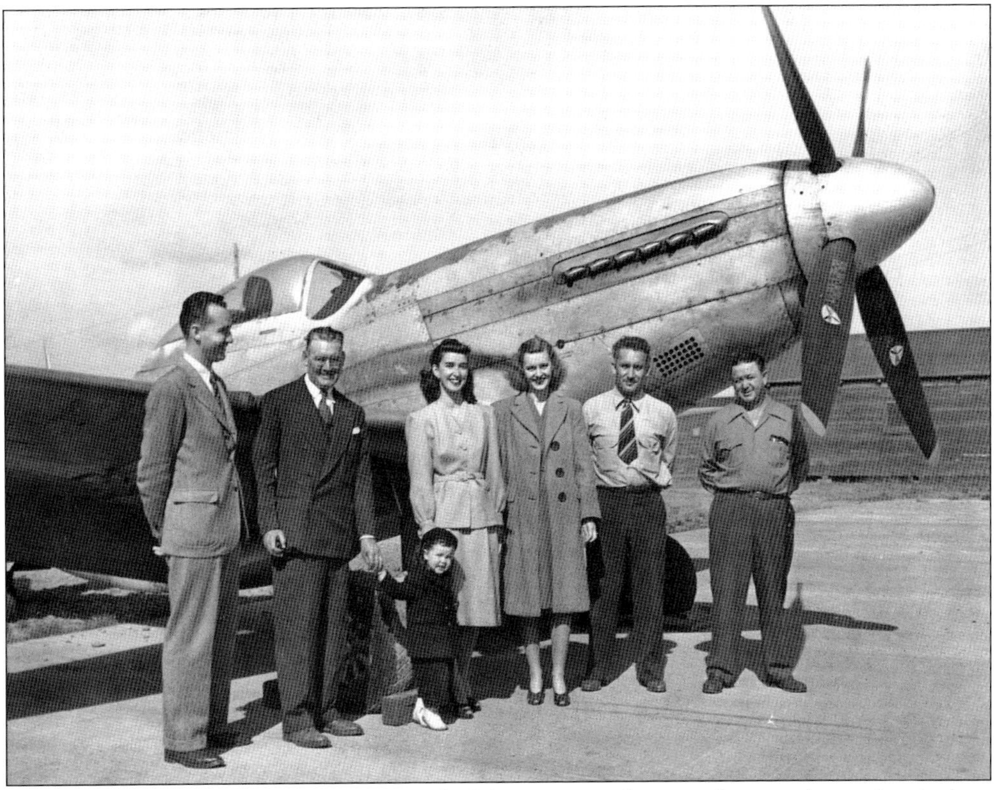

After the City of Corvallis regained control of the airport, it began to host air shows. An air show is an event where the public can attend to see aircraft that they may otherwise never be able to see. This P-51 Mustang, used as a fighter in World War II, is on the apron, allowing the public to come up and see it. (Benton County Museum, 1987-019.0001.)

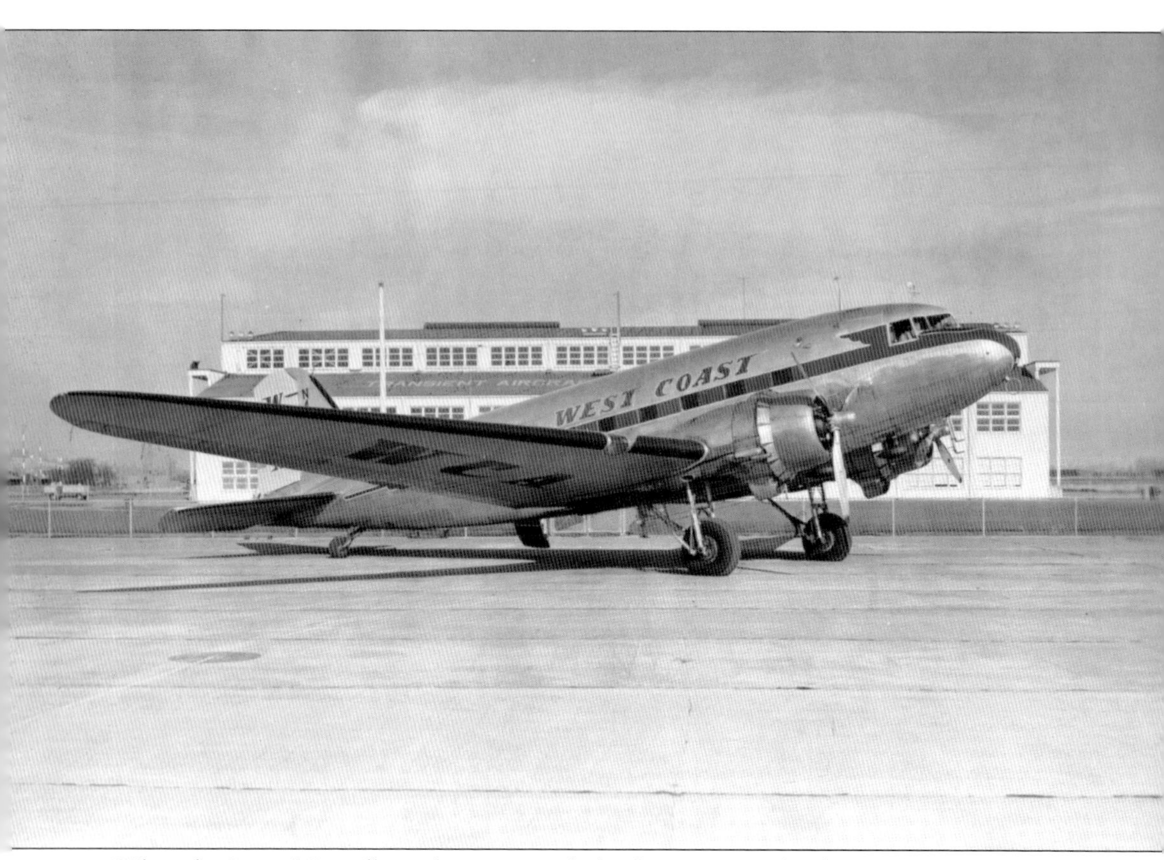

When the City of Corvallis took over control, the first company that leased the airport was West Coast, an airline that performed both civilian transportation and commercial cargo flights. The company moved into the Corvallis Airport in 1947, which increased the area's ability to engage in air travel. After the war, there were hundreds of companies that were quickly sold, merged, or went out of business as prices increased. West Coast was no different, with its history running through many mergers and acquisitions. West Coast first acquired Empire Air Lines in 1952. In 1968, Pacific and Bonanza airlines merged with West Coast to become Air West, which changed to Hughes Airlines in 1970. Then Republic Airlines bought it and merged with Southern Airways. Northwest purchased Republic and merged with Delta in 2010 to become Delta-Northwest. The name is gone, but the legacy of the company lives on through Delta-Northwest. (Benton County Museum, 2008-090-0608.)

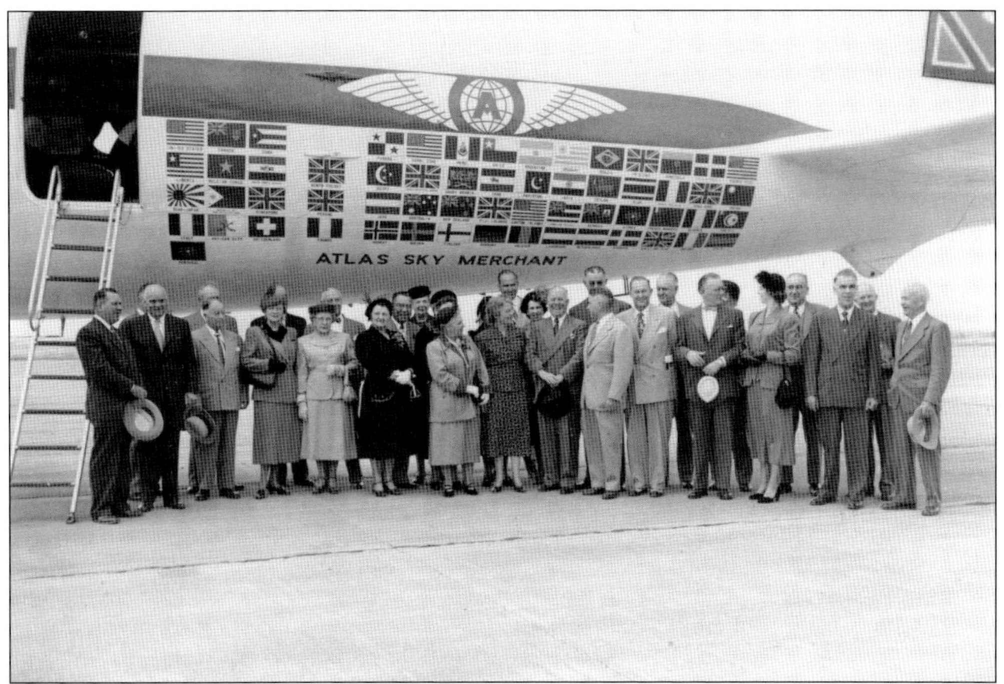

With Corvallis being a large airport and near the state capital, many different companies would use the airport when traveling. Atlas Sky Merchant flew around the world as a publicity stunt following World War II. It would collect postmarks from different states and countries and then add country flags. Gov. Douglas McKay (center, tan suit by man with black hat) and his wife, Mabel (center, floral dress, looking to her husband), are seen standing in front of the aircraft along with other officials. (Benton County Museum, 1999-104.0018.)

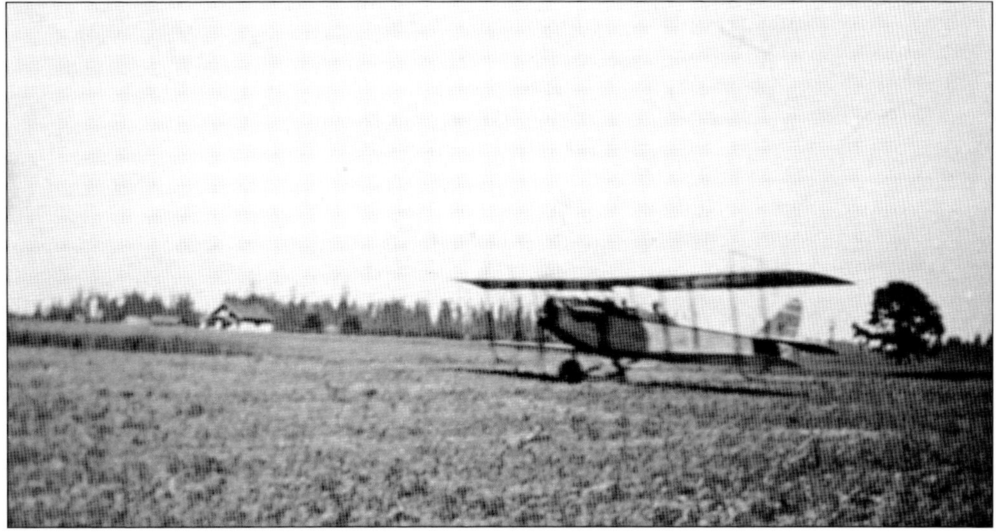

Founded in 1928, Hillsboro Airport was frequently used for commercial purposes. During World War II, the Army Air Corps determined that it would be used as an auxiliary airport for Portland AAB. With two runways and a hardpack surface, it was a close enough location that anyone traveling to Portland needing to divert could do so without serious consideration to fuel needs. It is now Portland Hillsboro Municipal Airport. (Pacific University.)

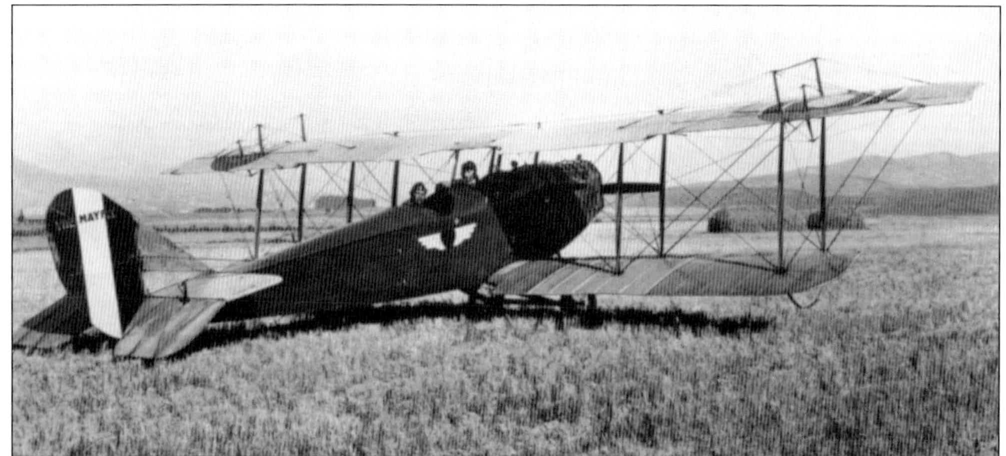

The land that eventually became Newell Barber Field was flat enough that aircraft had been landing there for decades by the time the US Army took over. This biplane, a Curtiss JN-4 "Jenny," landed in Medford on August 13, 1918, as one of the first aircraft to land on the freshly cultivated field. This was the start of a quickly growing interest in aircraft in the Medford region. (National Archives and Records Administration.)

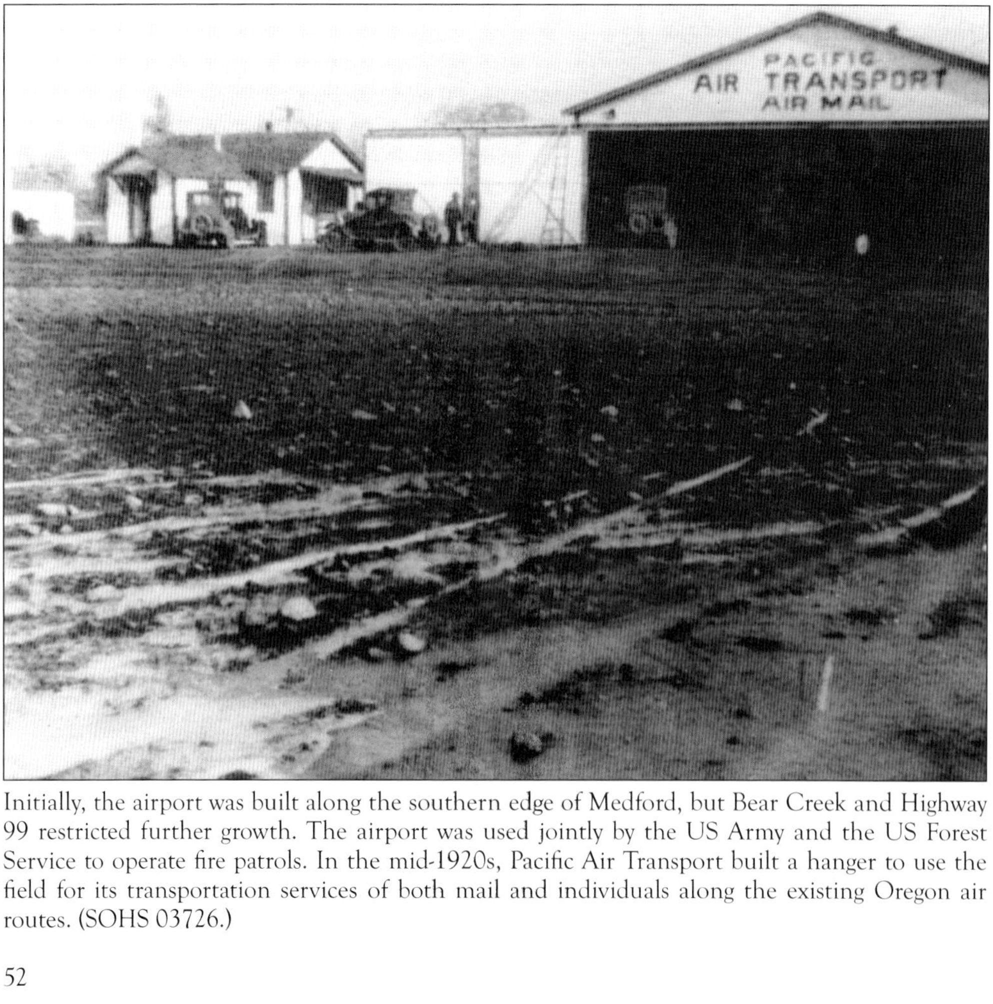

Initially, the airport was built along the southern edge of Medford, but Bear Creek and Highway 99 restricted further growth. The airport was used jointly by the US Army and the US Forest Service to operate fire patrols. In the mid-1920s, Pacific Air Transport built a hanger to use the field for its transportation services of both mail and individuals along the existing Oregon air routes. (SOHS 03726.)

Created in 1920 officially by the City of Medford, Newell Barber Field, named after a local pilot who was killed during World War I, was the first designated airfield in Oregon. In 2016, the City of Medford, along with the Jackson County Airport Authority, placed this stone at the end of the original runway. This monument marks the history of the field and further recognizes Barber. (Author's collection.)

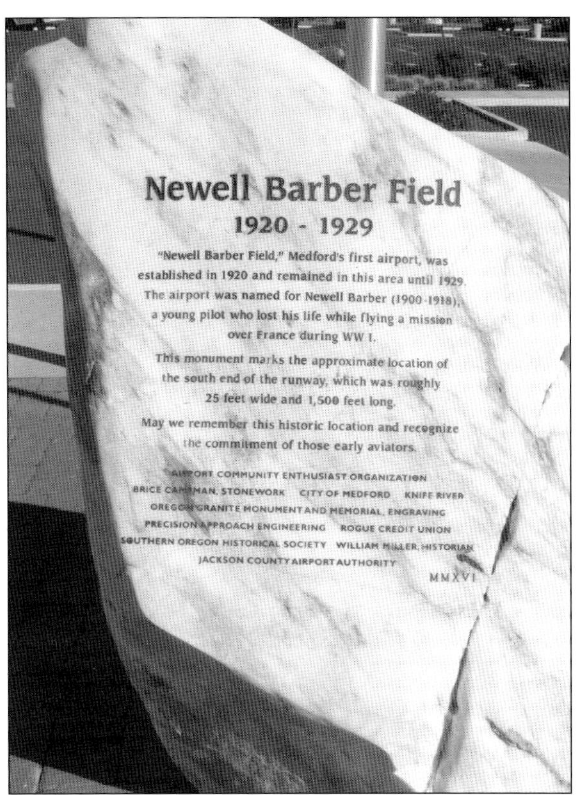

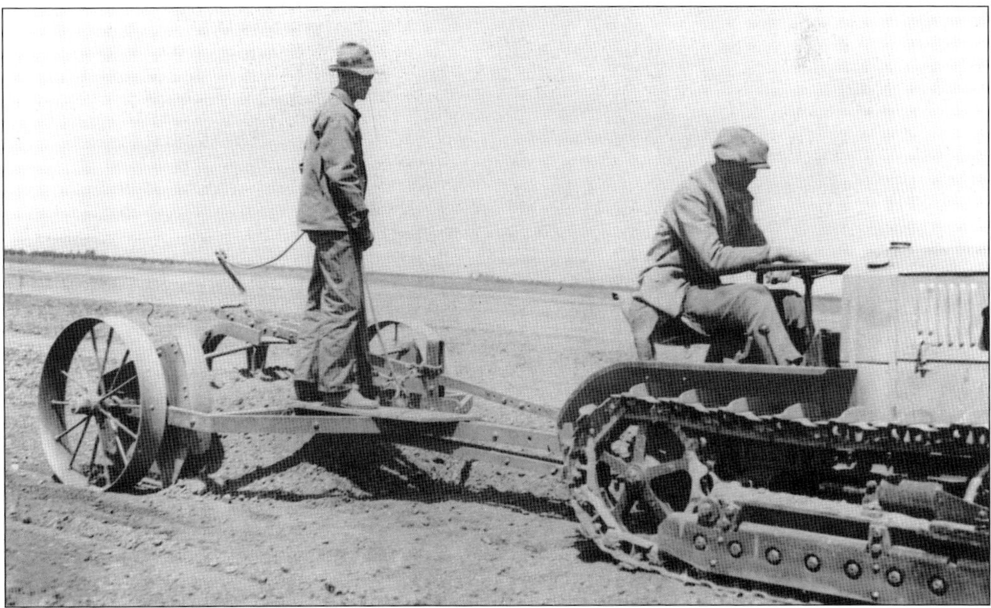

Even though pilots could land at Newell Barber Field, as aircraft became larger, Medford realized that it needed to have an established larger airport if it wanted to compete with other towns and cities in Oregon. In 1929, the City of Medford submitted a ballot measure to voters to create the Medford Municipal Airport north of Medford. It passed, with grading and construction beginning shortly. (SOHS 20707.)

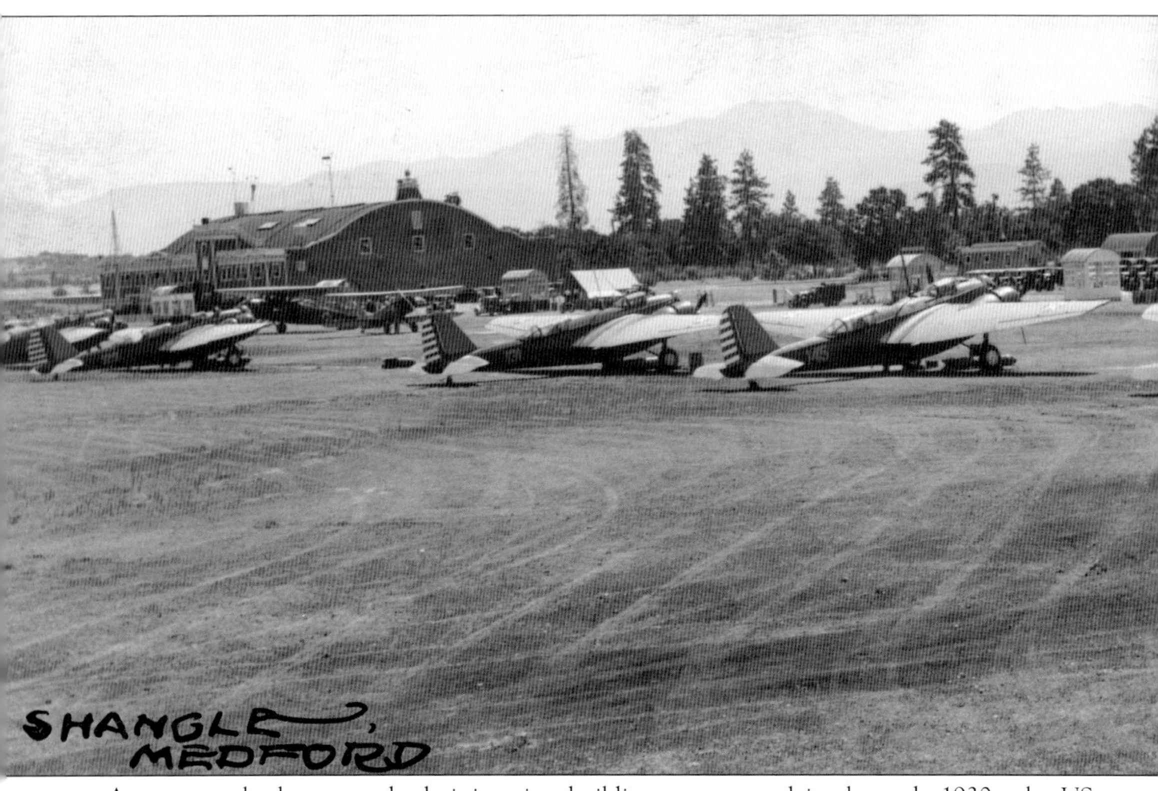

As soon as the hangar and administration building were erected in the early 1930s, the US Army began to station units for short training exercises. This unit of Martin B-10s with the 9th Bombardment Group was assigned to the 31st Bombardment Squadron. The first all-metal monoplane to be regularly used by the US Army was introduced to service in June 1934. This specific group of aircraft was stationed at Medford for a week in 1935 to perform bombing

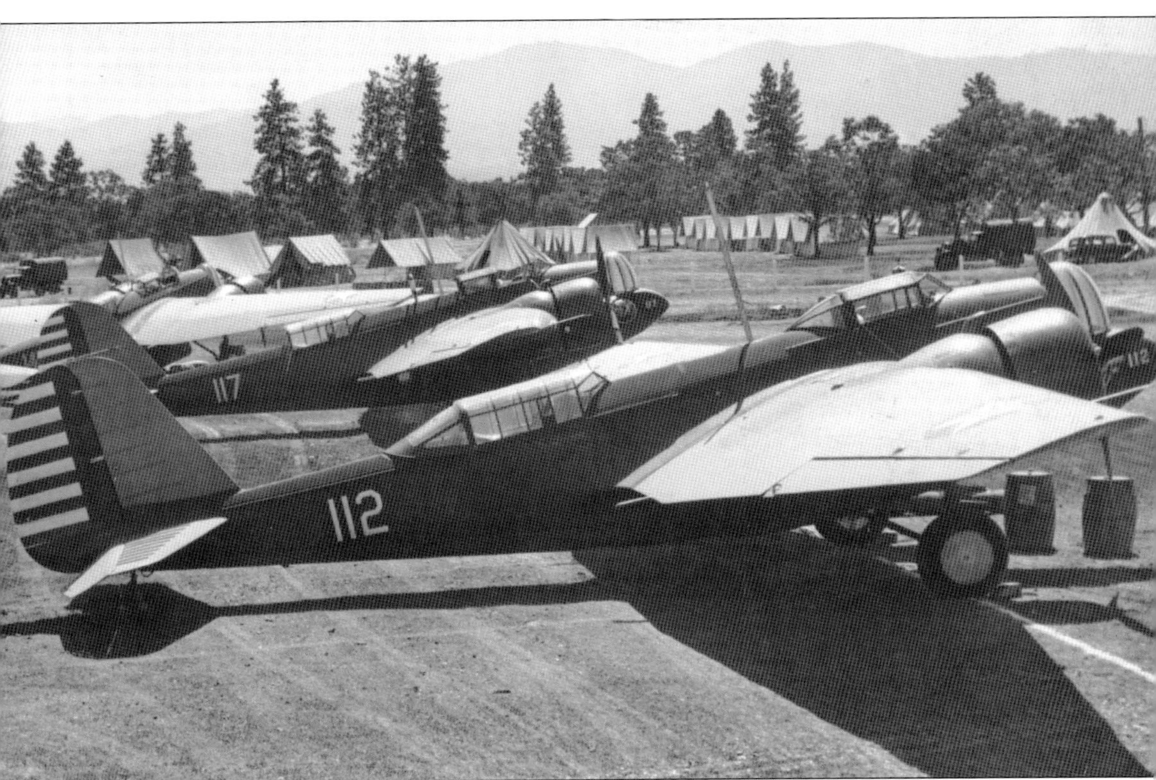

exercises. With few buildings constructed, the pilots and crews slept in tents that were set up just off the tarmac. It was not just the flight crews that gained experience, but repair and maintenance crews were given the opportunity to learn in noncombat situations. (Oregon Historical Society, OHS 0026P177.)

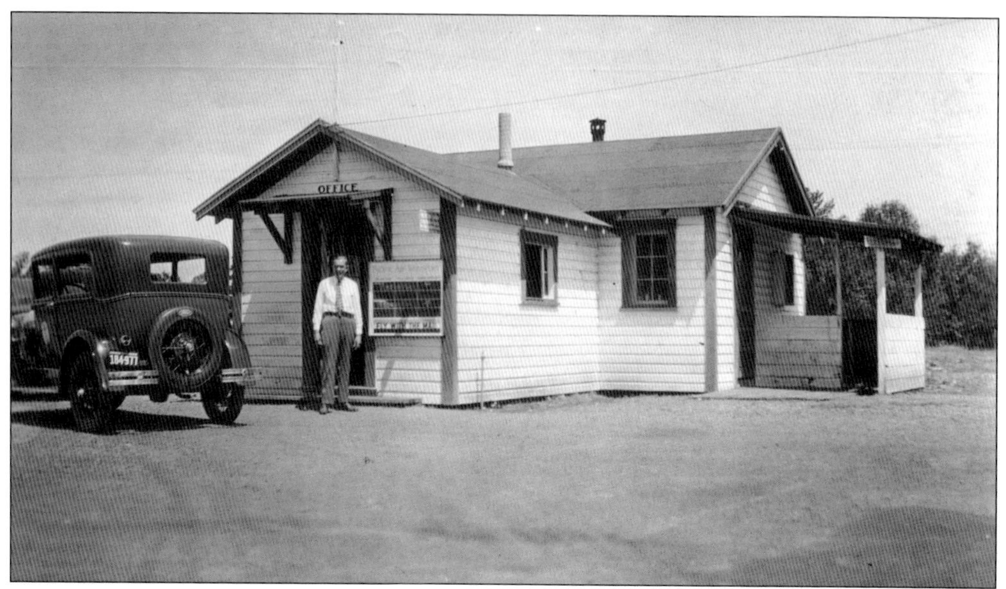

Sometimes, the newly built airport was small enough that the manager would also be a mechanic or other employee. With mail being transported by air, Medford was a hub for southern Oregon. Seely Hall stands in front of the airport office in the mid-1930s. The sign beside him shows the mail schedules and when someone could expect the arrival and departure of the aircraft. (SOHS 00957.)

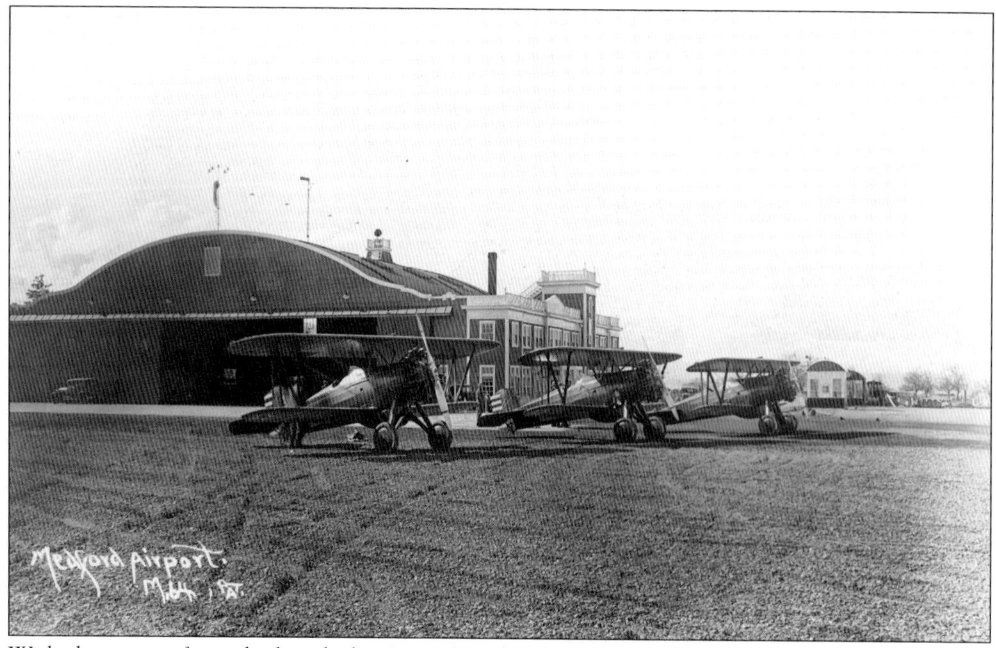

With the money from the bond, the City of Medford built a joint administration building along with a hangar. Three small aircraft sit on the leveled land in front of it. This photograph was taken by Doris Slater, who sent the image to her son Cecil Cross in Twin Springs, Idaho. Enlisting in the Navy at 17, Cecil served on a B-24 in the South Pacific. (SOHS 2005.3.1.)

MEDFORD

SURPLUS

HISTORICAL DATA - POST, CAMP, STATION OR AIR FIELD

NAME: Medford Army Air Field

Location: 4 miles north of Medford, Oregon

Post Office: Medford, Oregon Telegraph Office: Medford, Oregon Radio available: Yes [X] No [ ]

Railroad Station: Medford, Oregon Express Station: Medford, Oregon Acquired by:

Class Installation: III Assignment: GF [ ] SF [ ] AF [X] WD [ ] Capacity: Troops 688

Hospital Beds

Adm. Control: Air Materiel Command Storage (Sq. Ft.) 9804

Land Acres 190

Nearest Landing Field: Date Occupied 1945

HISTORY:

Airdromes and their installations at Medford, Oregon, are assigned to the Fourth Air Force - AG 580.82 (7-27-42)MR-AF-PM-M, dated July 30, 1942.

Air Facilities at Medford, Oregon, are designated by the 4th Air Force as "Army Airdromes, Med, Oregon" - assigned to the 4th Air Force - designated as an auxiliary field of Portland AAB - Hqs. 4th Air Force, GO #104, dated September3, 1942.

Airdromes and their installations at Municipal Airport, Medford, Oregon are assigned to the Second Air Force - per WD Memo No. W95-22-42, dated October 13, 1942.

The AAF station located 5 miles north of Medford, Oregon is designated as Medford Army Air Field - Post Office: Medford, Oregon - WD Memo No. W95-34-42, dated December 23, 1942.

Assigned to the Third Air Force - WD Memo No. W95-3-43, dated February 8, 1943.

Medford AAF Havingbeen assigned to the Third Air Force is reassigned to the Fourth Air Force - joint use by the Third Air Force - WD Memo No. W95-3-43, Changes #5, dated April 2, 1943. Also see WD Memo No. W95-17-43, dated July 7, 1943.

Sub-Post of Portland Army Air Base, Oregon.

Medford Army Air Field, Medford, Oreg. is assigned to the Air Service Command (joint use Third Air Force). - per WD Circular #46 dated 2 February 1944. Not fully utilized and available for reassignment.

Pursuant to instructions contained in letter, Hqs, AAF, dated 9 December 1943, Medford Army Air Field, Oreg. is transferred from the jurisdiction of the Fourth Air Force to the Air Service Command effective 20 January 1944. - per letters, Hqs, ASC, Patterson Field, Ohio dated 30 December 1943 and 21 January 1944 (C). **(Designation for Stand-by Status)**

Medford Army Air Field, Ore. placed on stand-by status. - per List of Temporarily Inactive Stations, AAF, as of 1 August 1944.

Medford AAF, Ore. is temporarily inactive - per List of Temporarily Inactive Stations, Army Air Forces as of 1 October 1944 (C).

Medford Army Air Field, Ore. (temporarily inactive) is assigned to the Air Technical Service Command - per WD Circular #29 dated 24 January 1945.

(over)

HISTORICAL DATA REFERENCE:

Military Reservations, dated [ ]

Construction and Real Estate Progress Report, C. of E, dated 4-30-43 [X]

Chief of Transportation Routing Instructions 10-15-43 [X] & Ch #58, 11-20-43.

Headquarters Army Air Forces Sta Housing Rept, as of 10-15-43 [X]

Headquarters Army Service Forces [ ]

Medford Army Airfield was assigned to the Fourth Air Force on July 30, 1942, before being moved around to different units. Before the eventual status of inactive in 1945, the base would be redesignated and assigned more than five times due to the needs of the Army and where most of the aircraft needed to be placed. Many of the units were transport and air mobility. (Air Education and Training Command History Office.)

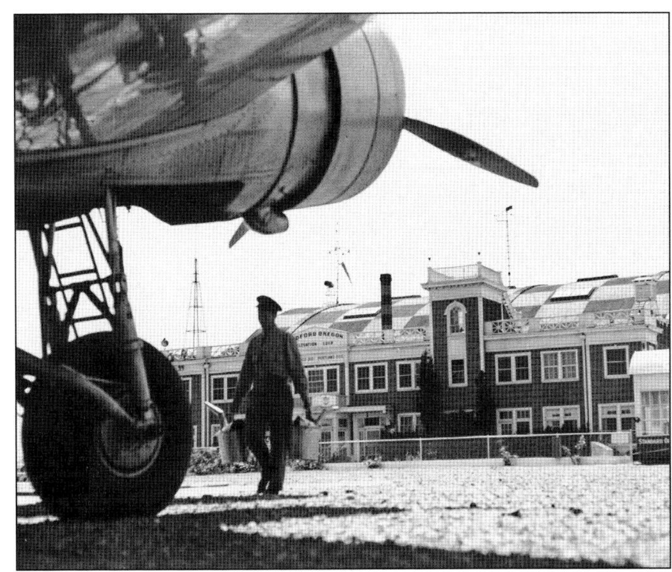

Before the United States officially entered the war, there were many units that were training for the eventuality that war was coming. The administration building, which also doubled as the hangar, was large enough for units that were transferring into their new station, or for those just stopping for a week or two for training. An unidentified man is seen walking from the administration building toward an observation aircraft. (Oregon Historical Society, OHS 0026P178.)

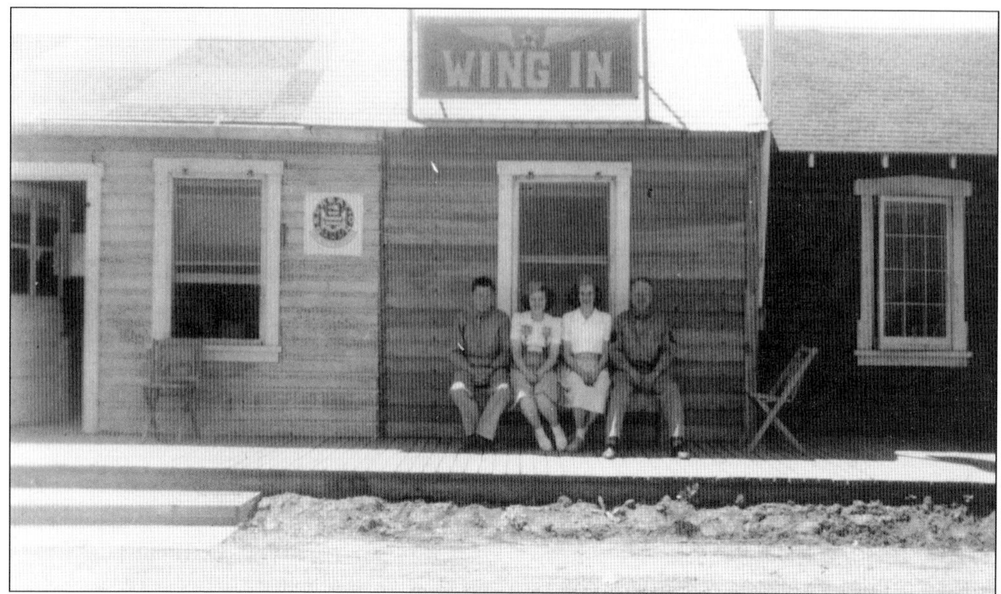

When the Army moved in, so did some of the comforts for pilots and other service members. The canteen, a recreational building, was a space for on-base civilian populations and military personnel to relax. Some canteens sold alcohol, and the majority were staffed by local civilians. Medford AAF built its own canteen, aptly named the Wing In. Pat Thompson, second from left, and possibly Kat Conroy, third from left, sit on a bench with two unidentified service members. (SOHS 16807.)

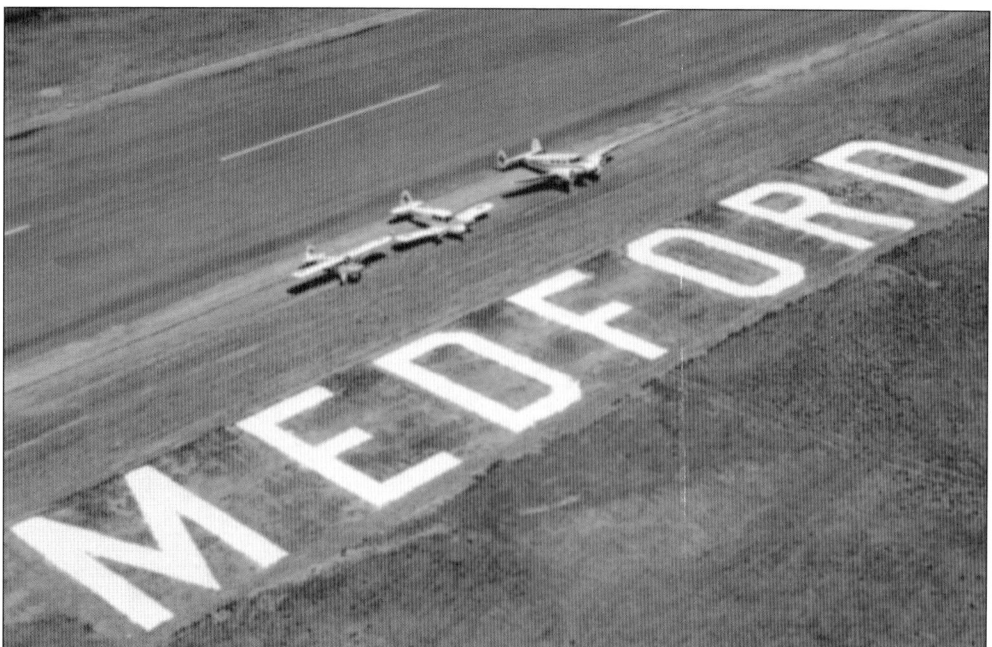

On October 1, 1944, the US Army put the Medford AAF on inactive status as it was no longer needed for training or repair and maintenance. On January 24, 1945, while still inactive, it was assigned to the Air Technical Services Command as a location for a command post. To this day, there are still some military activities at the airport. (MercyFlights.)

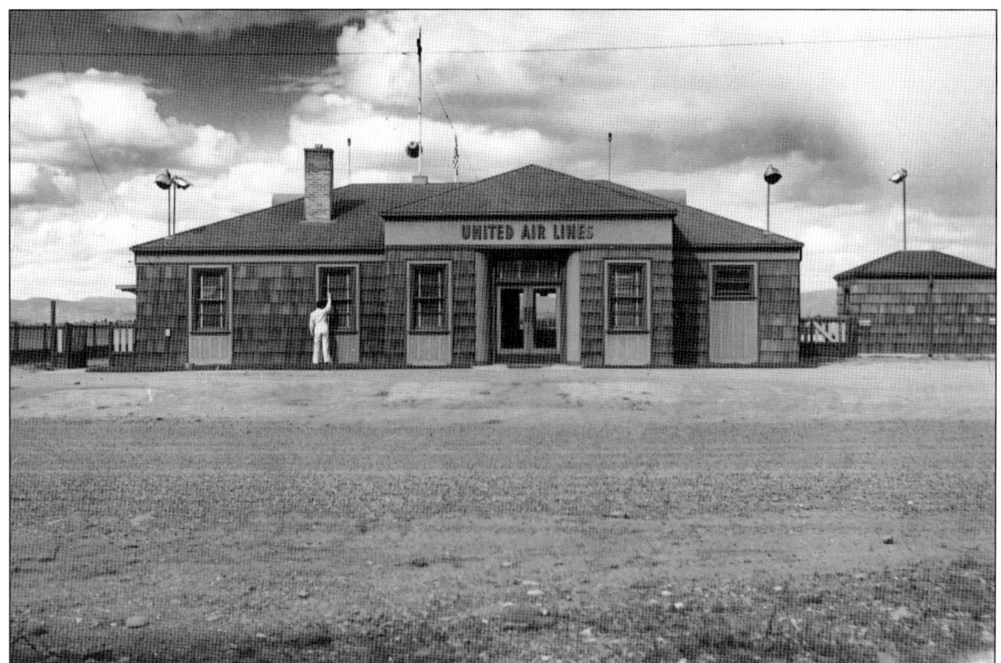

One of the first commercial aircraft companies to come into the Medford Municipal Airport was United Airlines. In the years after, multiple companies moved in, and the property grew. It was renamed twice, first to Medford-Jackson County Airport and then to the present name of Rogue Valley International Airport. In 2019, the airport was the third busiest airport in the state of Oregon, behind Eugene and Portland. (SOHS 16792.)

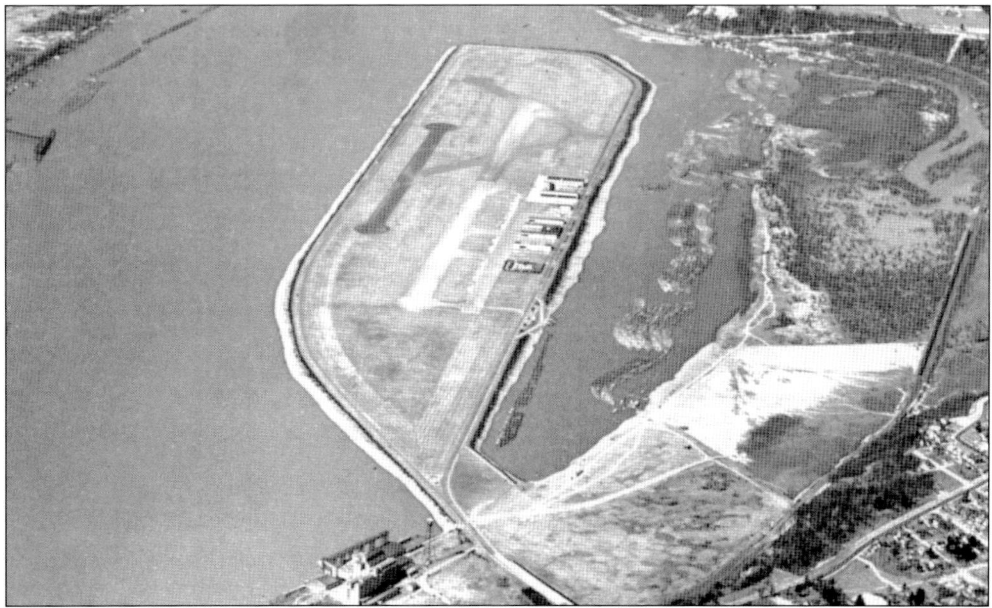

In 1926, the postmaster general of the United States threatened to cut mail service to Portland if the city did not build an airport close to Pearson's field in Washington. At the time, the US Navy was also looking around for an air base near the Columbia River. Enter Swan Island, a small piece of land on the Columbia River that was publicly owned. (City of Portland Archives.)

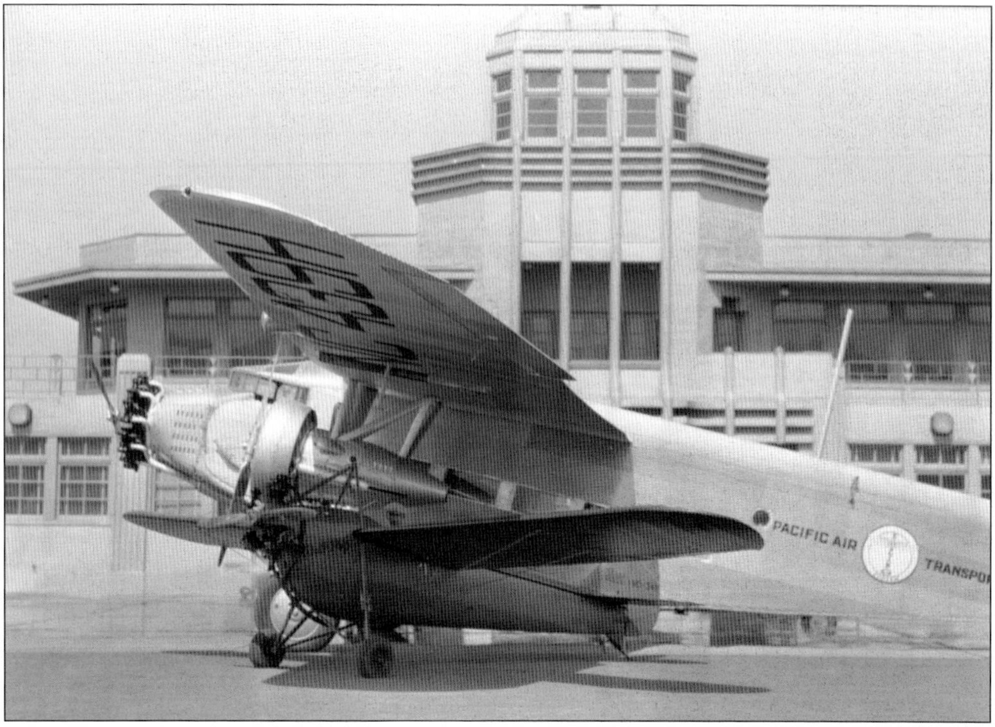

When Swan Island was officially dedicated in September 1927, the field was not finished, but the runways and buildings were. Pacific Air Derby helped to open the airport by having six Army aircraft perform for over 10,000 spectators. This image of a Buhl Bull Pup operated by Pacific Air Transport sits in front of the Swan Island Airport Terminal. The terminal was a U-shaped building that had this beautiful entryway. (Lee Corbin Collection.)

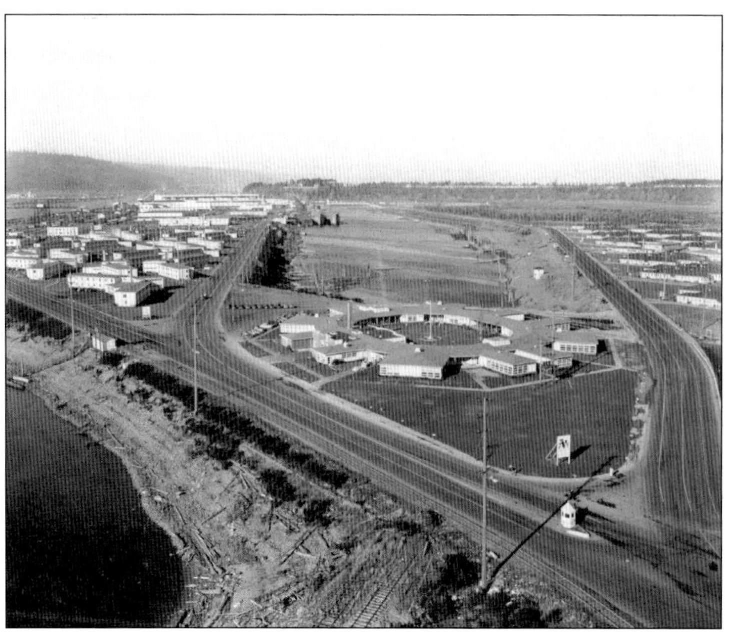

The land was quickly dredged and filled in, so transporting between the island and Portland proper was easier. Kaiser child service centers, the building in the center of the photograph was created using this dredging and filling. The center was created to care for over 300 children of both shipyard workers and air base personnel who were on or near Swan Island. (Oregon Historical Society, OHS ORHI78700.)

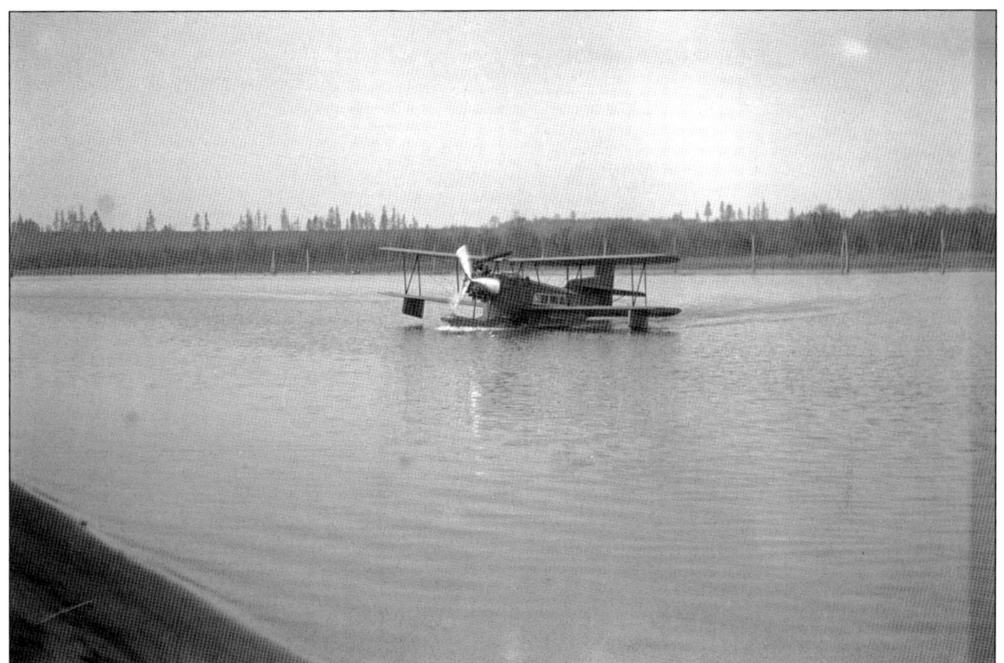

Being on the Columbia River, Swan Island, like other airfields near the water, had the capacity to accept aircraft that were suited for water landings, such as this Loening aircraft that is taxiing toward the base. This biplane held up to seven passengers in the enclosed center section while the pilot was above in the front under the top wing. (Pacific University.)

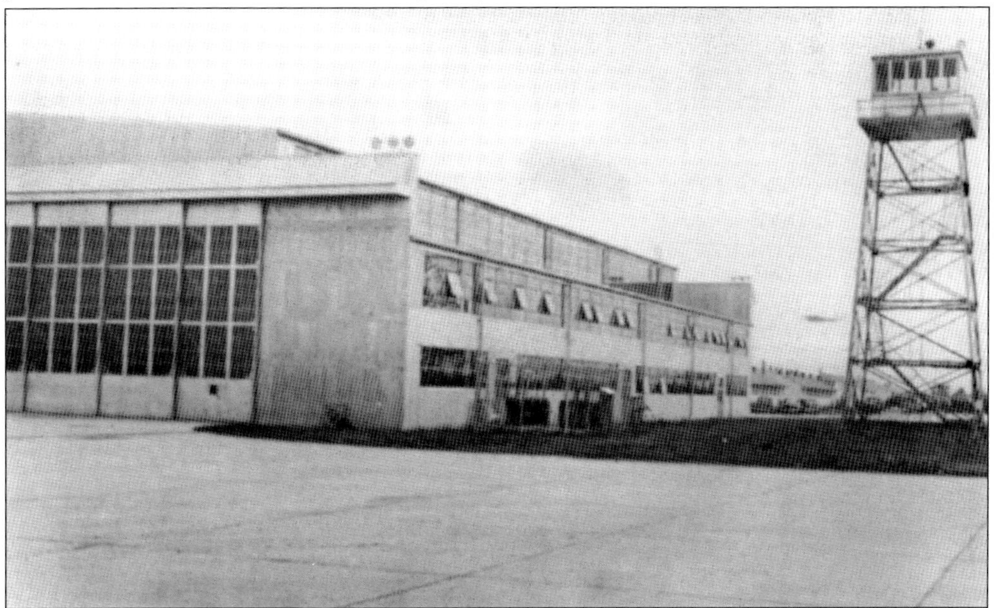

The Portland AAF functioned on Swan Island for quite a few years until 1940, when many of the air activities were moved to the new airport, and Swan Island was used for war production. This image is of the base maintenance hangar, along with the control tower, which was built for the smaller aircraft that were using Swan Island prior to and at times after the new airport was built. (Oregon Historical Society, OHS COLL849.)

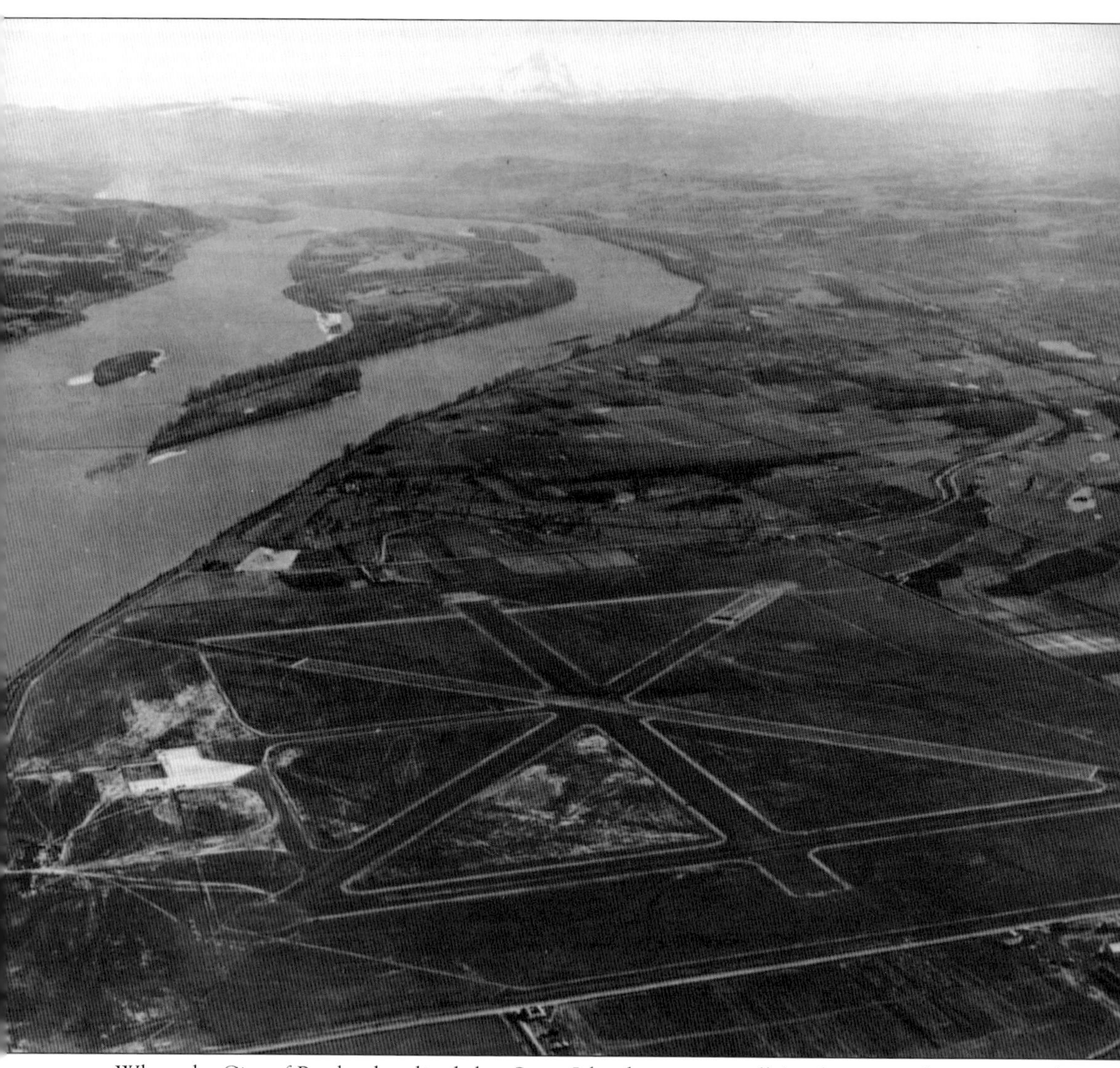

When the City of Portland realized that Swan Island was too small for the size and runway needs of the larger commercial air traffic, it set in motion plans to create a larger airport. The 700-acre piece of property was purchased in 1936 after the Portland City Council approved the purchase. In 1936, the City of Portland, along with the Port of Portland, requested a grant to develop the land into a "super airport." It was approved, and the construction project hired more than 1,000 men. The construction was completed in 1940, and two runways were capable of serving modern aircraft by 1941. The property is now the largest airport in Oregon, servicing numerous commercial flights as well as private aircraft and cargo. There is currently construction with a completion date of 2025 to provide more space to the main terminal. (Oregon Historical Society, OHS 014394.)

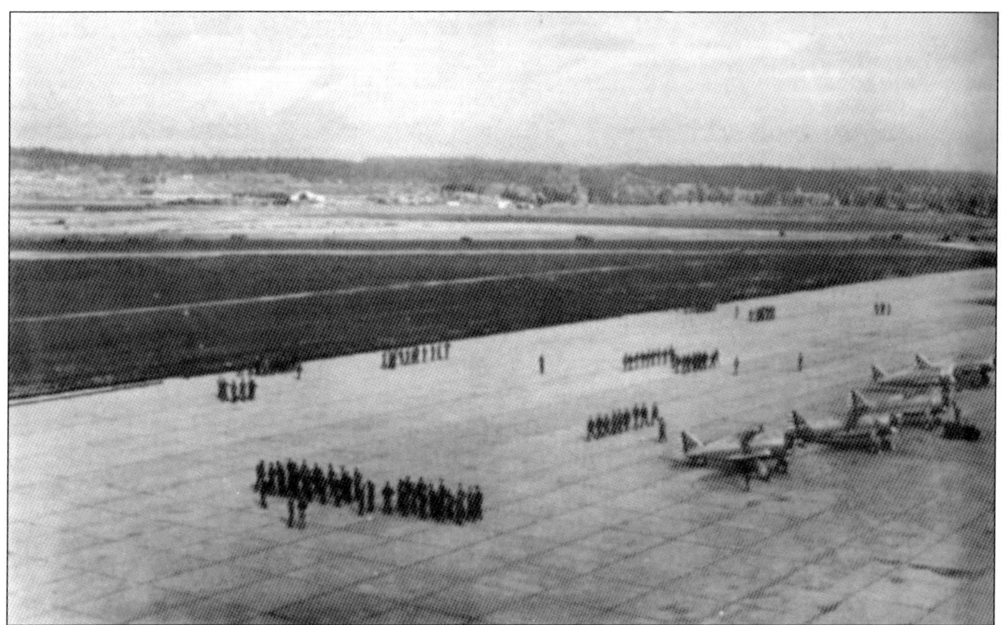

As part of any air base activity, troops drilled and prepared for when they were going to be deployed overseas. Many knew that it was only a matter of time, especially while training at an air base, before they would be sent to war with their unit. A majority—but not all—of the units that were stationed in Oregon were deployed to the Pacific theater. (Oregon Historical Society, OHS COLL849.)

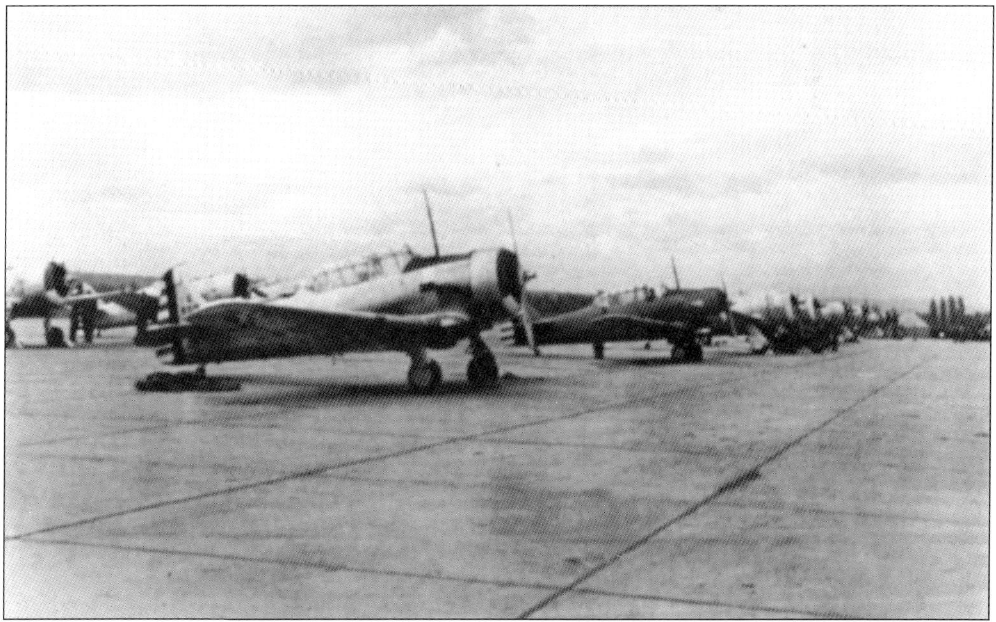

A group of North American T-6 Texans are lined up on the apron at Portland Army Air Base (PAAB) waiting to be used for training. The cockpit was large enough to allow for a pilot and an instructor to sit in tandem, allowing for the instructor to take over the controls if needed. These planes were used exclusively by the US Army Air Corps, US Army Air Force, and later the US Air Force as advance trainers. They are also known by the moniker SNJ. (Oregon Historical Society, OHS COLL849.)

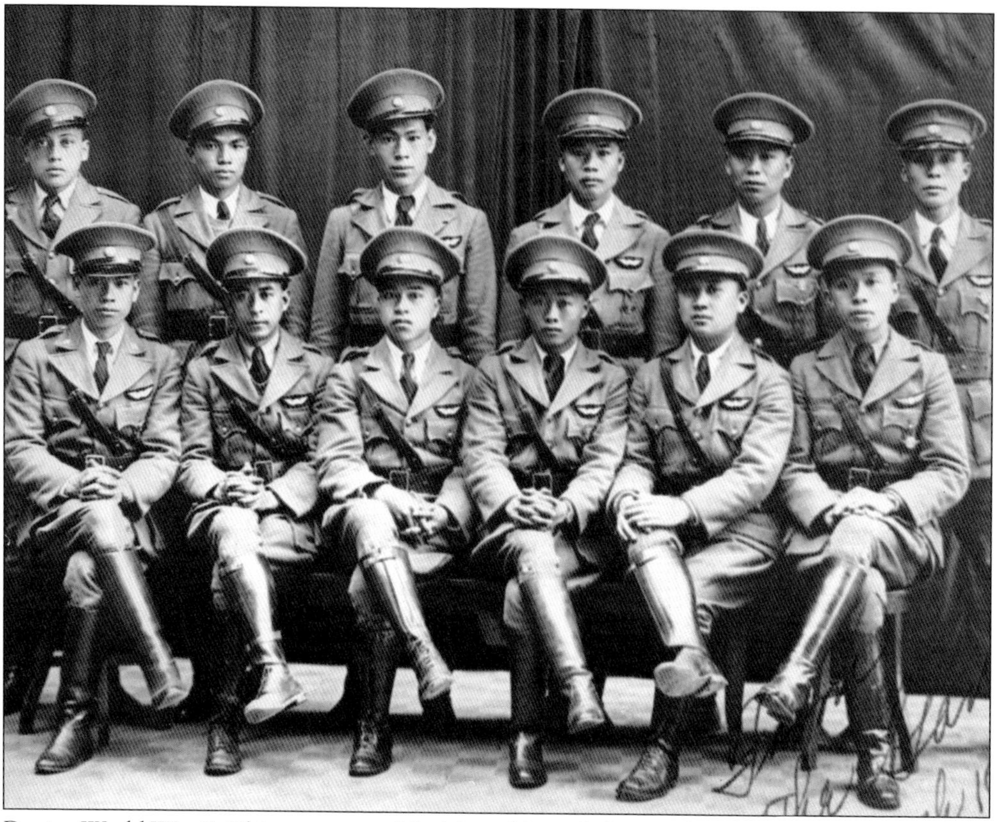

During World War II, China was one of the United States' allies. Before the United States officially joined the war, Chenault and the Flying Tigers were in China teaching the military how to pilot and work on aircraft. In the United States, those of Chinese American ancestry were segregated into their own units. These pilots were trained by A. Greenwood at Swan Island in support of World War II. (Oregon Historical Society, OHS 0022P197.)

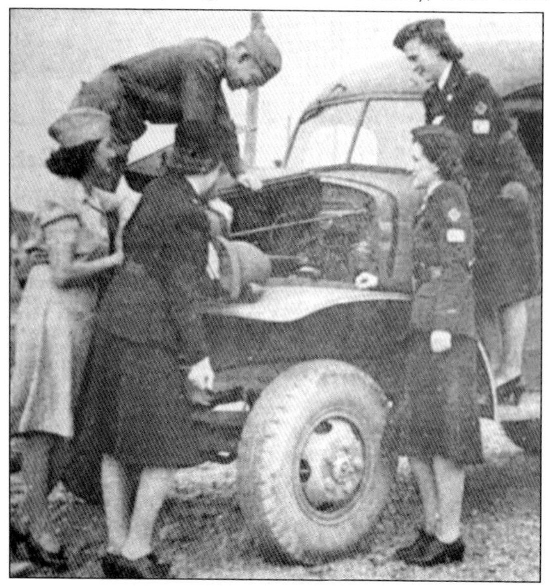

A year before the Women's Army Auxiliary Corps and the Women's Army Corps (WAC) were assigned to the PAAB, the American Red Cross established an office in mid-1941. The Red Cross recruited women to serve in uniform as part of the Red Cross Motor Corps, which was established in World War I. As drivers, these women received training from Army transportation personnel on what to do if the vehicle has issues. (Portland Army Air Base History, 142nd Wing History Archive.)

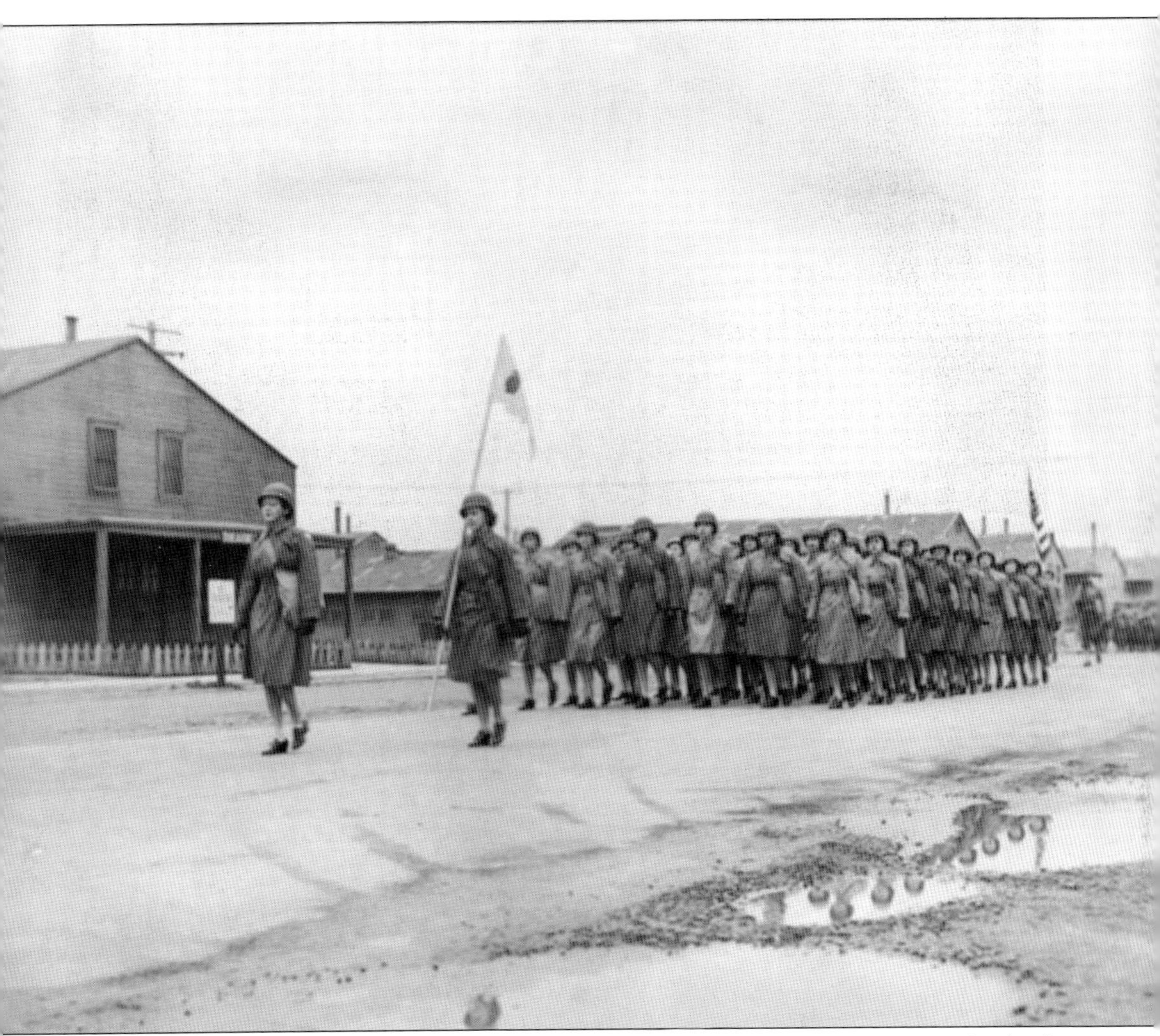

Prior to Pres. Franklin D. Roosevelt signing a bill into law on May 15, 1942, women on Portland Army Air Base were organizing themselves to assist with the war effort. In May 1941, the wives of many officers met across the river at Vancouver Barracks on how to create the Ladies' Auxiliary for the air base. By the end of 1941, there were at least 15 women meeting weekly for classes on how to support. By February 1942, there was a librarian, and in August 1942, women were organizing and having events on base. More women became volunteers but wore uniforms and served mostly as administration and nurses. By November 1943, there were 50 WAC service members at PAAB as part of the 807th WAC Post HQ Company. This unit is seen marching past the base theater during the afternoon base retreat parade in late 1943. (Portland Army Air Base History, 142nd Wing History Archive.)

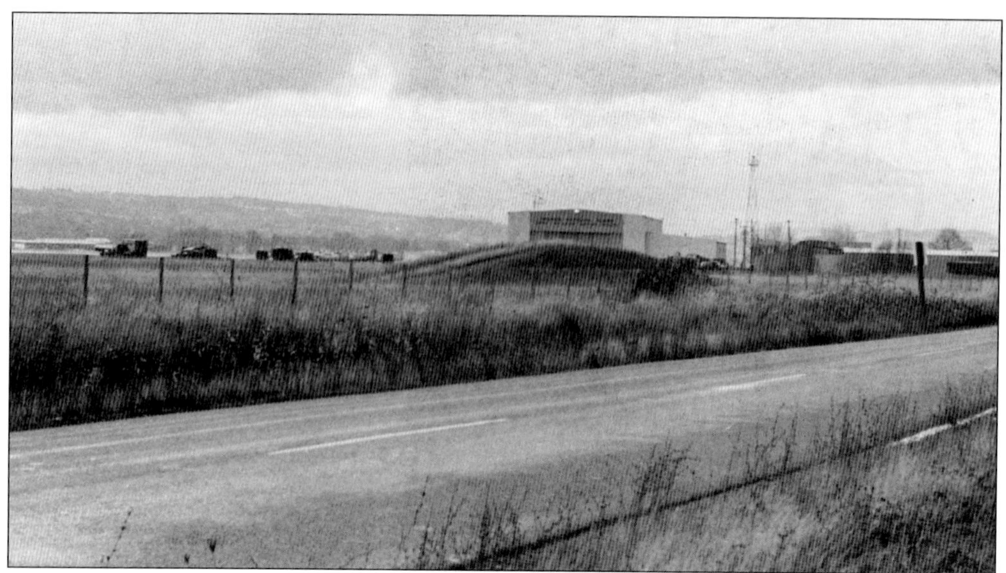

On May 8, 1910, a Curtiss model airplane was displayed in the D'Arcy Building on the new grounds of Salem Airport. Flight was successful on June 4, 1910, marking the beginnings of Oregon's capital city flight history The mount in the foreground was created as a defense against the Japanese during World War II. In the background is the hangar that was used during World War II. (WHC Collections, 2007.001.0299.)

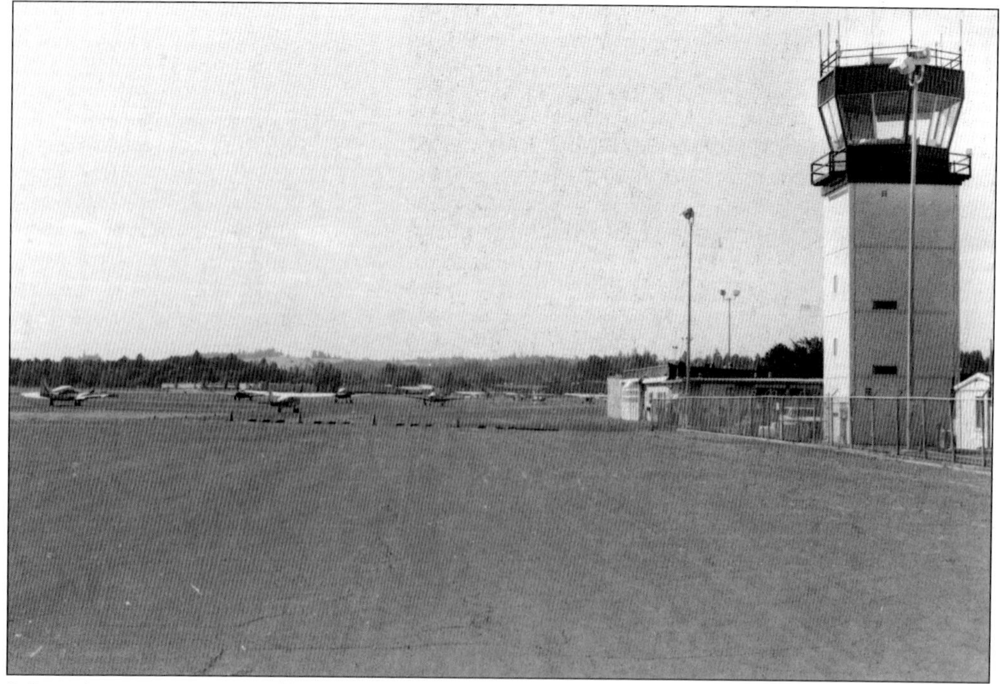

Salem Airport was originally used as a direct mailing airport, with the first direct mail being delivered on August 5, 1941, from an aircraft named the *City of Cleveland*, but soon as the military took over, it became home to the 356th Fighter Squadron of the 354th Fighter Group in order to train. Charles McNary was instrumental in securing the airport's designation as an Army airfield. (WHC Collections, 2007.001.0221.)

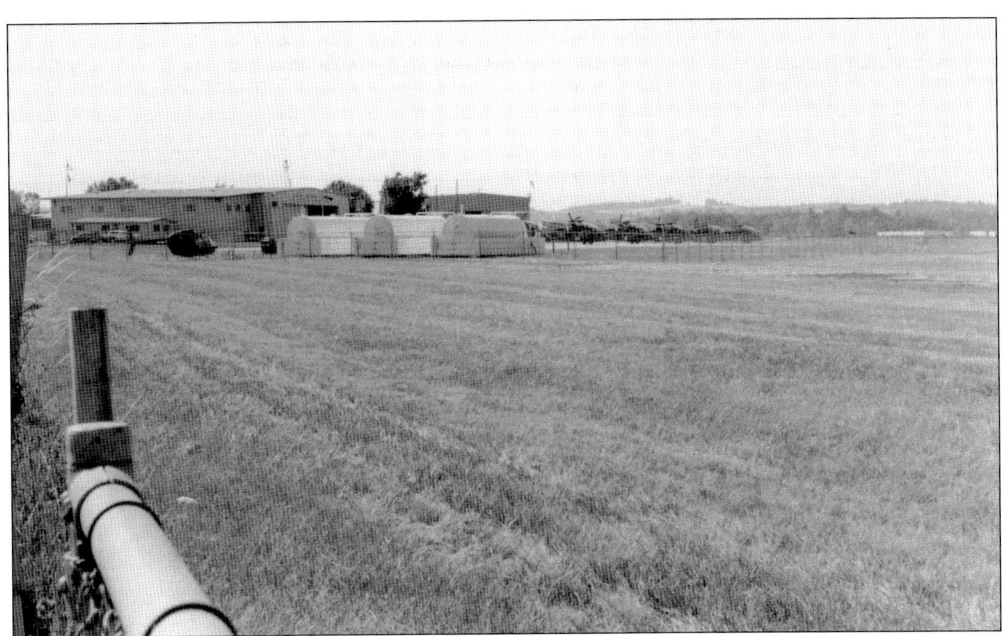

Although the military was still in partial control of Salem Airport, on March 6, 1944, the City of Salem officially changed the name to McNary Field, after the late Sen. Charles McNary, who was born near the airport. It was not until the military handed the airport back to the City of Salem in 1948 that the Navy signed a lease for partial usage in 1949. (WHC Collections, 2007.001.0237.)

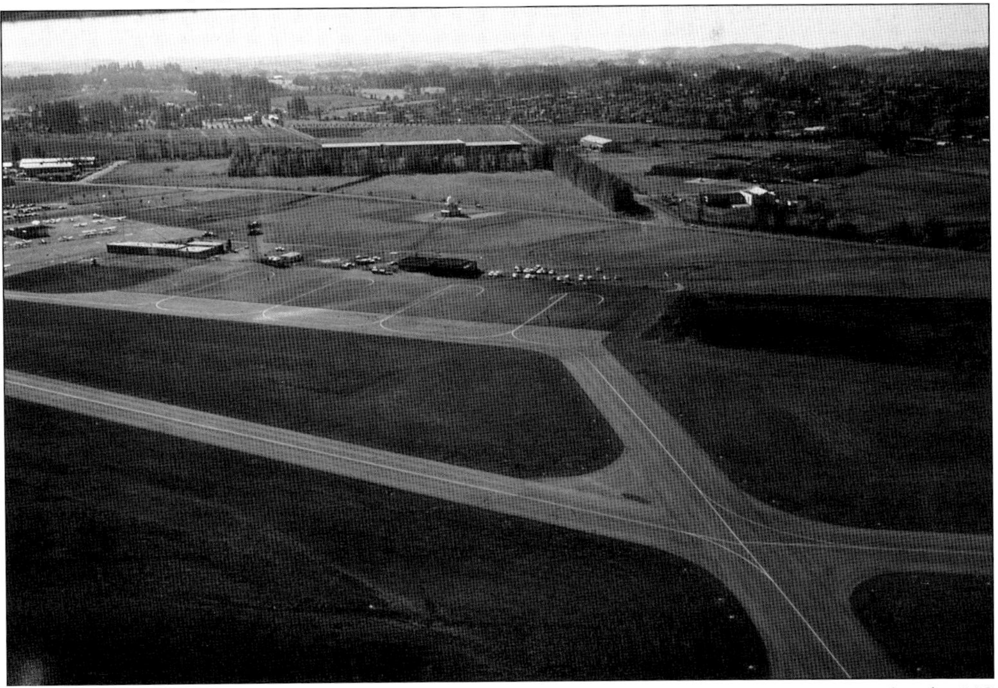

The first jet, an F-80, landed at McNary Airport on August 20, 1948, in preparation for the US Navy's creation of a naval facility. On August 5, 1949, the Salem Naval Air Facility was officially dedicated. The funds created by the lease allowed for a new aircraft tower as well as renovating the runways to allow for newer aircraft. (WHC Collections, 1998.013.0058.)

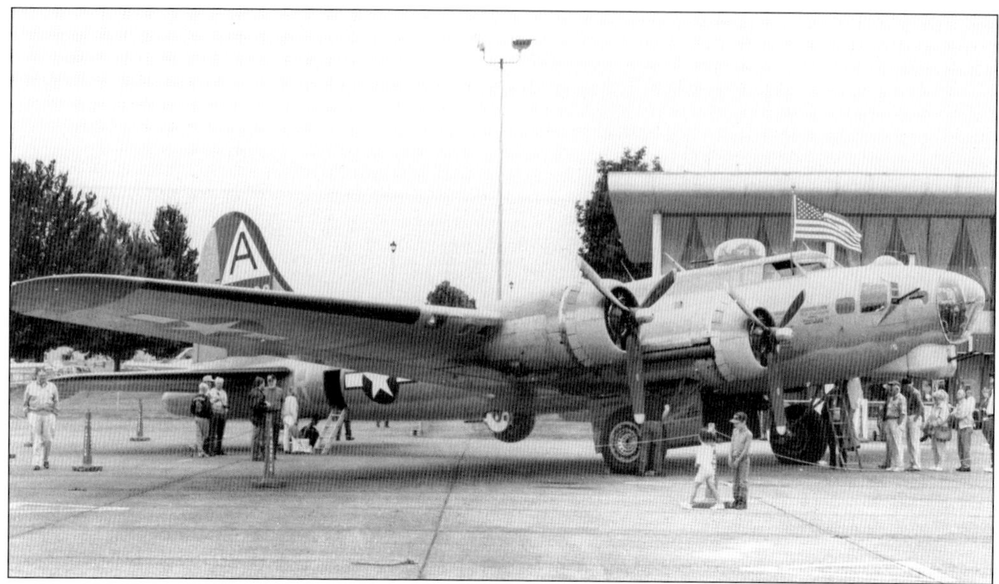

The size of the Salem Airport was increased as well as modernized to accept larger aircraft if needed. B-17s were not stationed at Salem Airport; therefore, they were not a common sight. In the case of an emergency landing, though, the airport was able to accommodate aircraft of this size. This B-17 landed at Salem Airport as a display for citizen viewing. (WHC Collections, 2004.010.0379.)

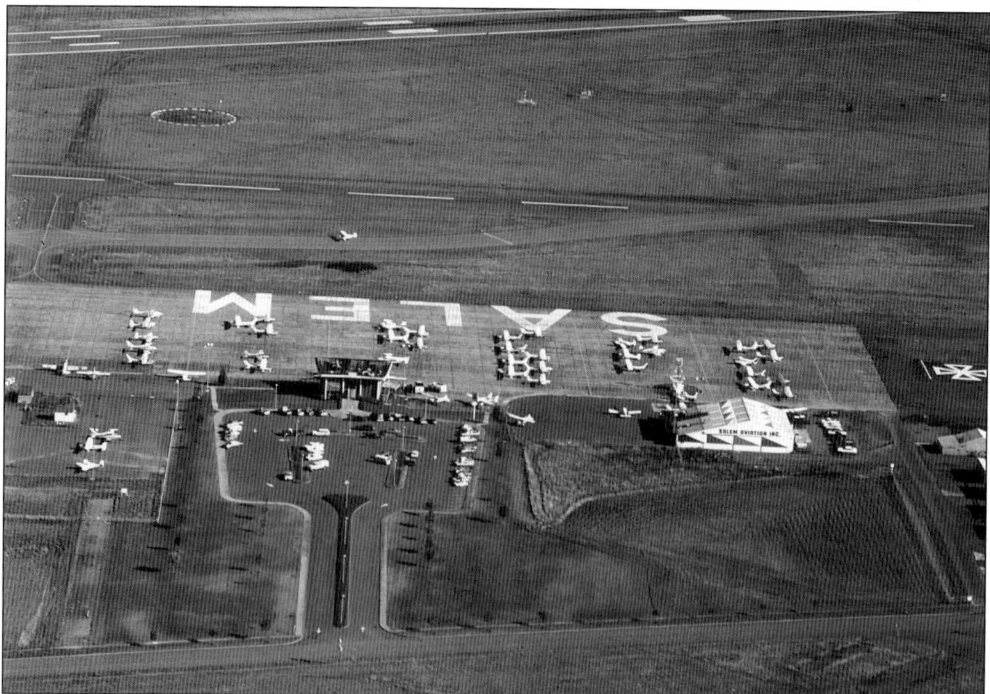

On October 14, 1960, an agreement was made between Marion and Polk Counties, along with the City of Salem, in the creation of a port agency. McNary Airport then came under joint control in hopes of streamlining some of the administrative functions and providing additional funding. With that, as well as the lease with the Navy, additional modernization has occurred at the airport. (WHC Collections, 1998.013.0086.)

Three

The Cascades

The Cascades is the geographical region that starts at the Washington border and ends at the California border. Sandwiched between the valley and Eastern Oregon, it includes the subregions of the Columbia River Basin, High Desert, Central Oregon, and the Klamath Lake Basin. While all part of the Cascades, these subregions tend to have marginally different weather and geographical features, which makes them different than others. For example, the Columbia River Basin is a lower elevation, averaging 2,100 feet, while the Klamath Lake Basin averages 4,140 feet above sea level.

This region is typically drier than farther western regions, with an average of 12 inches of rainfall throughout the area. Along the entire Cascades, however, there is a large amount of snow, with some areas receiving less than 16 inches a year on average, while others receive up to 40 inches. This is not counting the mountain ranges or Crater Lake, which are part of the Cascade Range and receive an average of over 40 feet of snow a year. Temperature averages in the whole region are similar, with a winter low of 21 Fahrenheit average to a summer high of 85 Fahrenheit. These temperatures also helped train flight crews on how to adapt to drastically changing weather conditions.

This location was suitable for bases because some of the airfields were already in use. The elevation average of over 4,500 feet above sea level gave pilots unique training opportunities as well as provided training for ground crews on how to adapt to higher elevations. Not only that, but given the location, aircraft could be easily flown from Eastern Oregon to provide additional training. Like with Eastern Oregon, during this time, the Cascades were not overly populated, so testing and larger air bases were possible that were not farther west. The airfields in the Cascades region include Bend, Fish Creek FS, Klamath Falls NAS, Madras AAF, Prineville Redmond AAF, Prineville, Madras AAF, and Klamath Falls NAS.

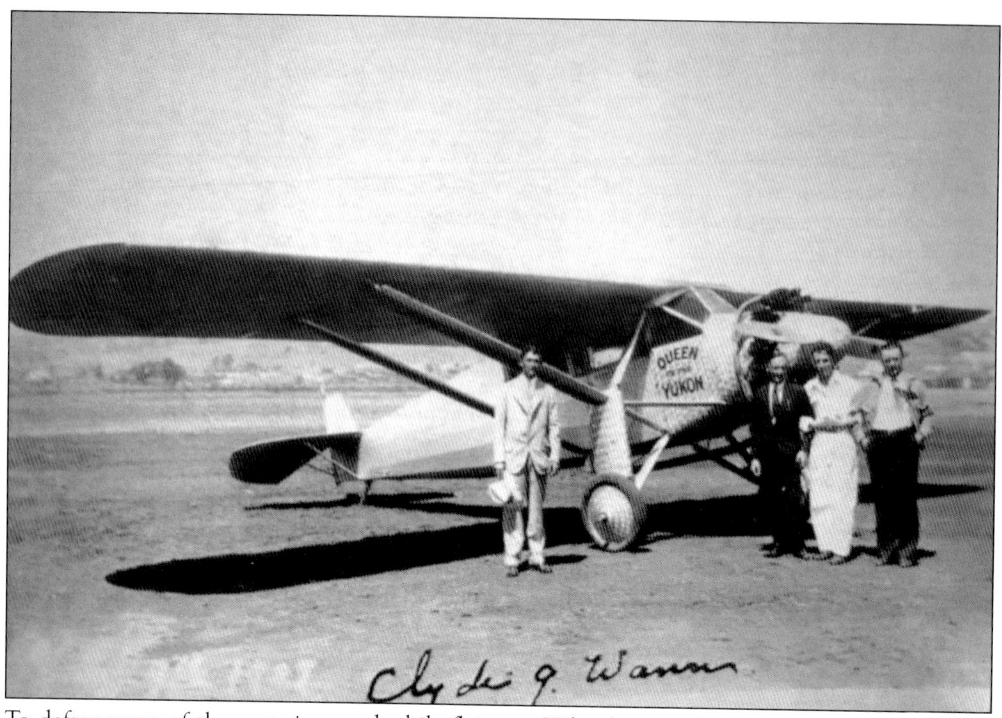

To defray some of the costs incurred while flying to Whitehorse, Alaska, the *Queen of the Yukon* landed at Knotts Field on September 7, 1927. The vice president of Yukon Airways, Clyde Wann, was on board and offered the plane for exhibition flights, allowing his pilots to take interested Oregonians up in the *Queen of the Yukon*. (DHM.)

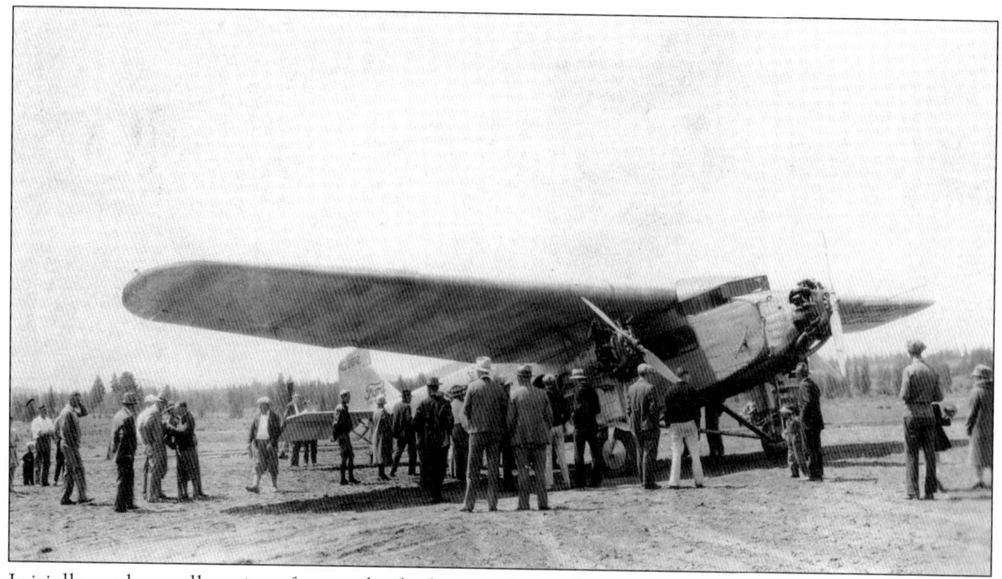

Initially, only smaller aircraft were built, but in the early 1930s, Ford began to construct larger aircraft. This trimotor named *West Wind* landed on April 30, 1930, at Knotts Field to a large celebration. It was the first time that the public in this area was able to see such a large aircraft. During the celebration, the public was taken on 20-minute flights before a large dance that night. (DHM.)

Due to the Knotts Field's size, officials knew that it was only a matter of time before it would outgrow this location. In 1931, Bend officials sought out and bought land owned by E.H. Brandenburg and renamed the property Long Butte Airport. Unfortunately, while the land was large enough, the location was less than ideal, with a cinder butte to the northeast of the runway, seen here. (USFS.)

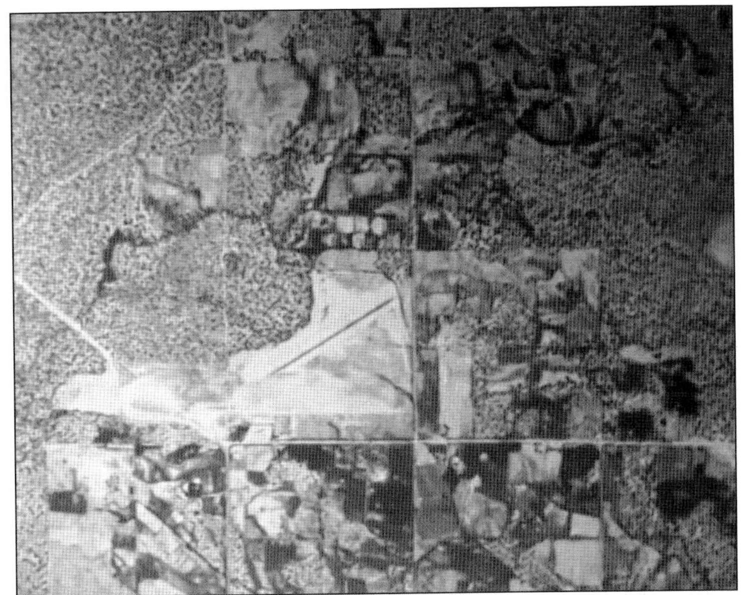

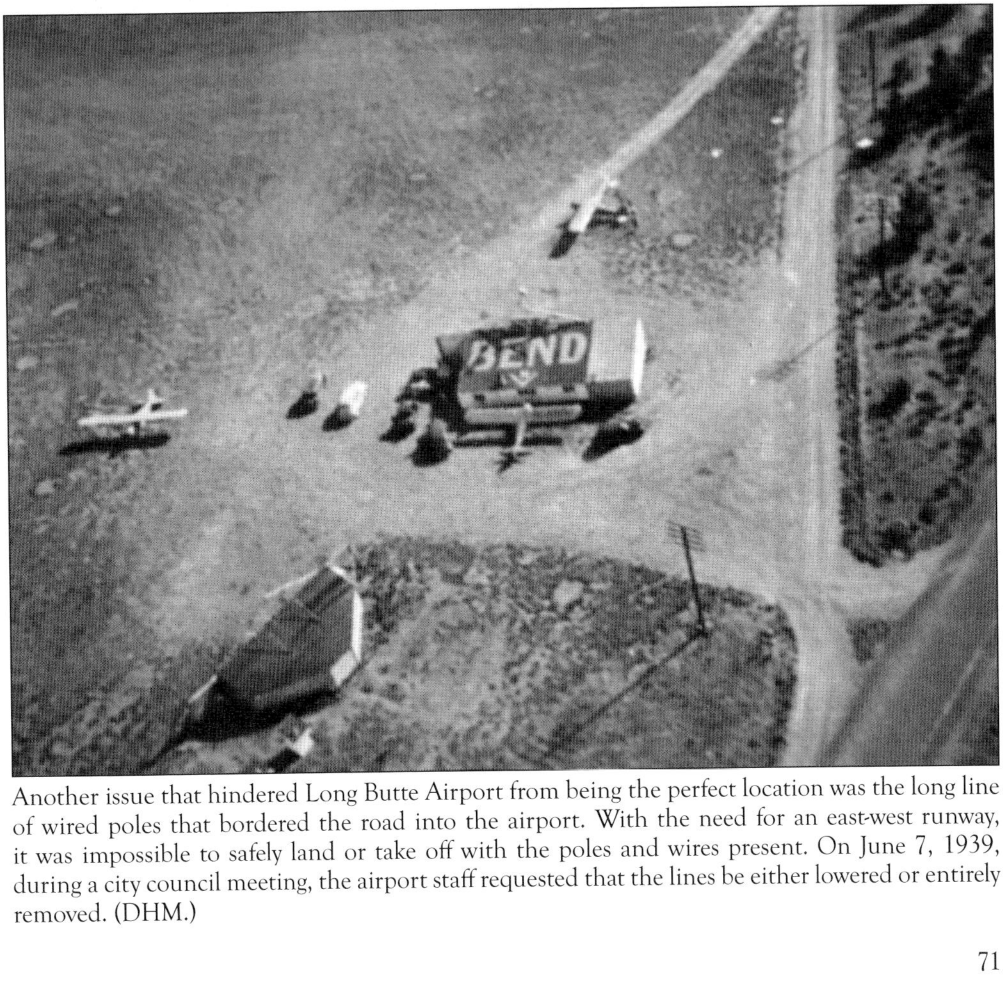

Another issue that hindered Long Butte Airport from being the perfect location was the long line of wired poles that bordered the road into the airport. With the need for an east-west runway, it was impossible to safely land or take off with the poles and wires present. On June 7, 1939, during a city council meeting, the airport staff requested that the lines be either lowered or entirely removed. (DHM.)

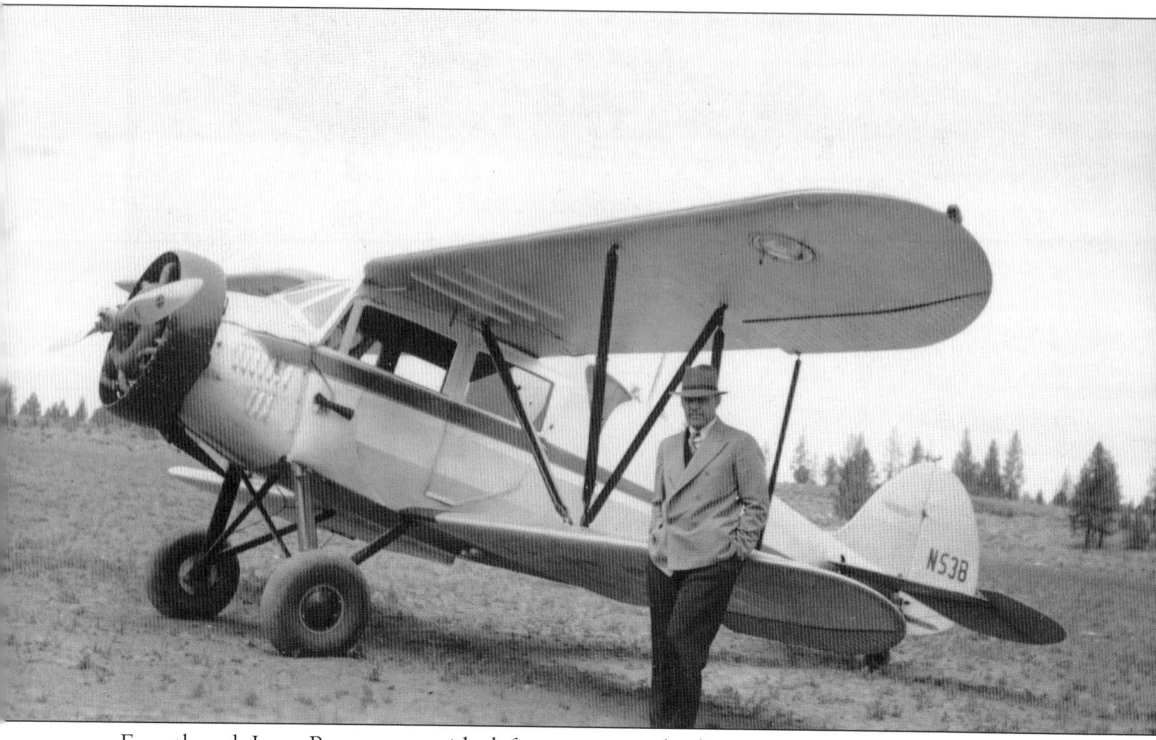

Even though Long Butte was not ideal, for many years, both Long Butte and Knotts Field coexisted, allowing pilots to choose what airfield to land at. With everyone starting airline companies and building aircraft, the US and state governments realized that if they did not start creating regulations regarding what could be in the air or where they could land, they might begin having large accidents. The Air Commerce Act of 1926 created an aeronautical branch of the Department of Commerce (DOC). The DOC oversaw testing and licensing of pilots as well as the certification of aircraft. Another aspect was the investigation of accidents, which at the time were frequent. With two airports in the immediate Bend area, the DOC came to test and license the numerous pilots. Robert D. Bedinger, an inspector for the DOC aeronautical branch, is seen near his Waco UEC at Knotts Field. (DHM.)

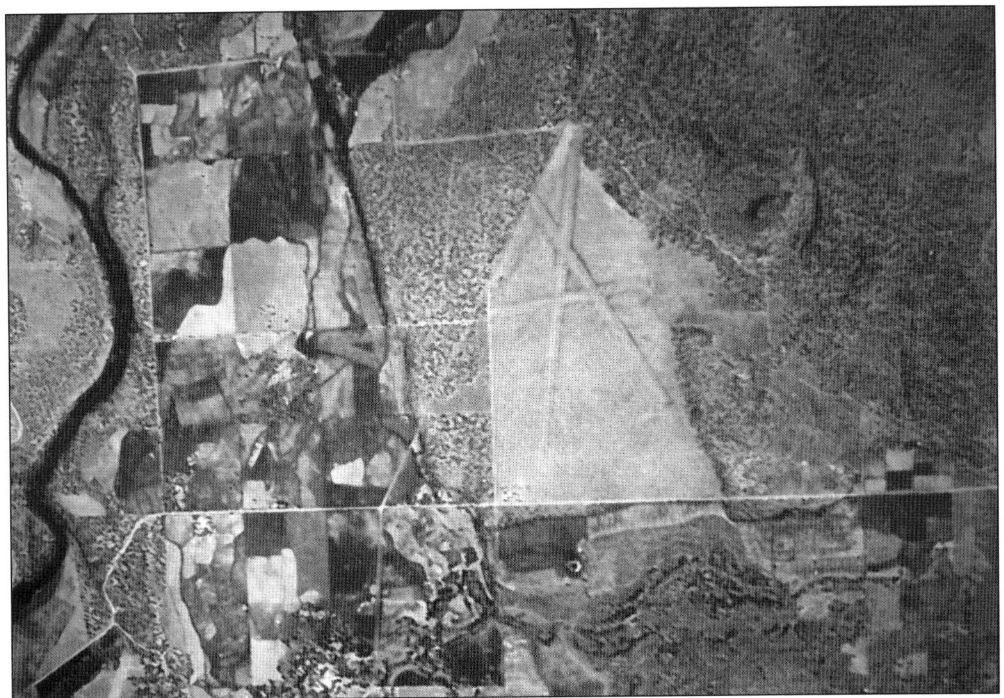

With the new airport created near Butler Market Road, Tilse Flying Service, owned by local Al Tilse, received approval to train pilots under the civilian pilot training program. Tilse, along with partner Oliver Bowman, trained pilots and then ran the airport from 1945 to 1951. In May 1946, the hangars and four aircraft were lost in a fire. New hangar construction began shortly afterward. (DHM.)

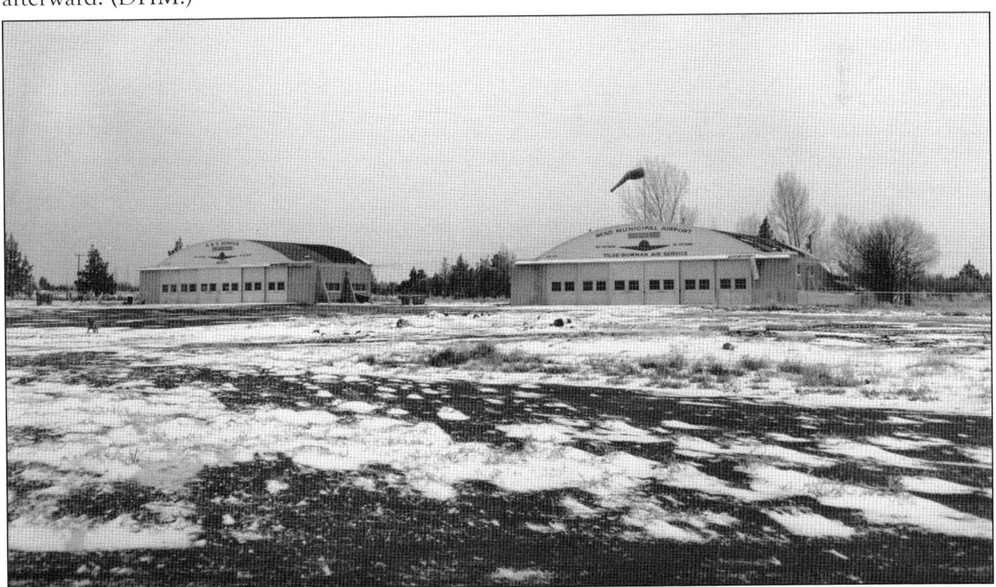

Although Bend was not a good location for a military base, with Redmond so close, many felt that the airfield should be utilized by the government as a pilot training school. The only issue was that Long Butte airfield was not set up for a training school. Thomas Brooks pushed the city to find an adequate location, which they did, and through an approved bond, they bought property. (USFS.)

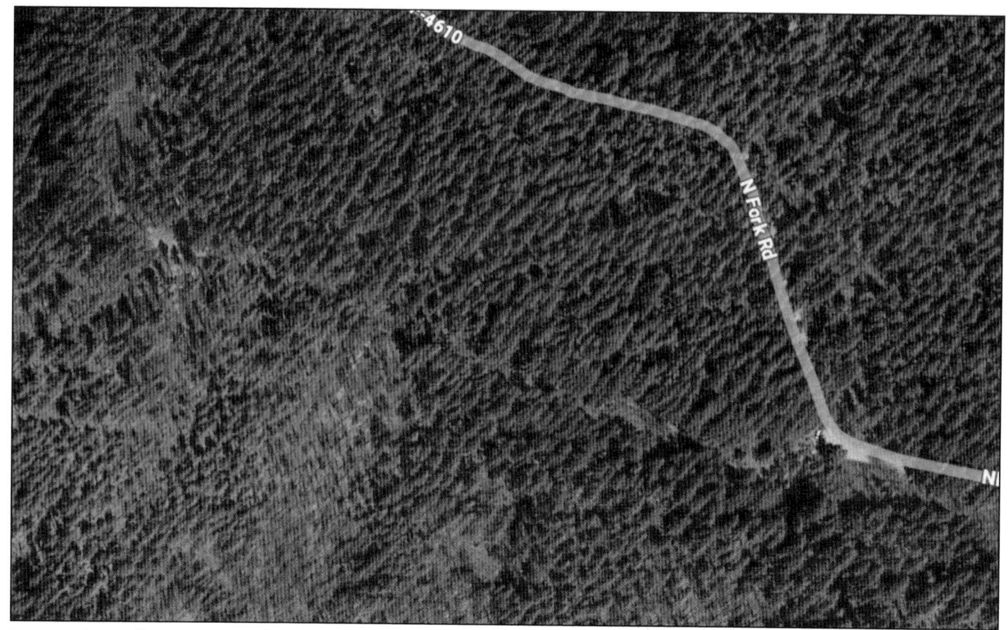

Located in the mountains overlooking the Clackamas River southeast of Estacada, there was a small flight strip. According to an individual by the name of Merve who served during World War II, the flight strip was created in the event the Japanese began to attack the Oregon coast. Known as Fish Creek FS, it was used as an emergency landing as well as a storage flight strip to move aircraft to. (USFS.)

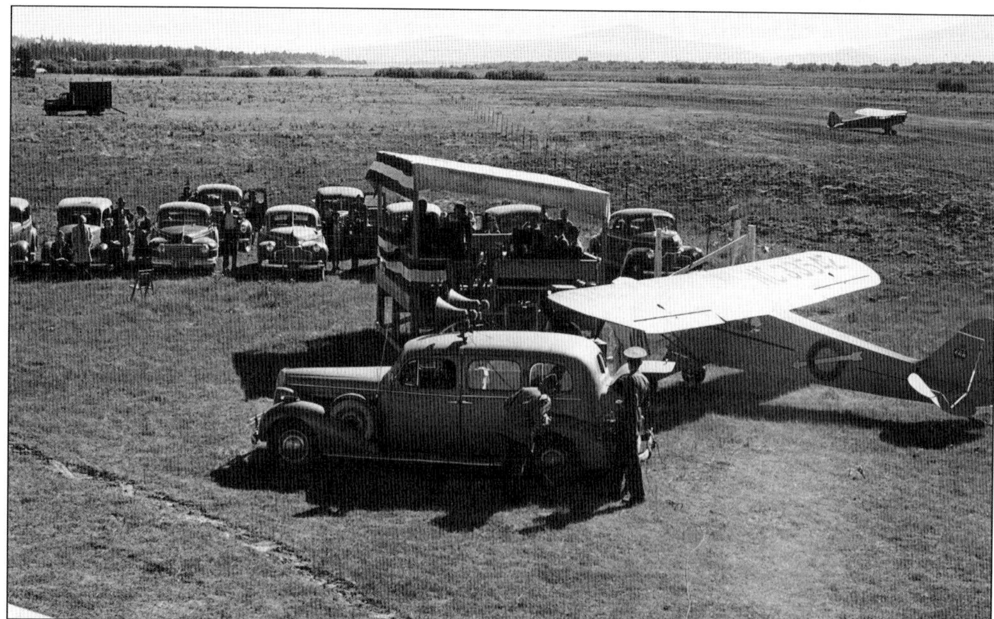

Air shows were so popular that Klamath Falls would construct a press box, allowing noteworthy individuals the ability to sit in the shade while partaking in the festivities. The organizers enlisted the help of police and other emergency services in the event of an accident occurring. The vehicle at the front of the picture was used by organizers to announce the next aircraft and pilot. Note the speakers on top of the vehicle. (KCM.)

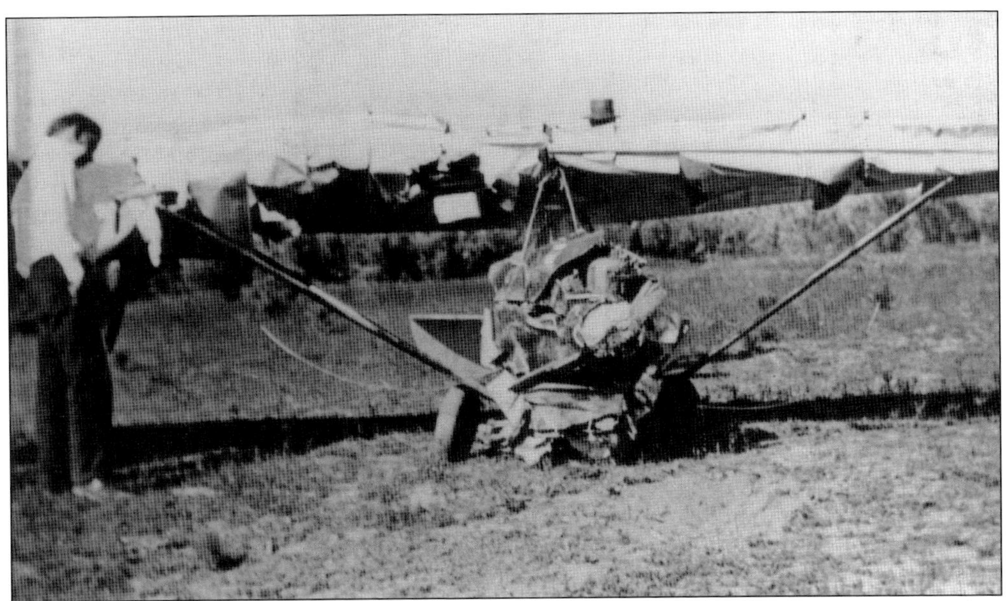
The early years of flying saw many accidents. Individuals created aircraft out of parts found around the airfield and garages. That, combined with inexperienced pilots wanting to fly, and accidents were almost expected. This small aircraft that was involved in a severe accident is being surveyed by an unidentified individual at Klamath Falls Field. Due to the fragility of these aircraft, many pilots suffered serious injuries and death. (KCM.)

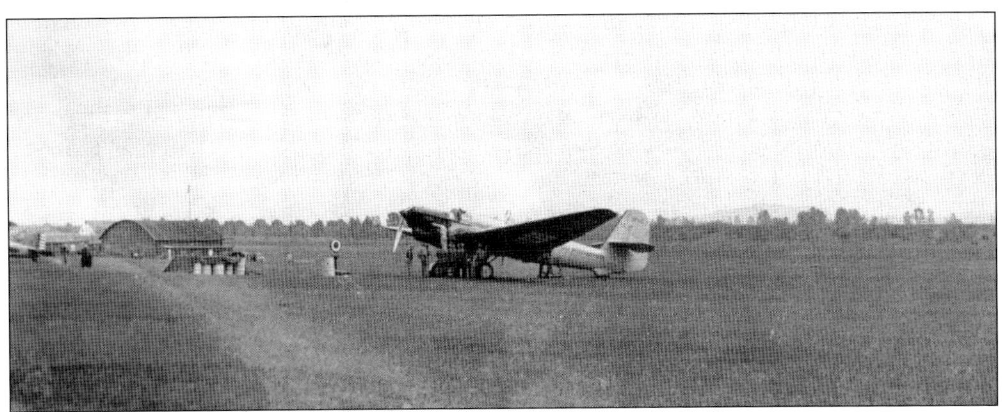
In the 1930s, it was common for many people to see aircraft take off and land in Klamath Falls. Around June 21, 1937, the public was surprised to see a craft unlike one they had seen before. Valery Chkalov, Georgiy Baydukov, and Alexander Belyakov made the first nonstop flight from Moscow to the United States, crossing over the North Pole. They traveled over 5,000 miles en route to California. (KCM.)

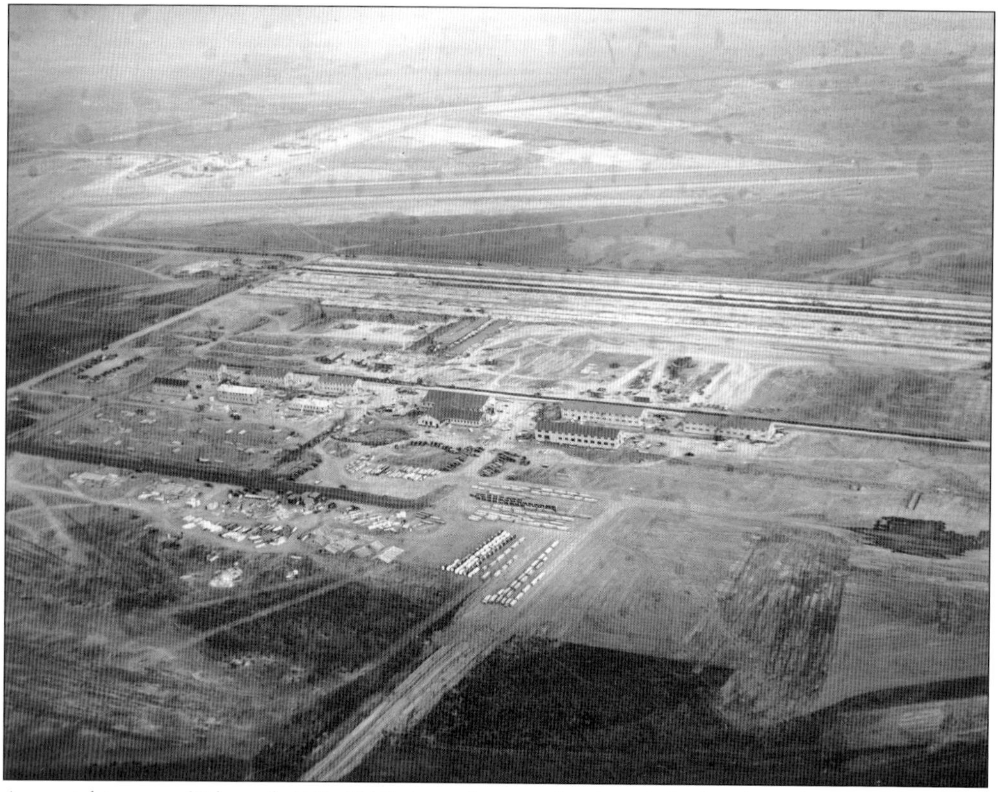

An aerial image of Klamath Falls NAS shows how undeveloped the land was before the military moved in. This image was taken after the construction of the main buildings, including barracks and the administration building, began. Due to the escalation of the war in the Pacific, the military wasted no time in building up the base and filling it with service members and aircraft. (KCM.)

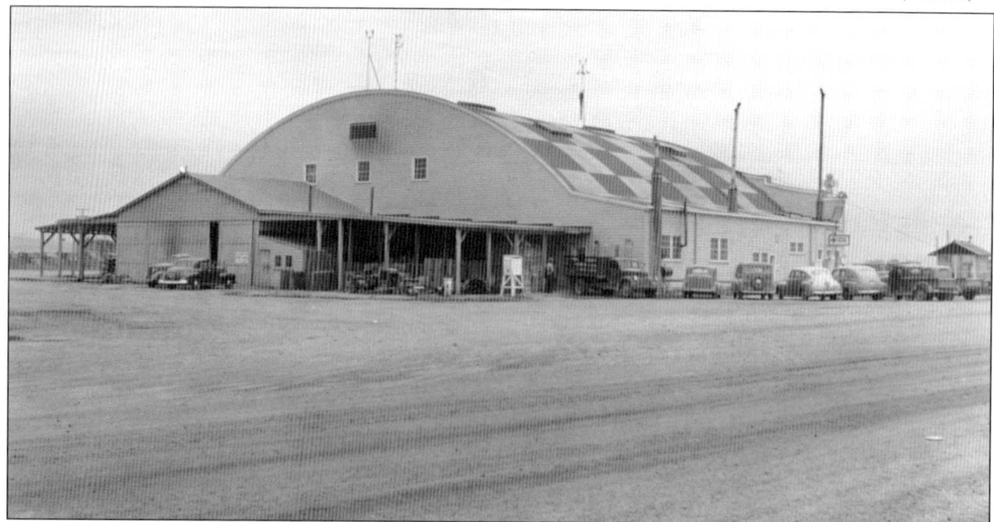

One of the first hangars built at the Klamath Falls NAS, this exhibited the common checkboard pattern on the roof. The pattern was used so that in poor or dark conditions, what normally would be an unbroken surface would be broken up and visible to pilots and other air crew. This specific hangar also had a first aid station located near the large hangar doors. (KCM.)

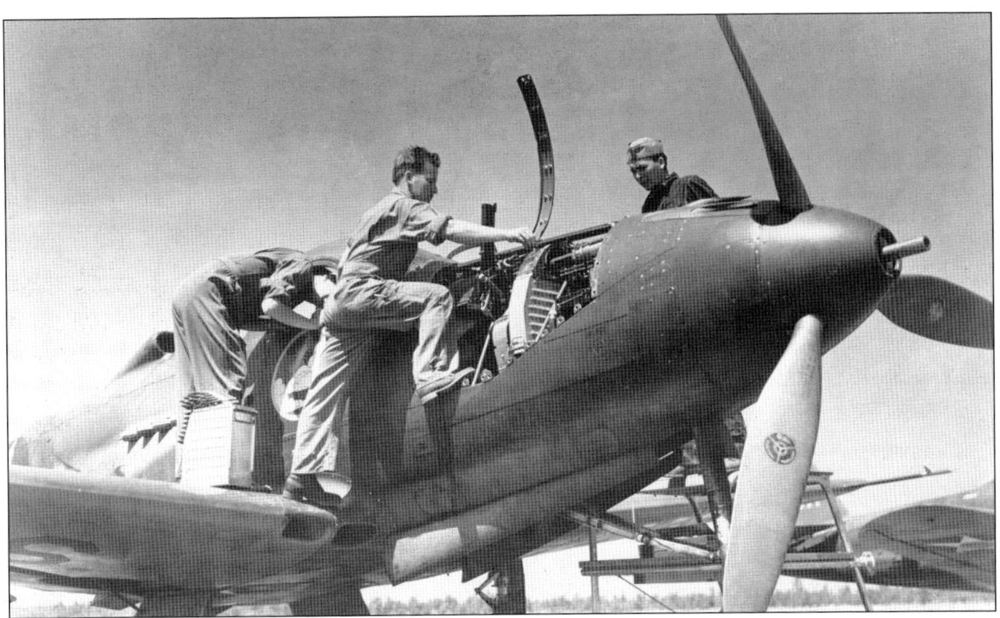

Three unnamed mechanics work on the munitions and engine bay of a Bell P-39C Airacobra. This aircraft was known for its quick maneuverability, which, while designed as a bomber interceptor, was also utilized frequently for ground attack, specifically in the Pacific. When stateside, these aircraft were used in war games to instruct pilots on how to evade enemy aircraft if necessary. (KCM.)

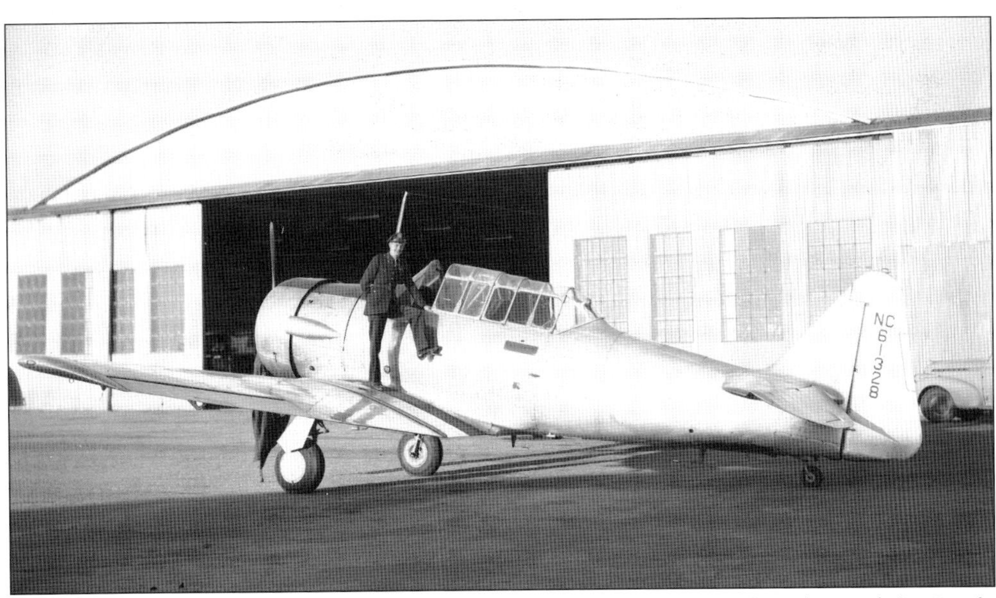

Klamath Falls NAS was used by the Navy as a training facility for pilots destined for Pacific deployments. This unidentified Army Air Corps pilot poses with a training craft in front of the aircraft hangar. It was not unheard of for cross-training to occur, especially between the Air Corps and the Navy. The SBD Dauntless was commonly used on aircraft carriers, and Klamath Falls NAS trained pilots on how to fly them. (KCM.)

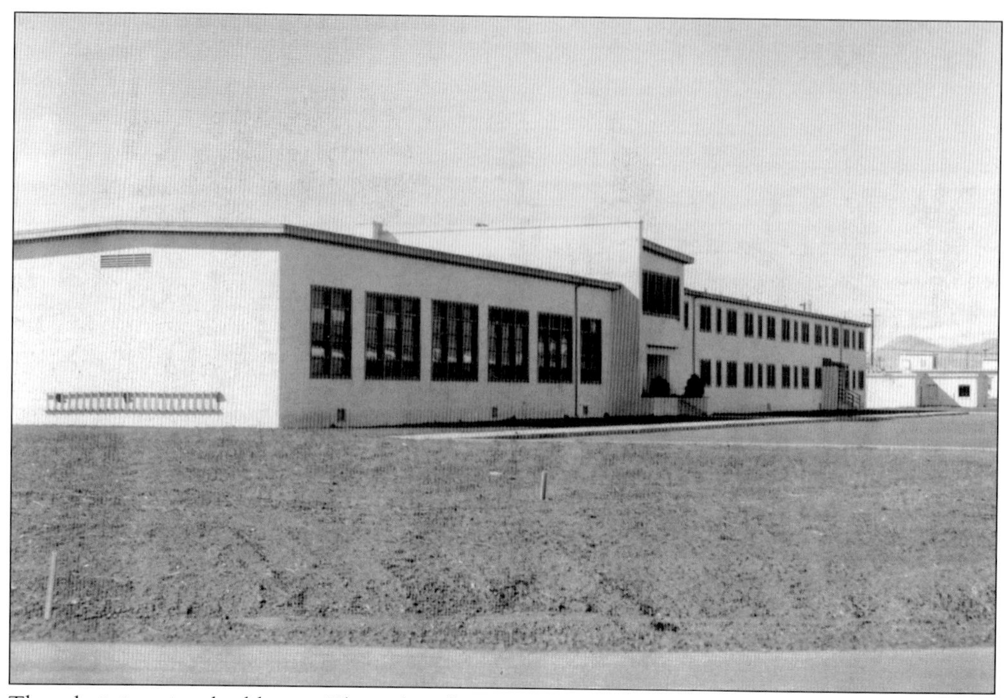

The administration building at Klamath Falls NAS was built after the military took over the area. As a halfway point between Portland and San Francisco, this base saw hundreds, if not thousands, of service members transitioning between those two bases. To keep the base running, a smaller, but still large, group of service members was needed to provide day-to-day administration. (KCM.)

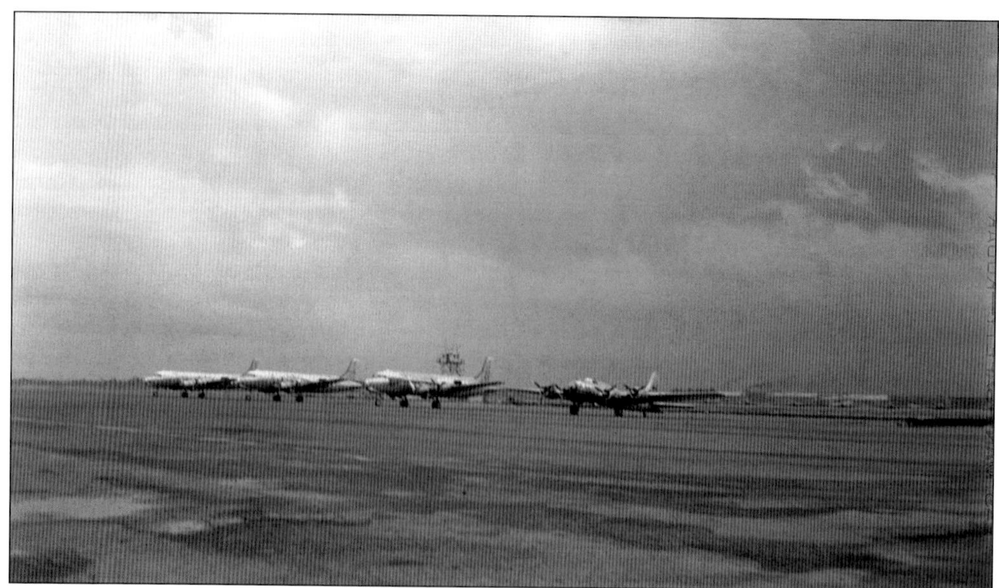

The old aircraft control tower can be seen in the distance with four large troop carriers parked on the apron. Due to their size and the fact that there were at times multiple aircraft at Klamath Falls NAS, it was not uncommon for aircraft to be stored away from the runways in the elements. (KCM.)

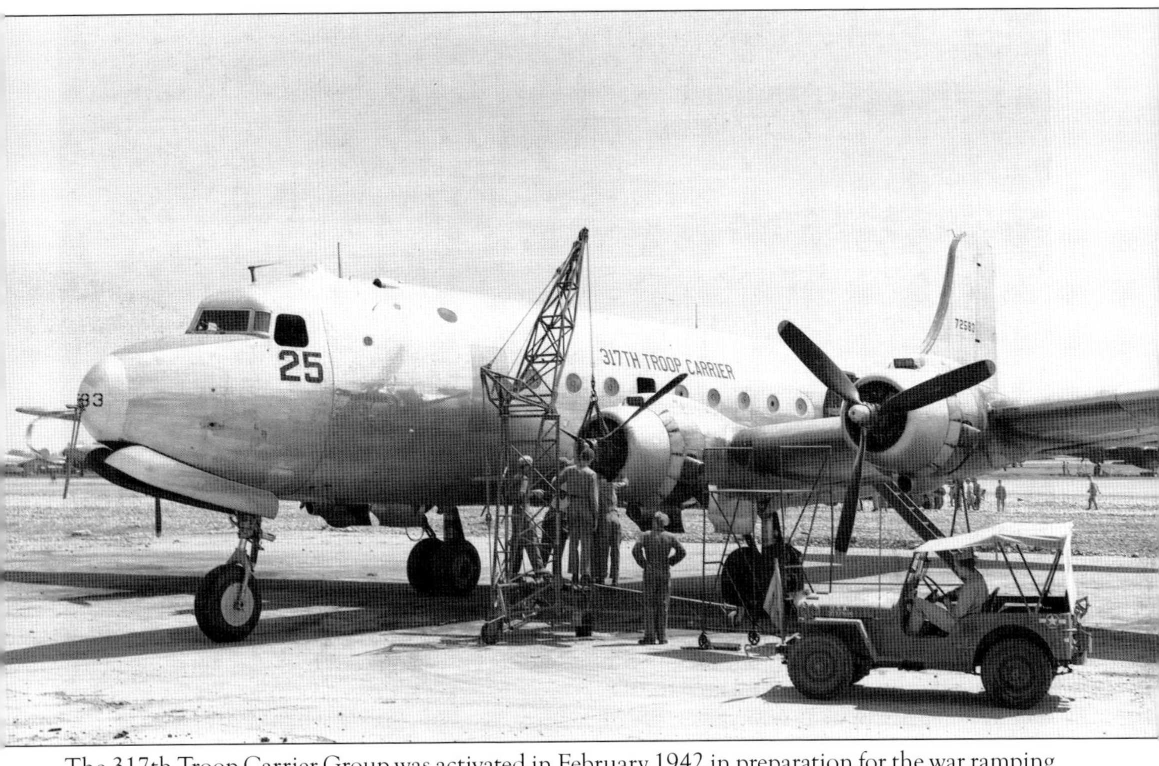

The 317th Troop Carrier Group was activated in February 1942 in preparation for the war ramping up. The main goal of the 317th was to tow gliders, but the military soon saw their usefulness for other things. Originally, the fuel tanks allowed the aircraft to travel domestically without major issues. However, the US Air Corps wanted it to become a troop carrier and transport troops to their deployment locations in both the European and Pacific theaters. To accomplish this task, the military equipped those aircraft destined to travel overseas with long-range fuel tanks. This specific Douglass C-47 Skytrain landed at Klamath Falls NAS in 1942 for what turned out to be an engine repair before traveling to the Pacific theater. While stopped, the troops that had been on the aircraft were able to stay in the visitors' barracks and get a bit more stateside time before deploying. (KCM.)

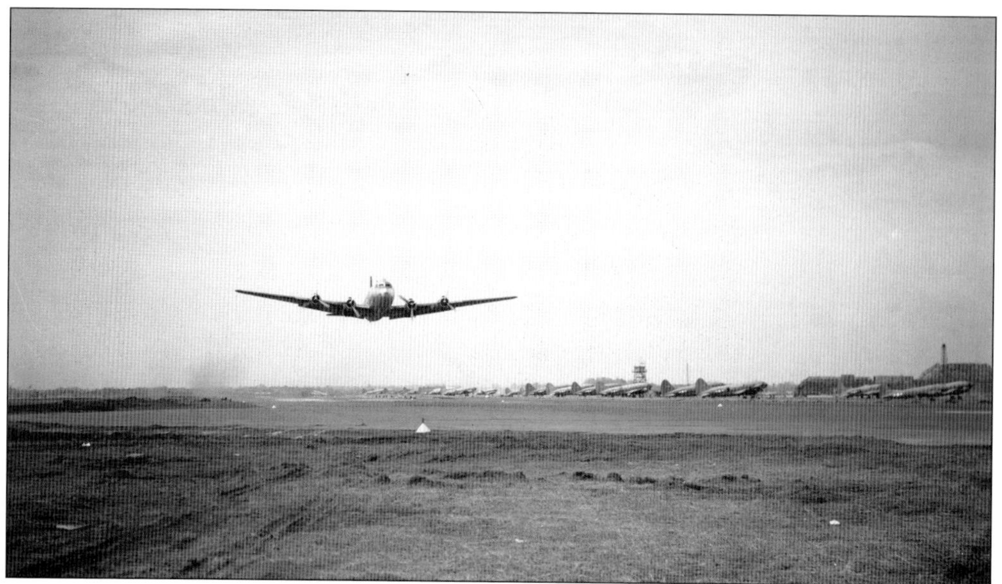

Taking off from one of the runways, this large aircraft was used for transporting materials and troops to other bases both domestically and internationally. In the distance are multiple aircraft prepped and ready to take off when needed. The runway may have been hard-packed; right off the runway was soft dirt, so it was important for the pilot to get the aircraft up as fast as possible. (KCM.)

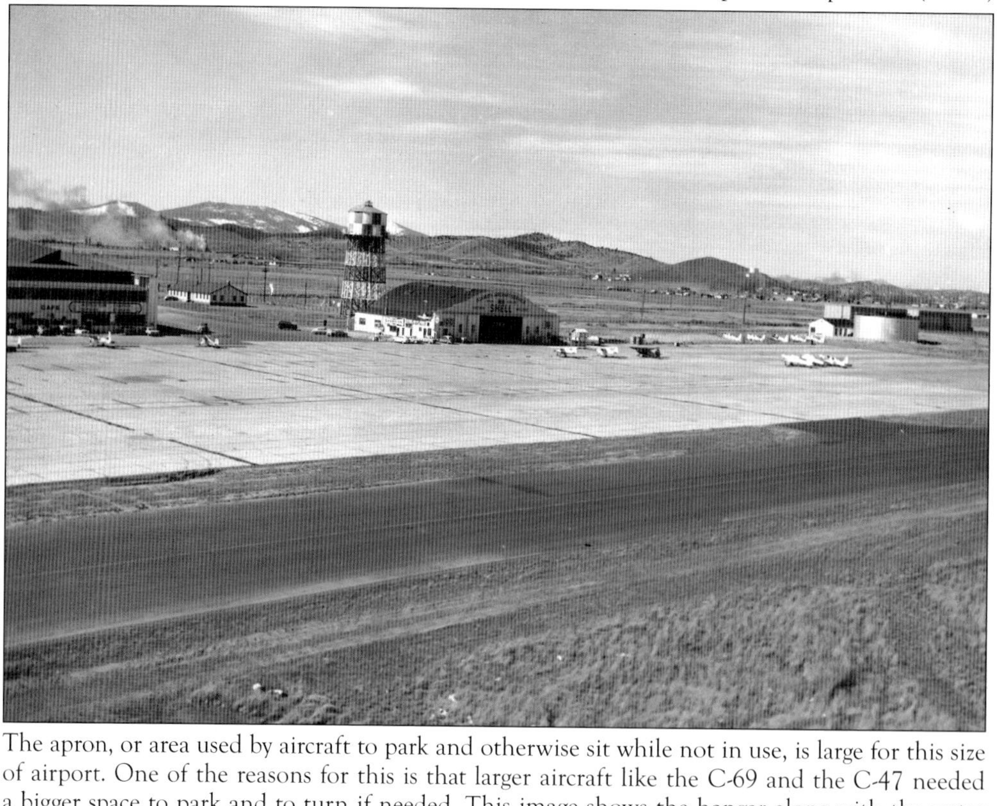

The apron, or area used by aircraft to park and otherwise sit while not in use, is large for this size of airport. One of the reasons for this is that larger aircraft like the C-69 and the C-47 needed a bigger space to park and to turn if needed. This image shows the hangar along with the water tower. (KCM.)

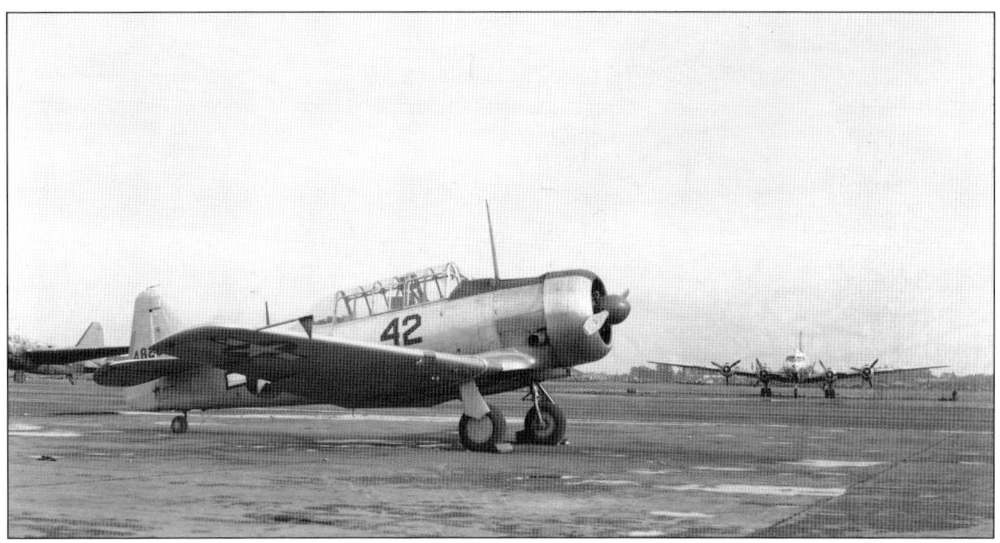

Another SNJ aircraft is sitting on the apron at Klamath Falls NAS. The large aircraft on the left rear was used as a troop carrier for the 317th domestically. In the distance, two rows of two-engine aircraft can be seen. Having a large enough field to accommodate multiple sizes for various needs allowed service members the opportunity to train on many different aircraft frames. (KCM.)

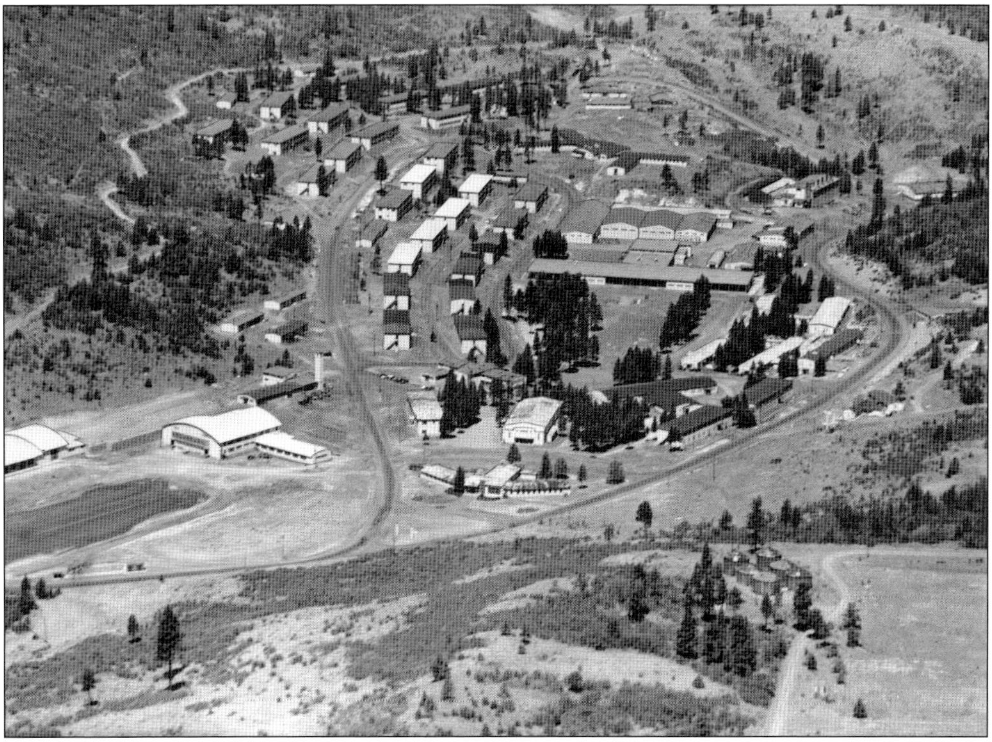

The Navy was not the only branch of service stationed in the Klamath Basin; near where the Oregon Institute of Technology is now a US Marine base sat. Many of the Marines worked at Klamath Falls NAS, while others trained for future deployments overseas. The image shows the entirety of the base, including barracks, administrative buildings, and entertainment facilities. (KCM.)

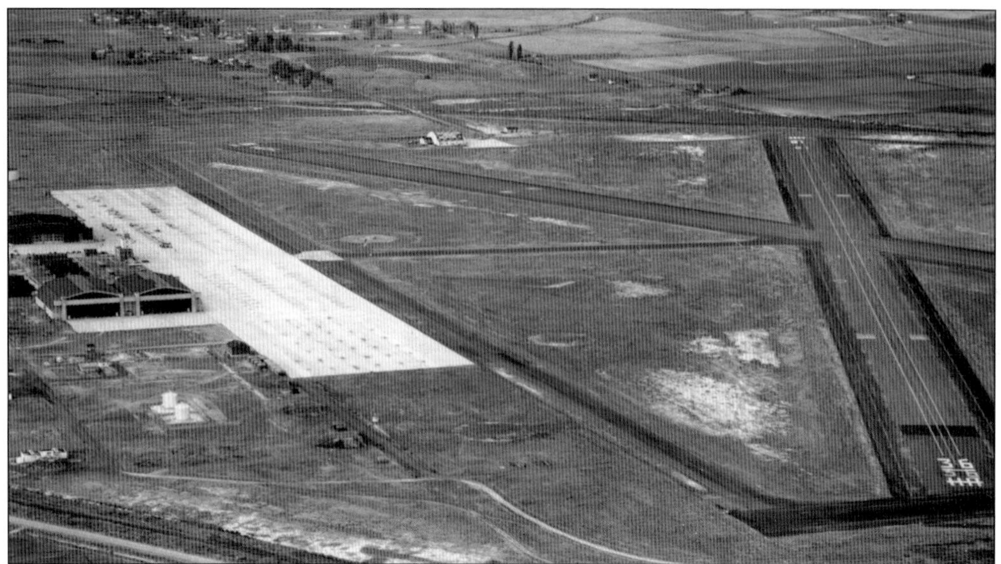

When the military initially left Klamath Falls in 1946, all the buildings remained intact. The military had paved major runways and provided enough structure for the city to easily transition to a municipal airport. This image was taken by the US military in preparation for a future transition to an active Air Force base. (KCM.)

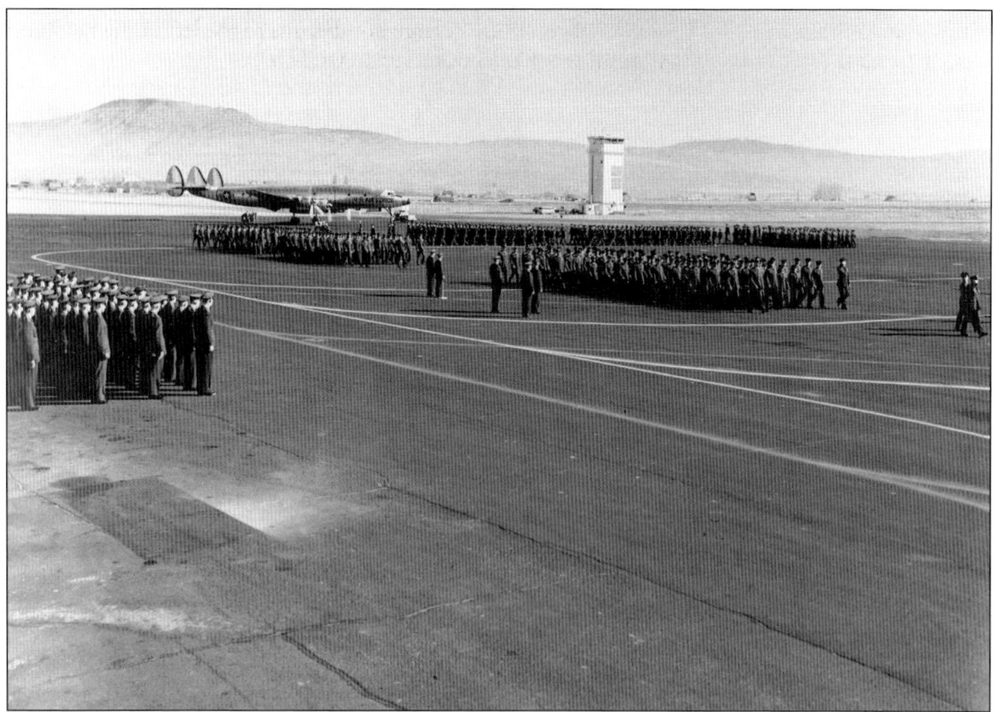

Due to its large nature, Klamath Falls NAS was able to accommodate aircraft that smaller military installations were unable to. This image shows multiple units marching in uniform in front of the air traffic control tower and a Lockheed C-69 Constellation. The C-69 was used during World War II as a military transport; this image was taken after the war as the C-69 displays the US Air Force insignia, which did not exist until September 1947. (KCM.)

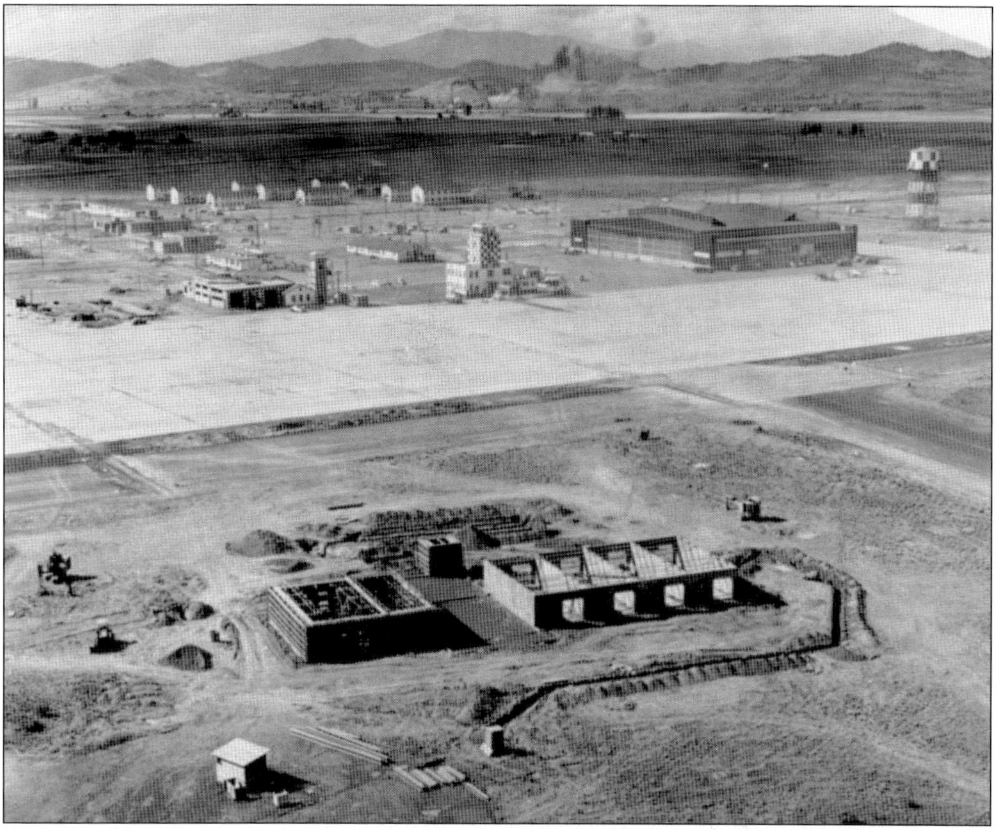

After the US military deactivated the base, it went into civilian control for a short amount of time before the newly created Air Force chose Klamath Falls as a base for all-weather interceptors. With the new squadrons coming in, additional buildings needed to be constructed to accommodate the new mission. The building in the foreground, in the middle of construction, was slated for rocket storage. (KCM.)

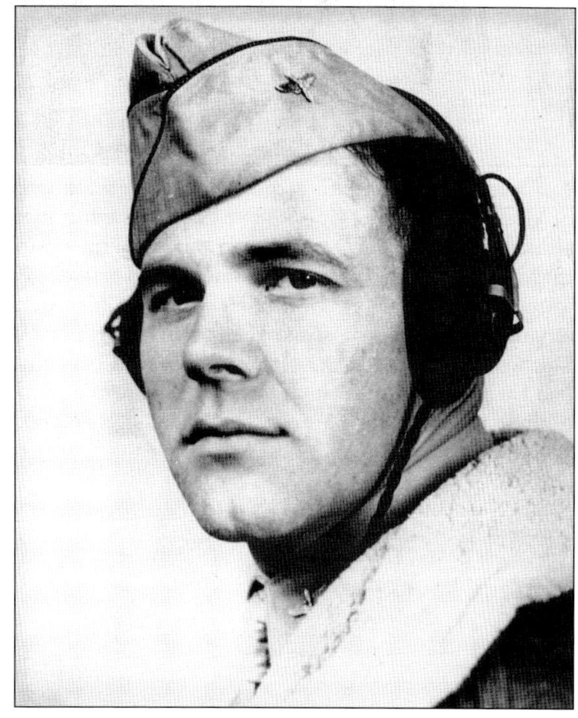

On July 3, 1956, the military officially dedicated the joint civilian-military airport as Kingsley Field. Second Lt. David R. Kingsley, an Oregonian, was killed in action on June 23, 1944, during the United States' bombing of the oil fields of Ploiesti, Romania. He joined the US Army Air Force in Portland in 1942. He was a bombardier with the 97th Bombardment Group. (KCM.)

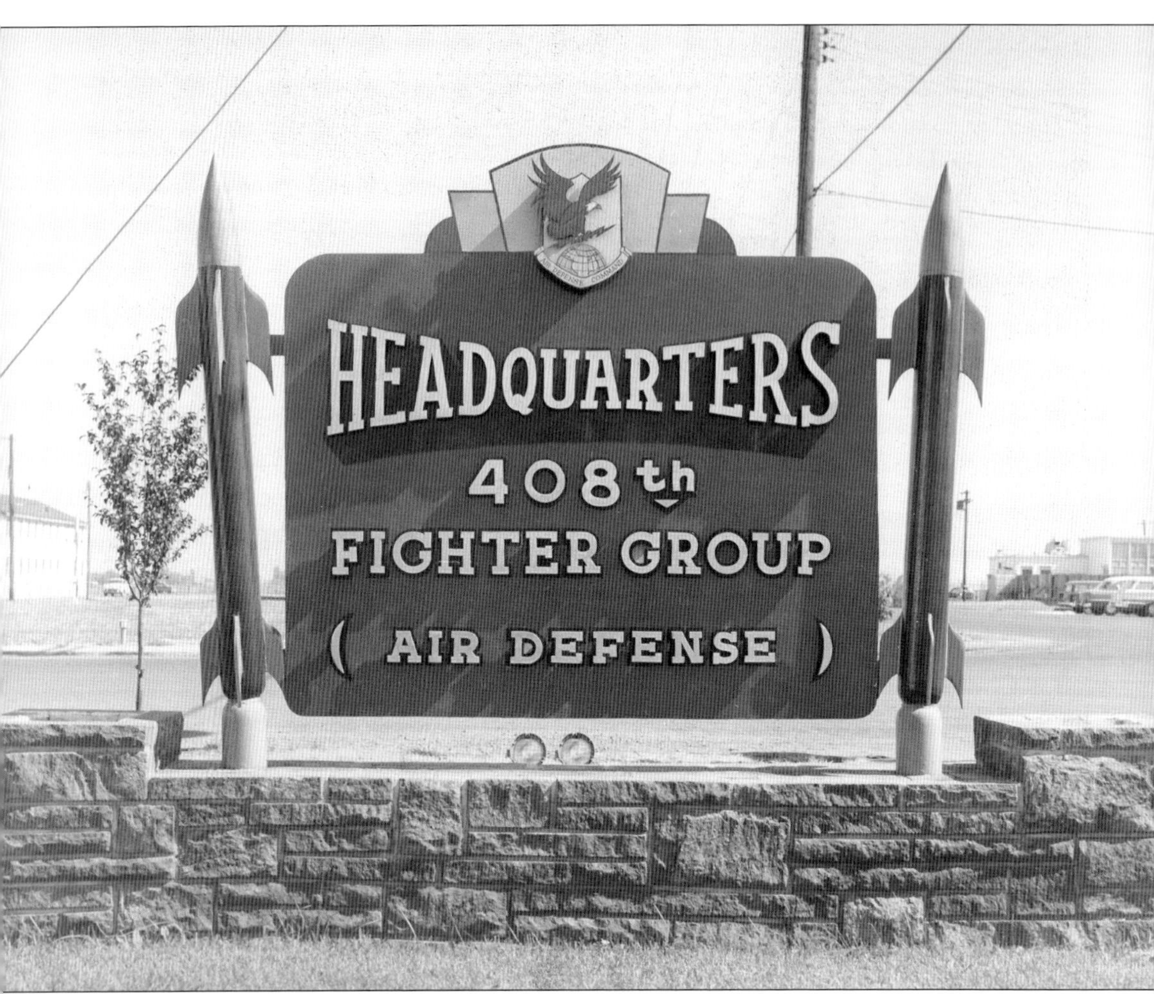

Following deactivation in 1946, the US Air Force selected the Klamath Falls municipal airport in 1954 as an ideal site for an all-weather fighter squadron with an aircraft control and warning squadron attached. The 408th Fighter Group was reactivated and moved to Klamath Falls in 1956 to rebuild and provide support to units being moved to the base. The group stayed until it was inactivated in 1970. In 1978, the US Air Force transferred the facilities from active duty to the Oregon National Guard, where it has remained ever since. The 173rd Fighter Wing of the Oregon National Guard was formed in 1996 at Kingsley Field to be the host organization and parent unit for the 114th Fighter Squadron, which moved from Portland to Kingsley Field. Every year, Kingsley Field hosts the STARBASE camp to bring STEM to basin students in a fun manner. (KCM.)

Prior to the military taking over the Madras airfield, it was open to the public. This biplane is shown with numerous individuals who were also pilots or training to be pilots. The individuals are wearing common outfits for flying in an open cockpit biplane: goggles, leather helmets, and leather jackets with boots. Leather was preferable, as it provided warmth and was flexible. (Jefferson County Historical Society.)

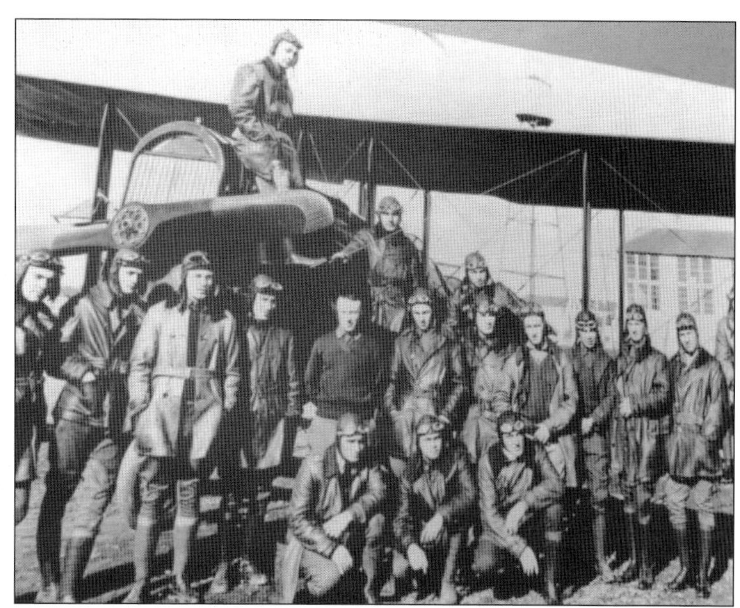

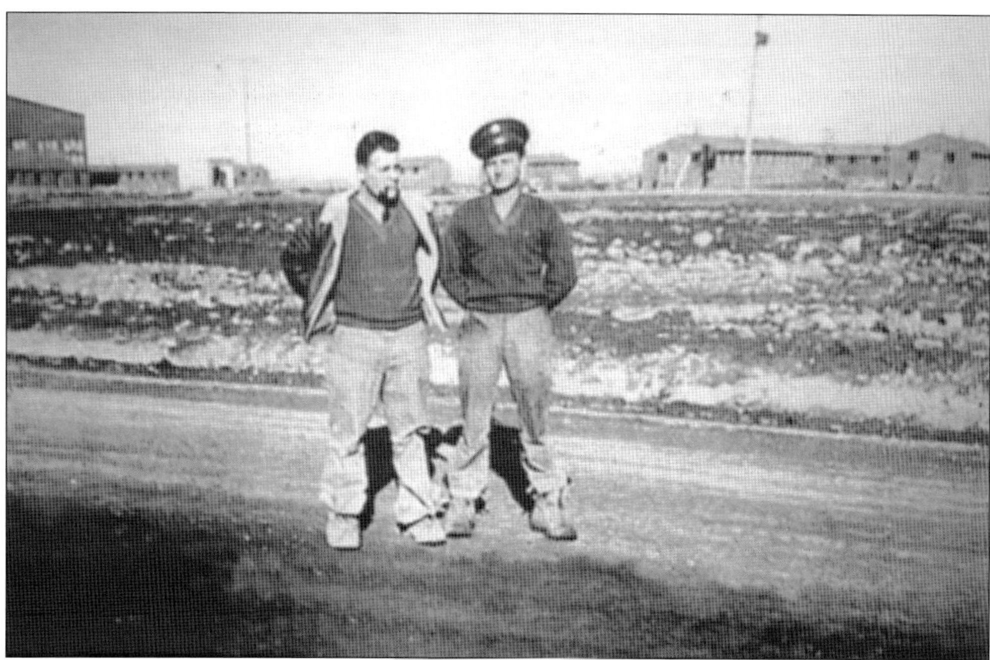

The initial steps to build an airport in Madras began in 1934 when Jefferson County purchased 40 acres of land. Due to budget constraints, it was another five years before construction began. The US military had already selected numerous locations in Central Oregon and decided that Madras would be a good location as well, and it quickly went from a rudimentary airfield to a large military air base. (Jefferson County Historical Society.)

SURPLUS

MADRAS

HISTORICAL DATA - POST, CAMP, STATION OR AIR FIELD

NAME: Madras Army Air Field

Location: 2.3 miles north of Madras, Oregon

Post Office: Madras, Oregon | Telegraph Office: Madras, Oregon | Radio available: Yes ☐ No ☒

Railroad Station: Madras, Oregon | Express Station: Madras, Oregon | Acquired by:

Class Installation: III | Assignment: GF ☐ SF ☐ AF ☒ WD ☐ | Capacity: Troops 1623

Adm. Control: Air Technical Service Command | Hospital Beds 10

Storage (Sq. Ft.) 34300

Land Acres 2140

Nearest Landing Field: | Date Occupied

HISTORY:

Airdromes and their installations at Madras, Oregon, are assigned to the Second Air Force - AG 580.82 (7-1-42)MR-AF-PS-M, July 6, 1942. Also see WD Memo No. W95-22-42, dated October 13, 1942. Also see WD Memo No. W95-3-43, dated February 8, 194

Army Air Field located 2 miles northwest of Madras, Oregon is designated Madras Army Air Field - Post Office: Madras, Oregon - WD Memo No. W95-9-43, dated April 8, 1943.

Sub-base of Walla Walla Army Air Field, Washington.

Satellite Base, AAB, Madras, Oregon, is assigned to Geiger Field, Washington. - per GO #179, Hqs, Second Air Force, Colorado Springs, Colo. dated 28 November 1943 (R).

Madras Army Air Field, Madras, Oreg. is assigned to the Fourth Air Force - per WD Circular #46 dated 2 February 1944.

The Precision Bombing Range, Madras Army Air Field, declared surplus 15 March 1944. Retransferred to Department of Interior 2 May 1944 - per Monthly Progress Report, OCE, dated 31 May 1944 (C).

Madras AAF, Ore. is assigned as a sub-base of Portland AAB, Ore. - per Army Air Forces Installations Directory dated 1 October 1944 (R).

Madras Army Air Field, Madras, Oreg. is assigned to the 4th Air Force - per WD Circular #29 dated 24 January 1945.

Madras Army Air Field, Madras, Oreg. (under Fourth Air Force) To ATSC 15 May, is temporarily inactive. -per List of Temporarily Inactive Stations, Army Air Forces, as of 1 May 1945.

Madras Army Air Field, Madras, Oreg. is assigned to the Air Technical Service Command - per WD Circular #166, dtd. 6 Jun

Madras Army Air Field, Oregon, is placed in the category of surplus, effective as of 15 Nov. 1945. - per AG 602 (26 Nov OB-I-SPMOC-M, dated 1 Dec. 1945. See also ASF Cir. #439, dated 7 Dec. 1945.

Announcement is made that the Air Technical Service Command is relieved of command responsibility for Madras Army Air F Madras, Oregon, effective as of 16 January 1946, subject station being transferred to Portland District Engineer as of that d - per Ltr., Hq., Air Technical Service Command, Wright Field, Dayton, Ohio, dated 29 Dec. 1945. & GO #4, Hq. Spokane ATSC, Spokane, Wash., dated 14 Jan. 46.

For a base that was used frequently by the US Army Air Corps, there are unfortunately not a lot of images available. On July 6, 1942, the Madras Army Airfield was assigned to the 2nd Air Force initially as a sub-base for Walla Walla. However, it was soon moved around to various other units before being its final military transfer on January 16, 1946. Following deactivation, the airport stayed open and became a civilian airport. In 2000, the airport began to collect vintage aircraft and started to have air shows for the community. The Erickson Aircraft Collection was originally stored at the Tillamook Air Museum. In May 2014, the collection moved to the Madras Airport. The museum not only has complete aircraft that can and do fly, but it is also one of the only facilities in the United States that can repair large vintage aircraft. The museum has the ability and resources to bring in experts and acquire original parts to repair a variety of airframes. The aircraft repaired are from both other organizations and private collectors. (Air Education and Training Command History Office.)

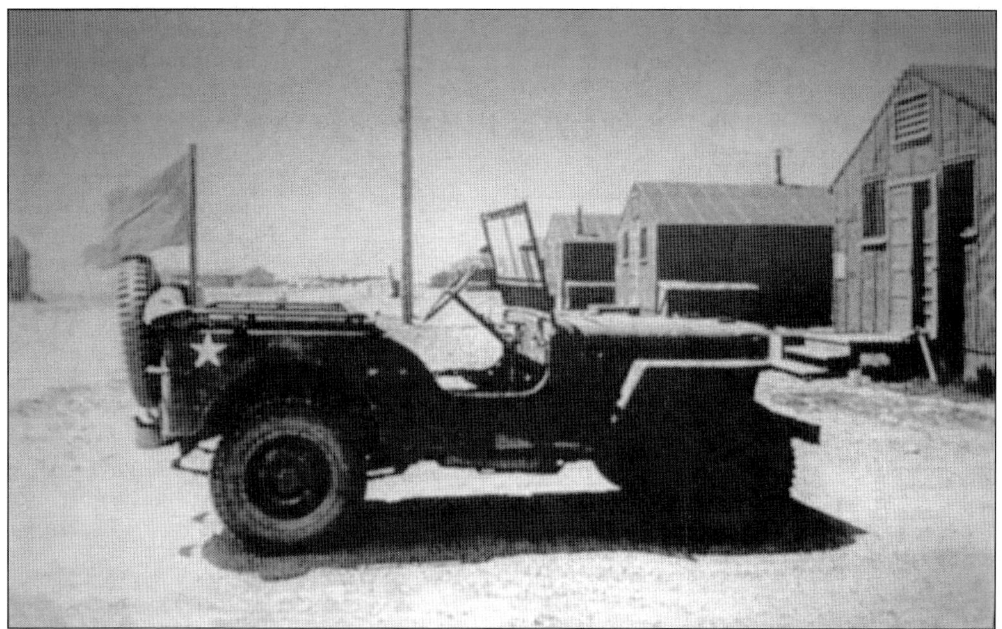

The hangars were state-of-the-art for the time, needing to be large enough for the B-17 Flying Fortresses and later for the P-30 Airacobra, P-63 Kingcobra, and P-38 Lightning. The runways at Madras were the largest of any military base in Oregon, measuring 7,400 feet. With the quick increase in personnel, some buildings were quickly constructed, such as these in the background. (Jefferson County Historical Society.)

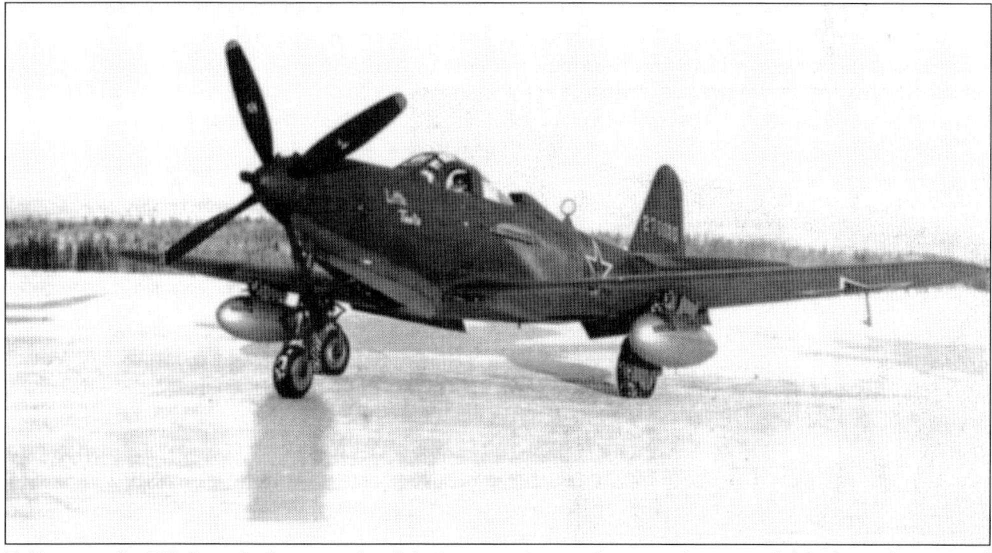

Following the US Army's decision that Madras was the perfect spot for an airfield, the military used it for training on the Boeing B-17 Flying Fortress and the Bell P-63 King Cobra. With how many people rotated through Madras, a lot lived in the community, commuting by military bus to the base. In 1944, the military transferred training for both aircraft to Redmond. The base's mission changed in September 1944 to aircraft maintenance. (Jefferson County Historical Society.)

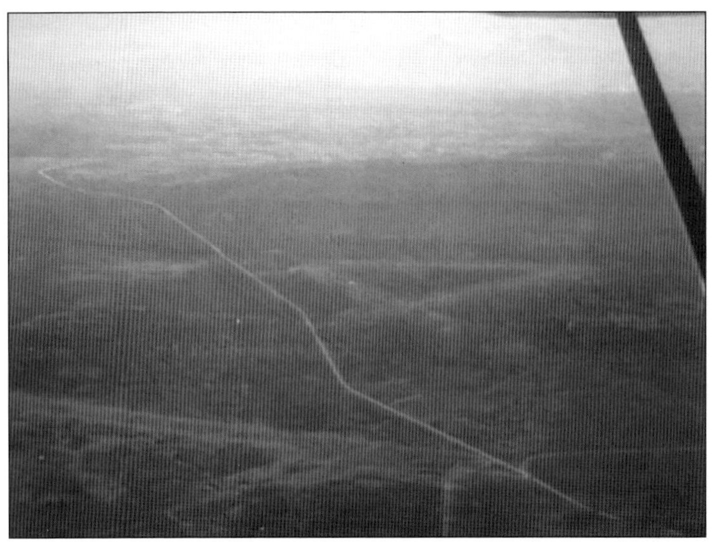

It was not long after Bend and Redmond gained airports that Prineville's residents wanted in on the action as well. In May 1920, a private citizen created a landing strip. The strip can be seen in the lower part of the picture. With how much aircraft enthusiasm there was, soon the City of Prineville bought the land and the runway from the private owner so it could be widely used. (Bowman Museum.)

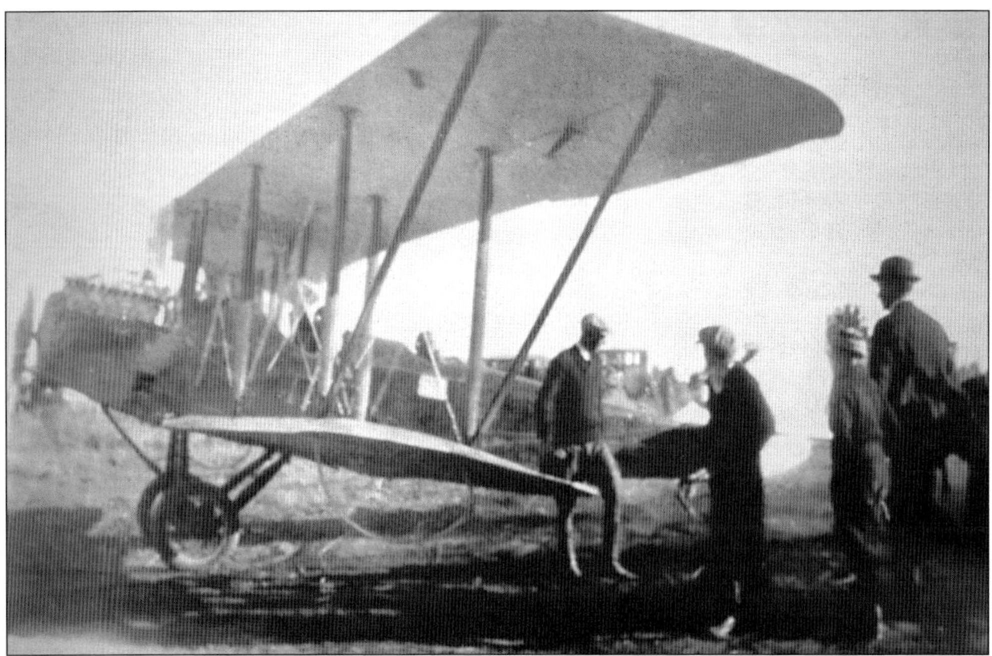

Soon after the property was purchased by the City of Prineville, aircraft began to land. On April 16, 1931, the first aircraft landed at the newly purchased property. The pilots allowed the public to view the aircraft and reported to the newspaper that it was a very nice field and would be recommended to other pilots. It still took three years before a fully functional airfield was built. (Bowman Museum.)

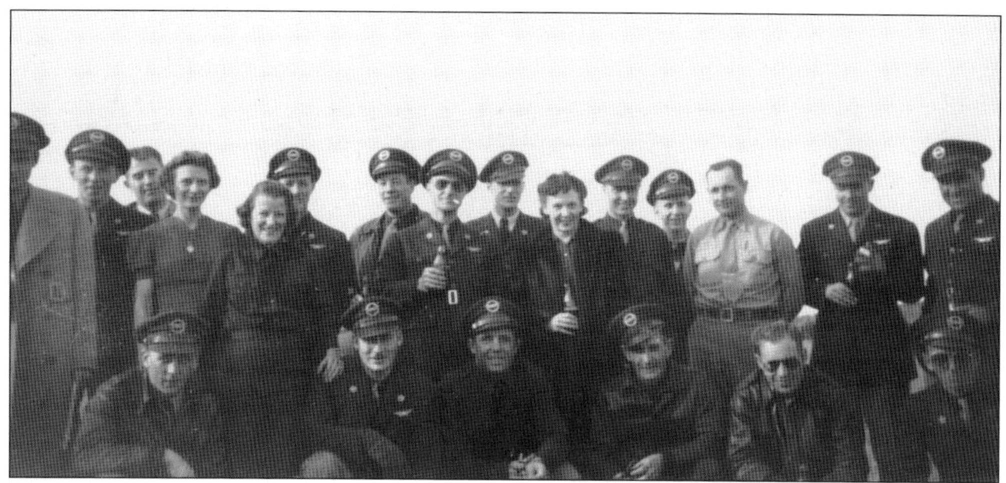

The Army was not the only organization that benefited from having a military base in Prineville. While the military got instructors and pilots trained, community members were employed, and the community saw a surge in income due to the service members being stationed there, even for small amounts of time. This image shows pilots as well as some of the instructors and administration celebrating. (Bowman Museum.)

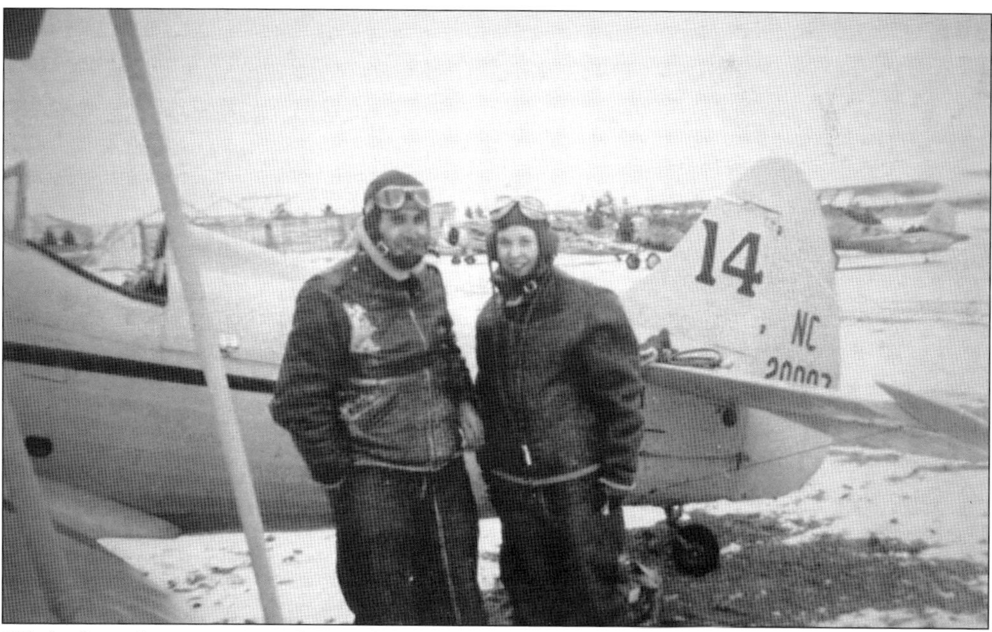

While the military was completing the renovations and construction needed, it was searching for instructors. Ralph Scroggin, a native of Western Oregon, applied for the position of civilian flight instructor. Soon after acceptance, he moved to Prineville with his wife, Grace. When the military sold the base back to the city in 1944, Ralph and his family stayed on, founding the Prineville Flying Service and teaching civilians how to fly. (Bowman Museum.)

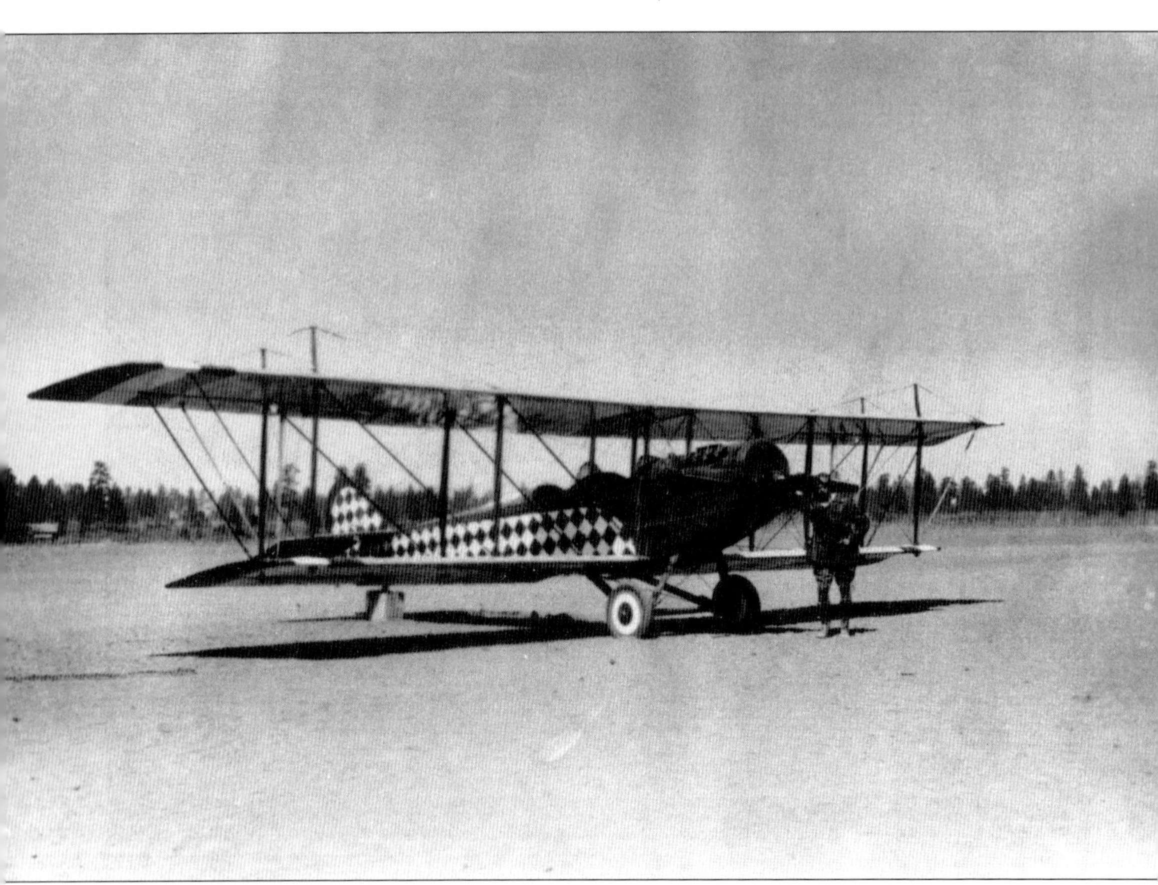

Everyone wanted to be part of flying, in the air or just being around the aircraft. Before Bend and Redmond had designated airfields, the community was building, buying, and flying their own aircraft. With the increase in aircraft came the desire to be around and socialize with other people who enjoyed the hobby. Even though not sanctioned by the city, it did not stop the community from putting on events. In May 1920, Central Oregon hoped to bring attention to the growing aircraft industry by holding the first air show in the region. The event was widely publicized throughout Central Oregon, allowing those who had never seen an aircraft in person to do so. The first aircraft the public saw in action was a Curtiss JN-4, a biplane with two seats. Roland Thompson landed in Redmond as part of the barnstorming event. (DHM.)

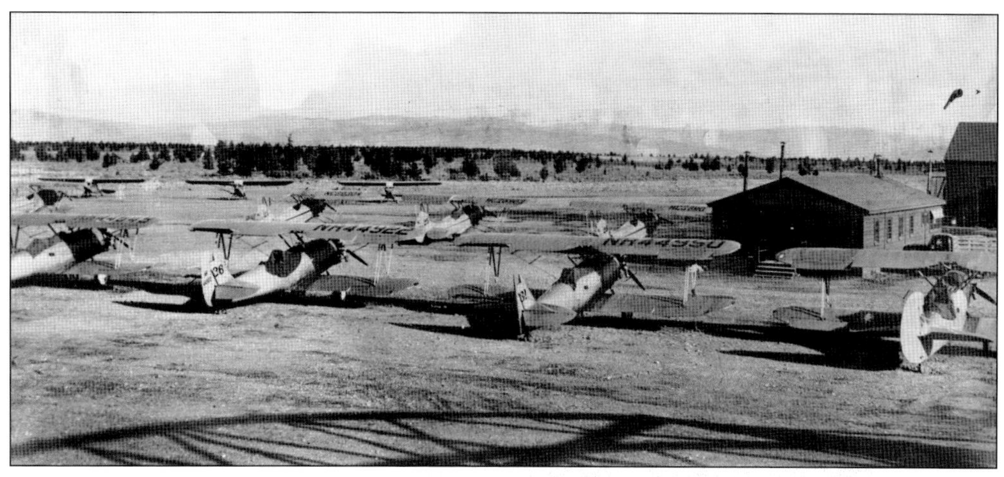

At the start of the war, the Prineville airport was being used by civilians, but with its proximity to Redmond, along with the other airports in the area, the military decided to use it as a training facility. This was common due to the airfields already being built up to some capacity. Both images are from when the Army Air Corps came into Prineville with its training aircraft. In the image below, one can see the multiple lines of aircraft as they sit, with a runway in the back. The image above is of similar aircraft but shows some of the buildings that the Army constructed to assist in the training and administration of the airport. (Both, Bowman Museum.)

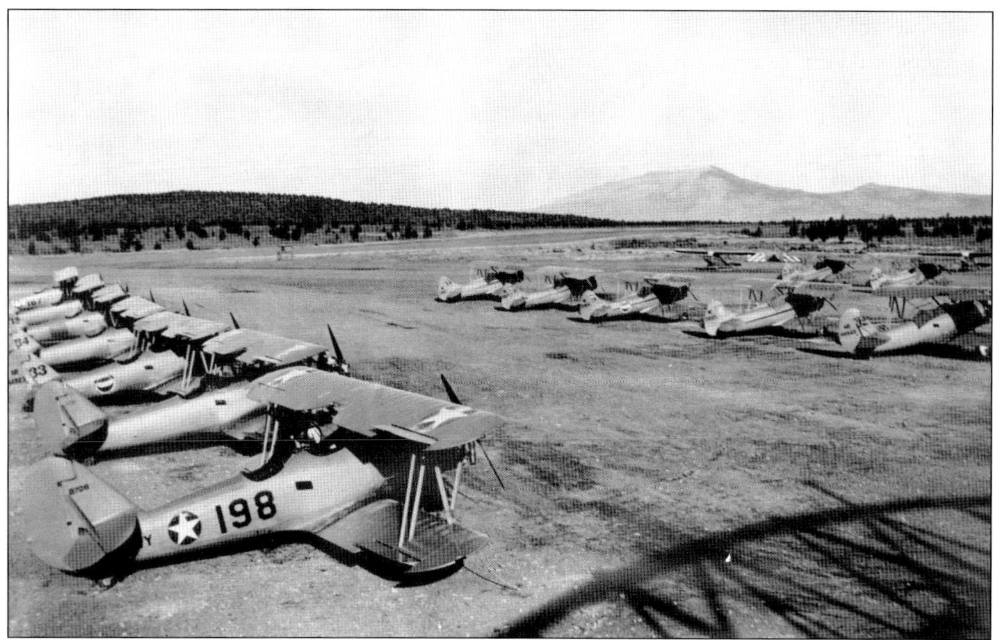

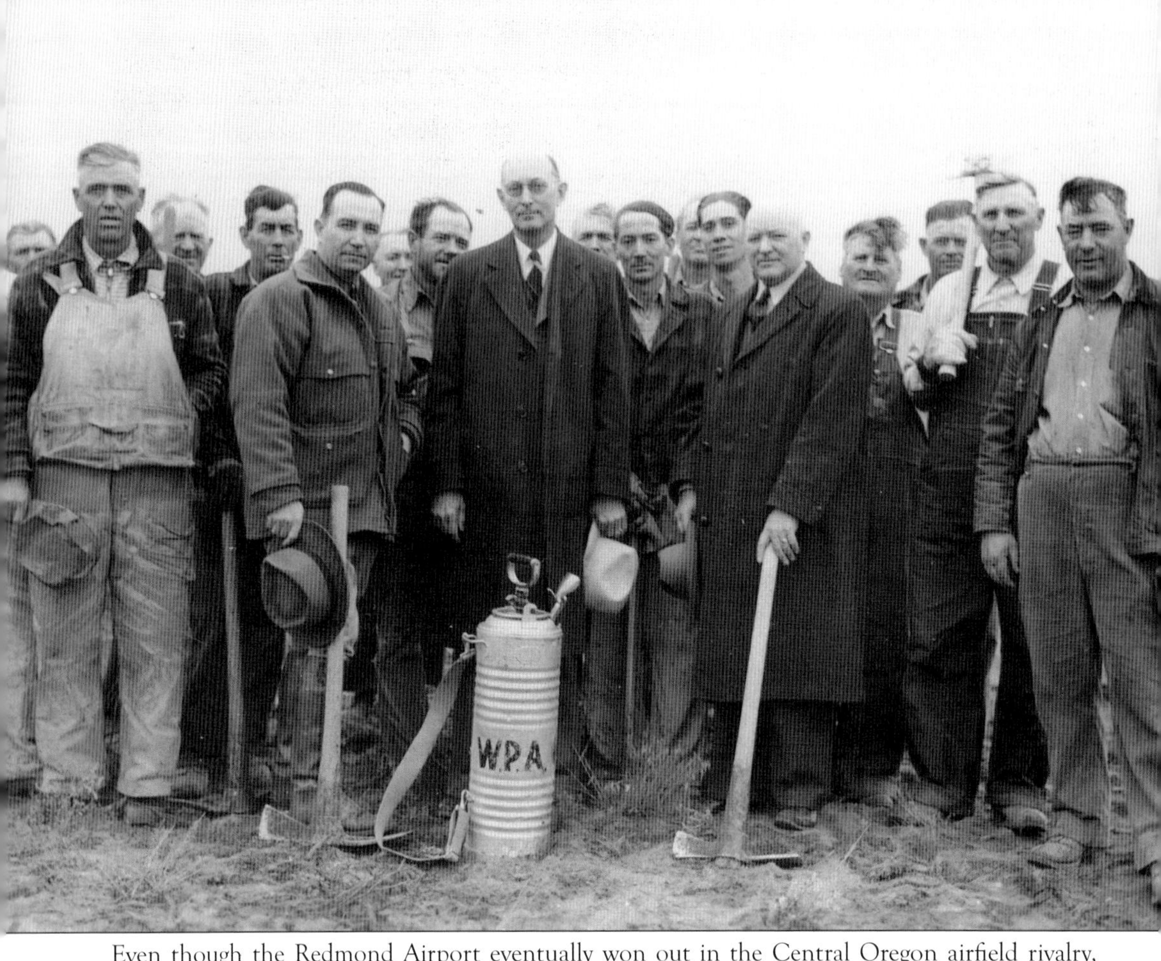

Even though the Redmond Airport eventually won out in the Central Oregon airfield rivalry, Bend was the first to have not one but two airfields. Seeing this, the residents of Redmond wanted their own. In 1928, the American Legion, along with the City of Redmond, began to advocate for an airport. The major hurdle was to secure funding for the airport. It took six years of working on grants and petitions before the airport plans were finally accepted in 1934. It took another two years before the Works Progress Administration (WPA) was able to allocate the needed funds. This image shows the WPA, along with some of the architects of the Redmond Airport, posed at the new location of the airport after funding was allocated. These men, along with numerous community leaders and members, helped to position the airport as the largest in Central Oregon. (DHM.)

Ten short months before the United States entered World War II, a Works Progress grant was approved by President Roosevelt's administration in the amount of $717,000 to expand the existing airport. Soon, construction began, which consisted of two runways and only the necessary buildings. The City of Redmond named the airport after J.R. Roberts, who worked with Senator McNary to secure the airport. This photograph shows the completed airport in 1941. (USAF Historical Research Agency.)

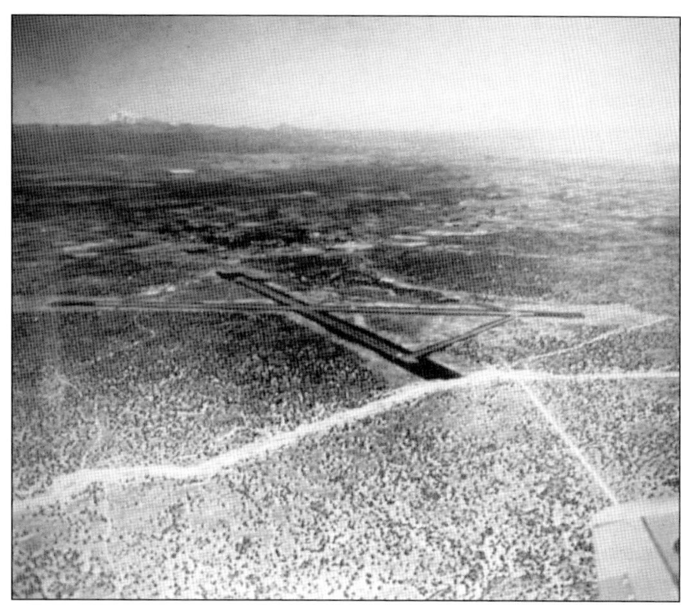

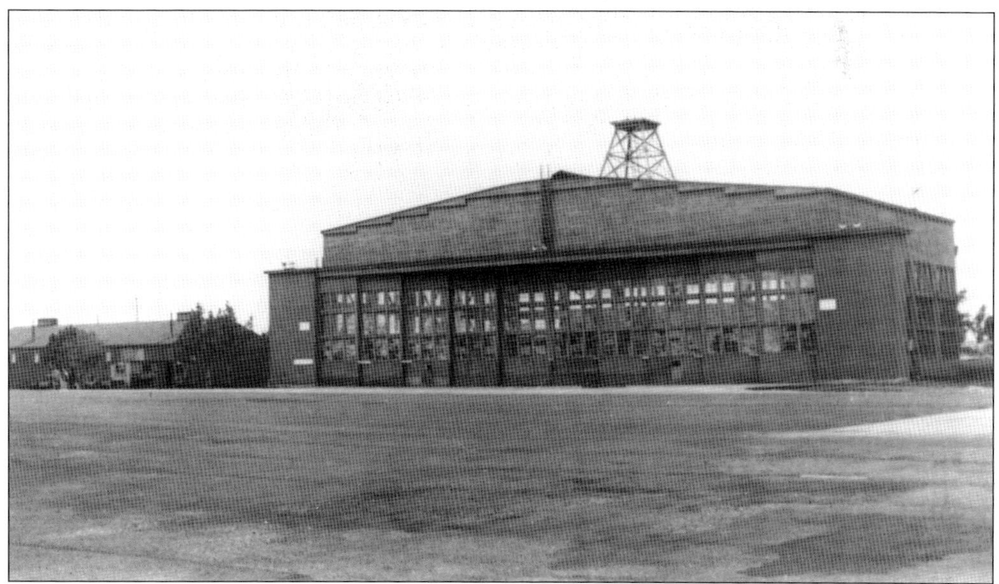

When Roberts Field became a full-fledged airport, a hangar needed to be built. This hangar was still used even after the US Army built a new hangar next to it. While not as large as the new hangar, the space was still needed, and it was utilized by the Army as a location for training and maintenance. An administration building can be seen to the left. (DHM.)

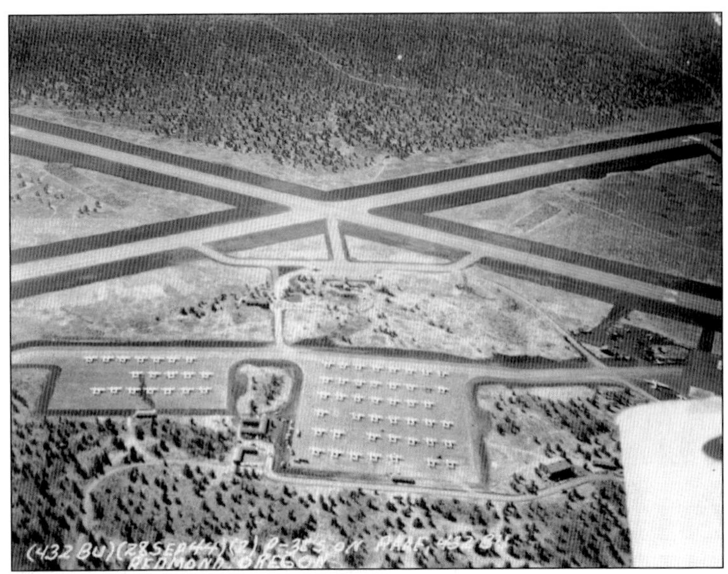

In this image taken by the US Army, Redmond Army Airfield is fully visible. The two main runways, along with the apron, were able to hold a large number of P-38s used for training flights as well as simulated combat situations. To the right are the main buildings that held the administration department as well as the hangars for smaller aircraft and other larger aircraft. (USAF Historical Research Agency.)

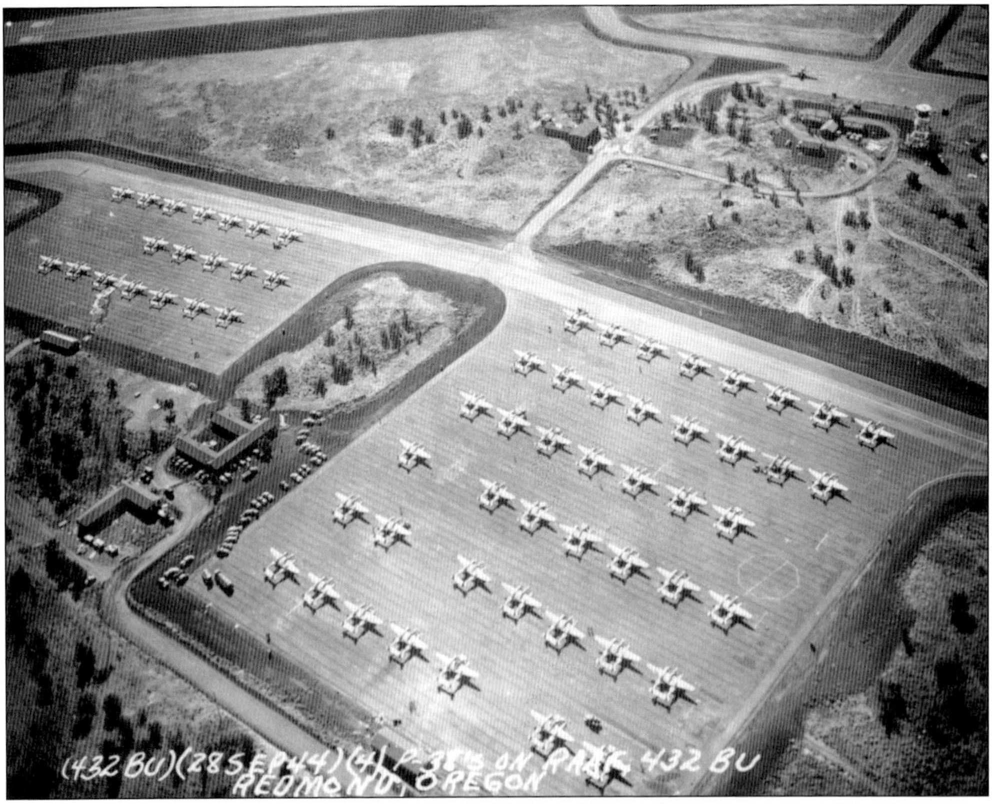

Shown here is a closer view of the apron that held the P-38s used. The majority of the P-38s were destined to be transported and used in active combat; a small contingent was maintained at the airfield to ensure that training for pilots and maintenance crews could continue without needing to bring in more aircraft. This image also shows the two main buildings used between the two storage aprons. (USAF Historical Research Agency.)

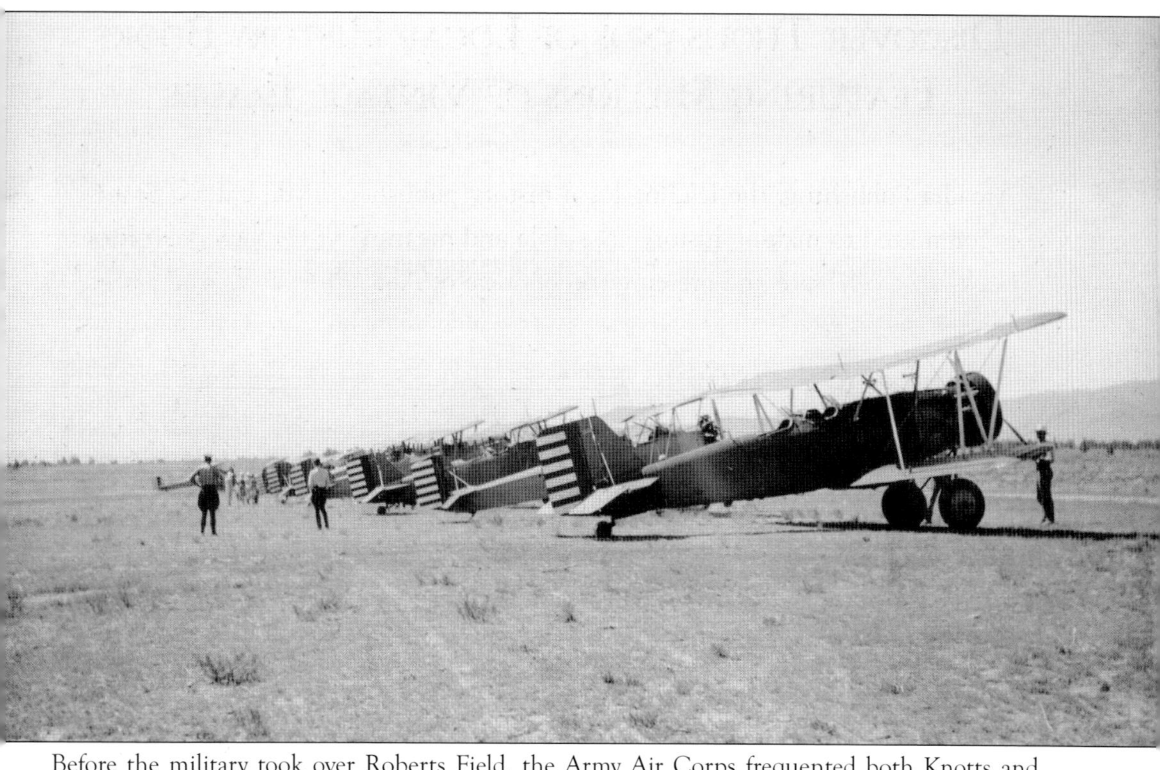

Before the military took over Roberts Field, the Army Air Corps frequented both Knotts and Roberts airfields while en route from one base to another along the Pacific coastline. These O-19 observation aircraft are lined up at Roberts Field during a stopover. The O-19 aircraft was the predecessor to the O-47 seen in other photographs. The biplane was specifically built by the Thomas-Morse Aircraft Company for the US Army Air Corps. It was a metal frame with fabric-covered wings and tail surfaces. While light, the fabric did tend to be replaced frequently as opposed to the later models, which were made entirely out of metal. Of the 176 O-19 aircraft built, they were used frequently by the US Army Air Corps as well as the Philippine Army Air Corps. During longer layovers, the military sometimes allowed citizens the chance to view aircraft not normally seen. (DHM.)

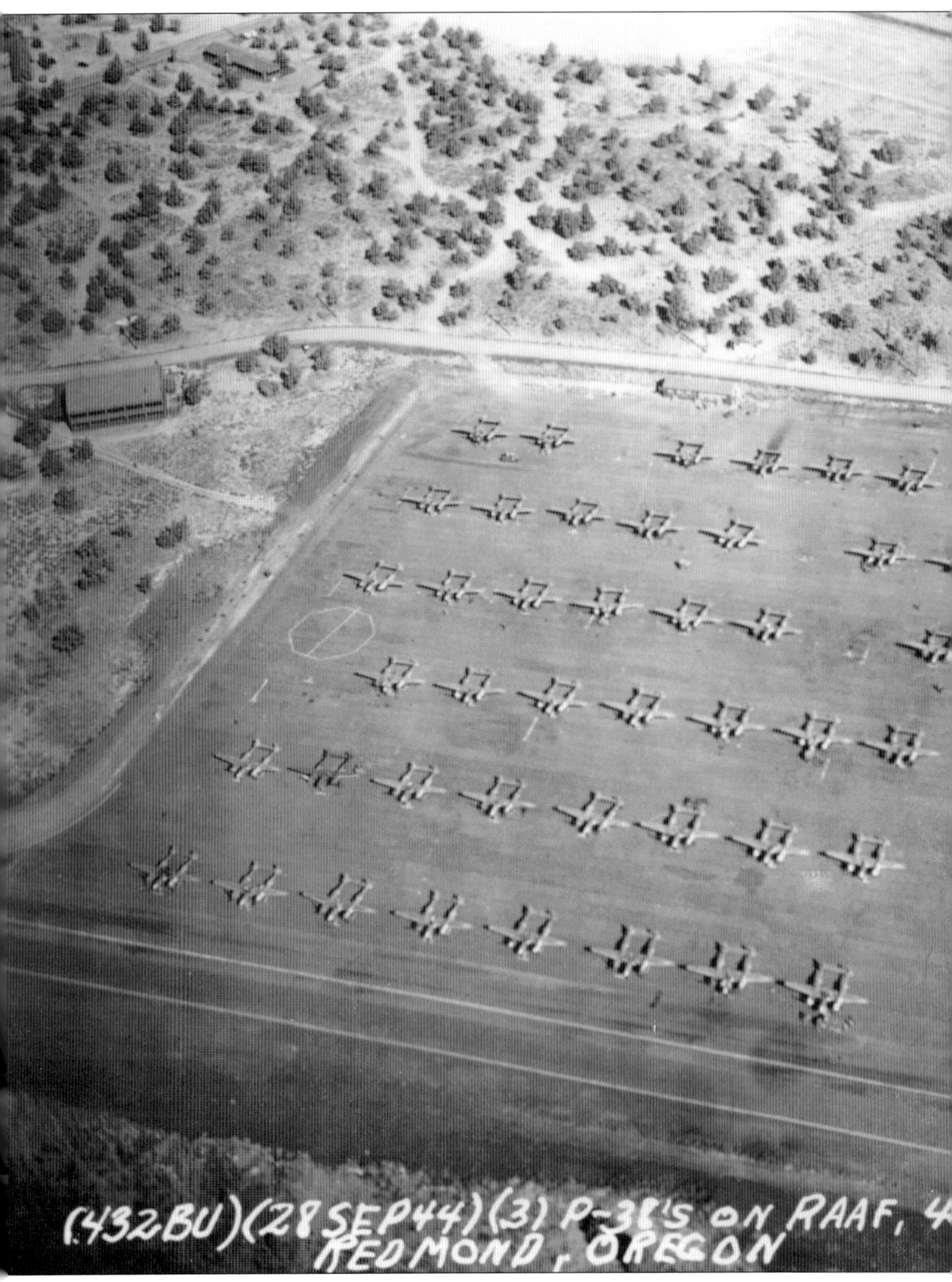
(432BU)(28SEP44)(3) P-38'S ON RAAF, 4
REDMOND, OREGON

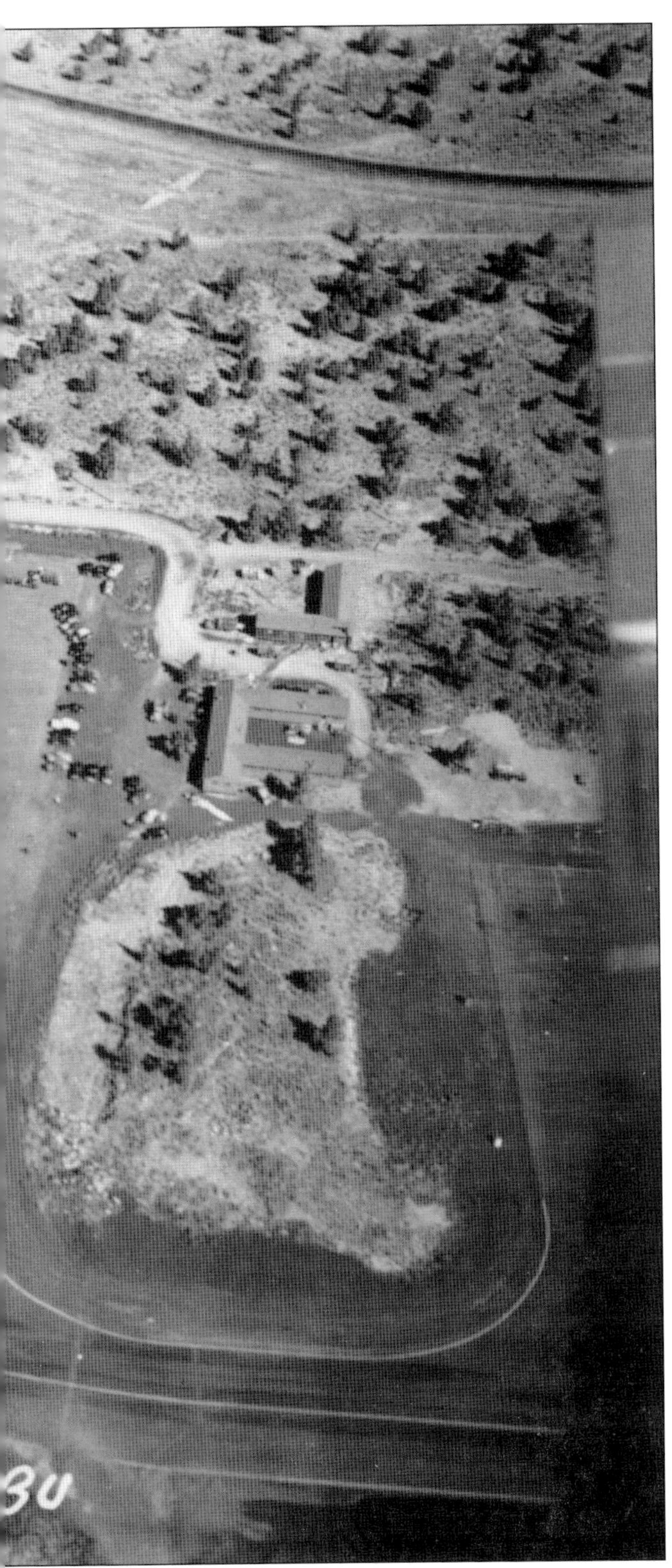

When the military took control of Roberts Field, it initially was a sub-air base to Portland Army Air Base. A sub-air base means that it can have its own commanding staff, but they answer to the main base at Portland Army Air Base. These sub-air bases were used for overflow aircraft, training, and dispersal. Another main reason that sub-air bases exist is for additional support functions that the main base did not have the resources or space for. This includes maintenance or repair for specific aircraft that were not normally attributed to the main base but were regularly in the area. Redmond was modified to store, train, and maintain the larger P-38s. The first thing that was needed was an increase in the runways and then larger aprons to hold the aircraft. This larger storage apron held aircraft not immediately needed. (USAF Historical Research Agency.)

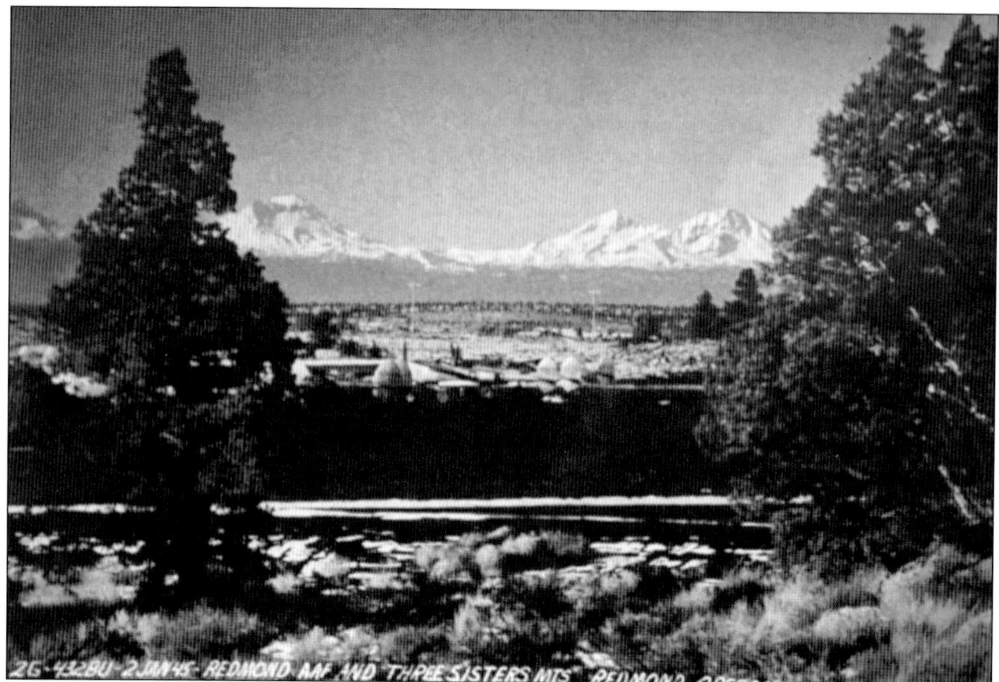

Roberts Field saw thousands of soldiers as they trained on the P-38s. Most of the individuals training at Roberts Field were sent to the Pacific theater to engage in combat. With the Three Sisters mountains in the background, the US Army performed hundreds of simulated battles here, dividing the base into two units, the Red and the Blue forces. These simulated battles took place between July and October 1943. (US Still Pictures.)

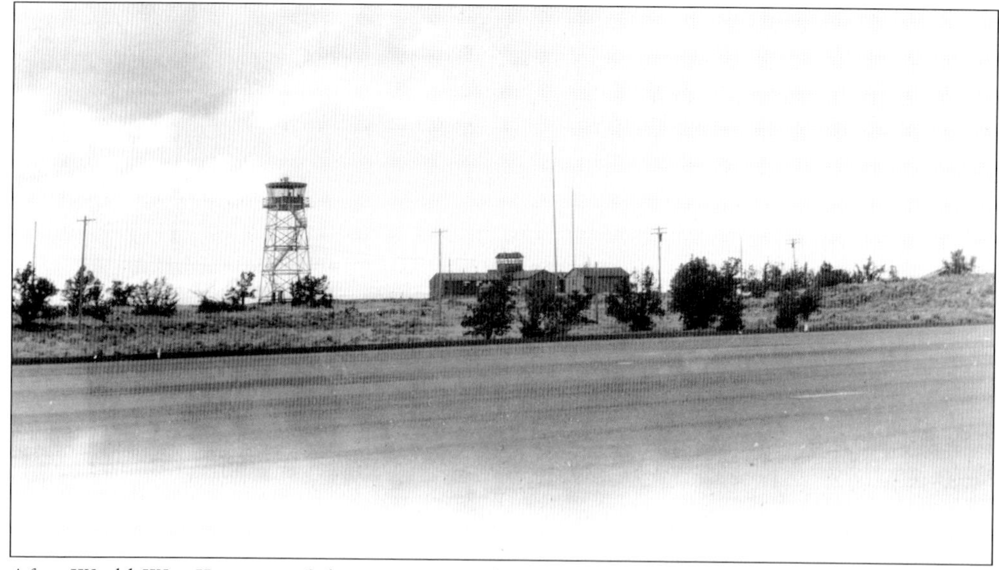

After World War II, many of the previous air bases were decommissioned. However, the Civil Aeronautics Administration (CAA) began to look at certain airports around the United States in hopes of finding well-maintained airports that could be transitioned into municipal, regional, and, in some cases, international airports. Roberts Field was on the list of properties that the CAA recommended for further development and use as a civilian airport. (DHM.)

Four

Eastern Oregon

Eastern Oregon goes by many names, such as "Outback," "High Desert," "Blues," and the Wallowas. The region spans the largest portion of Oregon, from the Washington border to the north to the California border to the south and west from the Idaho border to where the Cascade region begins. While the largest geographical region at 457 miles long and 262 miles wide, it is the least populated, with only about five percent of Oregon's entire population.

Geographically, Eastern Oregon varies. With an average elevation of over 3,500 feet, it has the most extremes from one area to another. Compared to the rest of the state, these regions are drier and receive less precipitation than others. The range goes from an average of less than 12 inches a year to places that see over 60 inches of snowfall that same year. This drastic variation extends into temperature as well. Some localized regions see ranges from 14 Fahrenheit in the winter to over 100 Fahrenheit in the summer, while others are more temperate, with their averages ranging from 40 to 85 Fahrenheit.

The military chose Eastern Oregon for multiple reasons. Given that there were large swaths of land that were mostly flat, the military saw it as a suitable location to train and test the large bombers of World War II. Using airfields in adjoining states as well, the military could transfer aircraft, personnel, and materials easily with the much larger aircraft. Another reason the military chose these locations was that it was sparsely populated, allowing the military to utilize more space and worry less about civilian populations being affected by testing craft accidents. The cost for land was relatively cheaper, and the communities welcomed the military jobs and personnel, giving new life to smaller communities. Not just testing of aircraft, but testing of munitions was also possible, which gave the military another aspect to its bases. Airfields of Eastern Oregon included Alkali Lake AAF, Lakeview NAAF, Ontario NAS, and Pendleton AAF. Documentation for the airfields at Baker, Boardman, and Memaloose FS exists; however, no historical imagery could be located.

SURPLUS

ALKALI

HISTORICAL DATA - POST, CAMP, STATION OR AIR FIELD

NAME: Alkali Lake Flight Strip

Location: Alkali Lake, Oregon

Post Office: ______ Telegraph Office: ______ Radio available: Yes ☐ No ☐

Railroad Station: ______ Express Station: ______ Acquired by: ______

Class Installation: III Assignment: GF ☐ SF ☐ AF ☒ WD ☐ Capacity: Troops ______

Adm. Control: 2nd Air Force Hospital Beds ______

Storage (Sq. Ft.) ______

Nearest Landing Field: ______ Land Acres ______

Date Occupied ______

HISTORY:

Airdromes and their installations at Flight Strip, Alkali Lake, Oregon, are assigned to the 2nd Air Force per War Dept. Memo No. W95-29-42 dated 11-13-42. See also WD Memo No. W95-3-43 dated 2-8-43. & W95-17-43 dated 7-7-43.

The airdrome and its installations at Alkali Lake, Oregon, having been assigned to the 2nd Air Force, is announced as a sub-post of Army Air Base, Walla Walla, Wash.; Base Commanders are not required to have personnel stationed at this airdrome unless the situation warrents such occupancy per Hq. 2nd AF, General Order No. 173 dated 11-24-42.

Alkali Lake Flight Strip, Alkali Lake, Oreg. - is assigned to the Second Air Force - per WD Circular #46 dated 2 February/1941

Alkali Lake Landing Strip, Wagontire, Oregon, declared surplus 8 October 1945 - per List of Airfields Excess to AAF, Continental US, dated 1 May 1946.

On February 2, 1941, a flight strip located at Alkali Lake near Wagontire was assigned to the 2nd Air Force as a sub-post for the Army air base at Walla Walla. An airdrome and buildings were created in the event that the flight strip was needed. During the war, no personnel was allocated to the flight strip as it was only minimally used. (Air Education and Training Command History Office.)

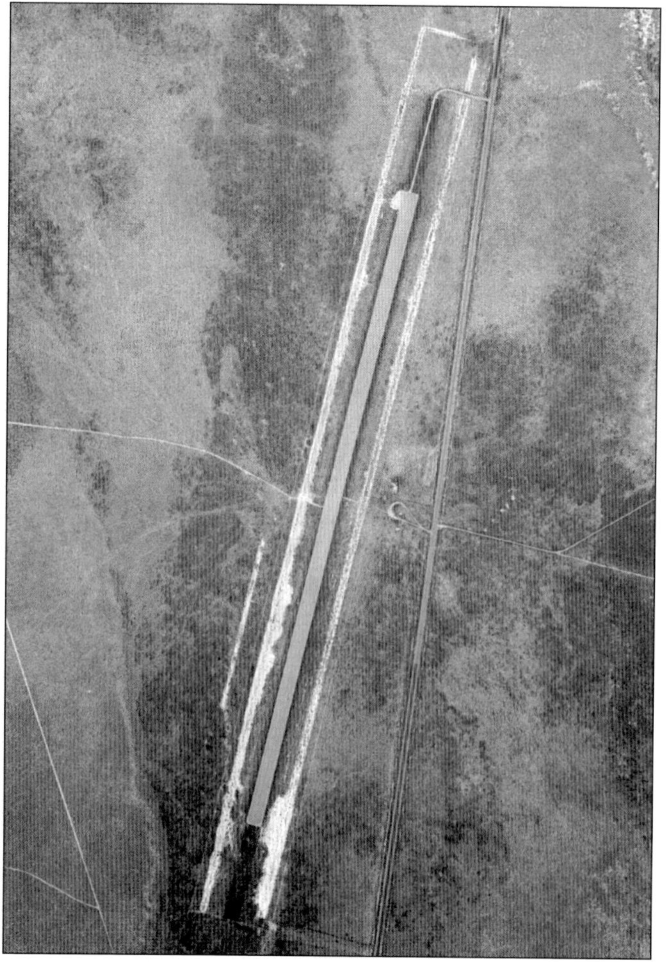

Alkali Lake flight strip originally consisted of one runway along with two small buildings. On May 1, 1946, the US Army Air Force considered Alkali Lake to be surplus and removed it from the continental United States list of airfields. The runway is still in use as a private permission-only airport, with additional buildings with fuel available. Its name changed from Alkali Lake to Wagontire Airport. (United States Geological Survey.)

SURPLUS

BOARDMAN

HISTORICAL DATA - POST, CAMP, STATION OR AIR FIELD

NAME: Boardman Flight Strip

Location: 5½ miles southwest (1 3/4 miles proposed) from Boardman, Oregon

Post Office: Boardman, Oregon Telegraph Office: Boardman, Oregon Radio available: Yes ☐ No ☒

Railroad Station: Boardman, Oregon Express Station: Boardman, Oregon Acquired by:

Class Installation: III Assignment: GF ☐ SF ☐ AF ☒ WD ☐ Capacity: Troops

Hospital Beds

Adm. Control: 2nd Air Force Storage (Sq. Ft.)

Land Acres 2562

Nearest Landing Field: Date Occupied

HISTORY:

The airdrome and its installations at Boardman, Oreg. having been assigned to the Second Air Force, is announced as a sub-post of Army Air Base, Walla Walla, Wash. Base Commanders are not required to have personnel stationed at this airdrome unless the situation warrants such occupancy per Hq. 2nd AF, GO No. 173 dated 11-24-42. See also WD Memo No. W95-29-42 dated 11-13-42 and W95-3-43 dated 2-8-43. &W95-17-43 dated 7-7-43.

Boardman Flight Strip, Boardman, Oreg. is assigned to the Second Air Force - per WD Circular #46 dated 2 February 1944.

Boardman Landing Strip, Boardman, Oregon, surplus 8 Oct 1945 - per List of Airfields Excess to AAF, dated 1 May 1946.

While there are no available images for the flight strip located at Boardman, the Army Air Force created a base there on February 2, 1944. Its airdrome was constructed for use as a sub-post for the Army air base in Walla Walla. Like with many smaller flight strips, personnel was not warranted unless the situation changed and frequent use was needed. The flight strip was deactivated on May 1, 1946. Boardman Flight Strip is now used by the US Navy as a Naval Weapons Systems Training Facility. (Air Education and Training Command History Office.)

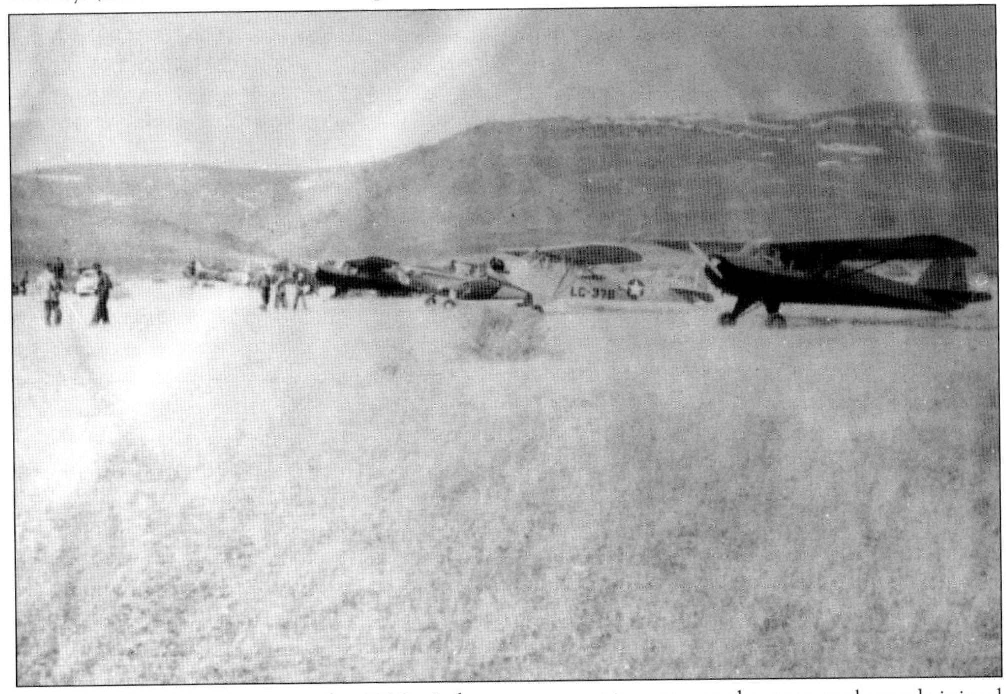

At the height of the air race in the 1920s, Lakeview was not immune to the craze and eagerly joined in. Even without a viable runway or buildings, local and visitors alike used a patch of flat land that later became the airfield to land planes and socialize. Compared to Klamath Falls, the events were small but always drew a reasonable crowd of people who wanted to see aircraft up close. (Lakeview Historical Museum.)

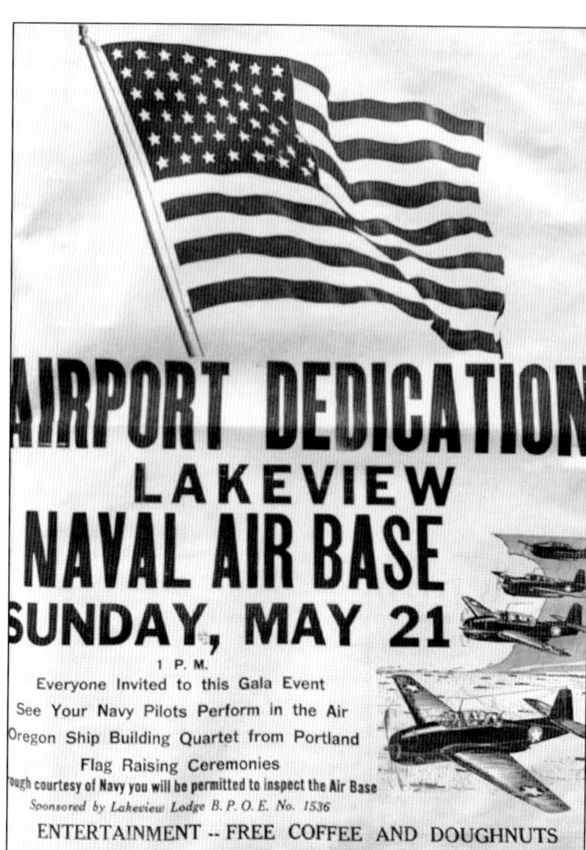

Lakeview is one of Oregon's tallest towns, in that it is at one of the highest elevations. Given the elevation, the Navy felt that Lakeview would be perfect for assembly, class "C" repairs, and some high-elevation training. To celebrate the new base, the Elks club sponsored the commissioning ceremony that was held on May 21, 1944. This flyer was posted in the newspaper as well as in local buildings and gathering places. (*Herald and News.*)

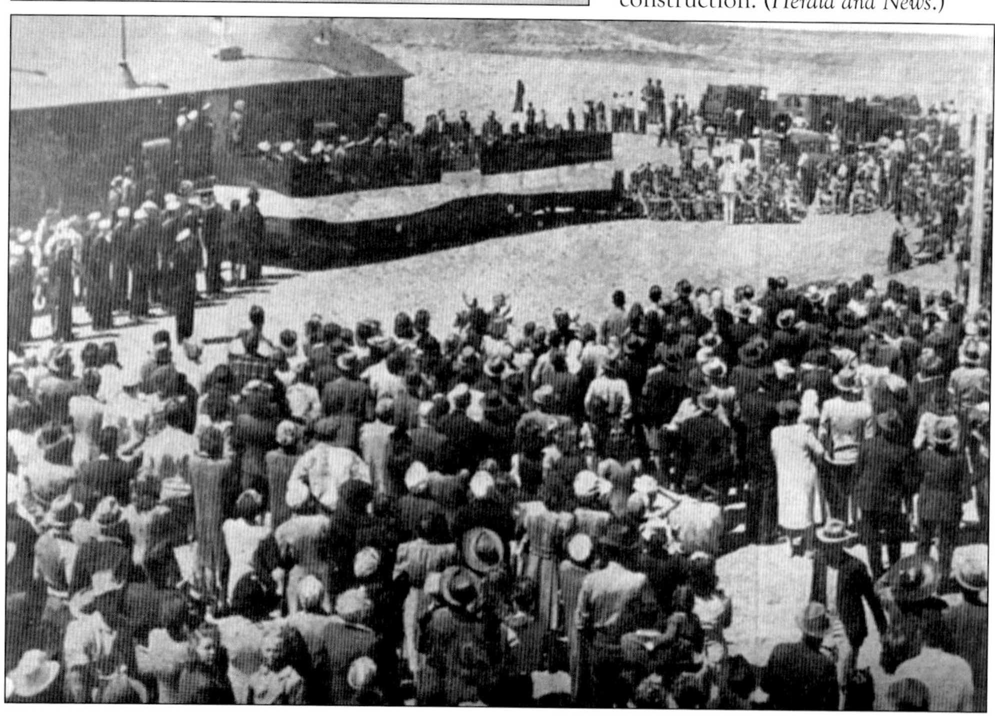

On May 21, 1944, the entire town of Lakeview was invited, with many showing up, to witness the commissioning of Lakeview NAAF. This image shows just one of three groups that were positioned around the speaker's stand, listening to them talk about the new NAS and what it could and would do for the community. In the background is a traveling house, allowing staff to remain on-site during the construction. (*Herald and News.*)

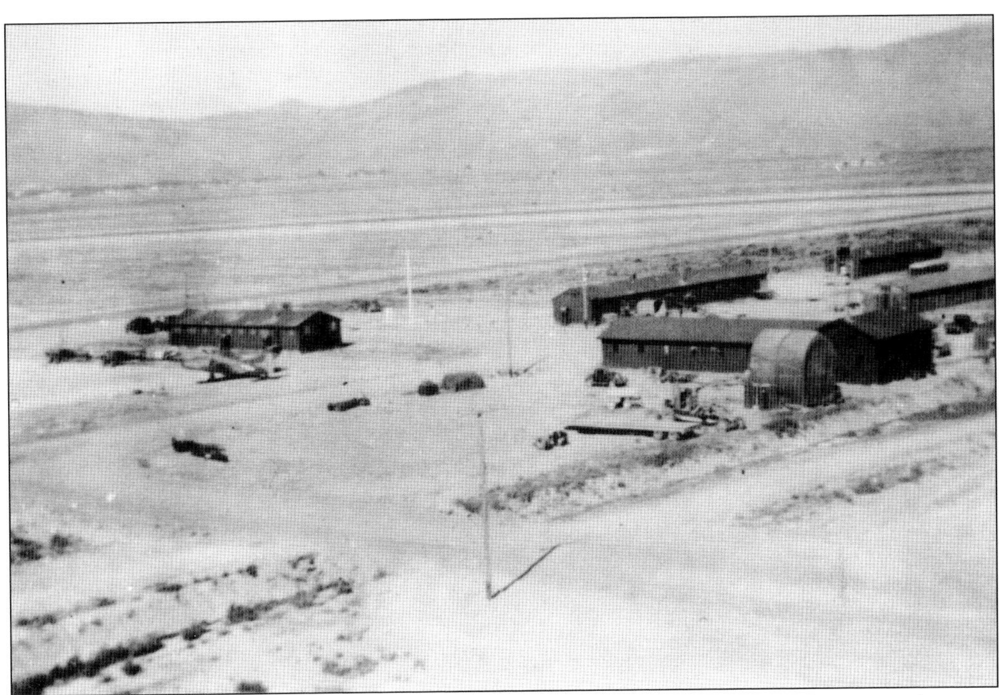

The base mostly consisted of the hangar, multiple repair and assembly buildings, two housing units, and the administrative building. This allowed traveling pilots to have a place to sleep if needed as well as all the fundamentals necessary to maintain an airfield. When the war ended, the Navy listed Lakeview NAAF as surplus, and the property was reverted to local control. (Lakeview Historical Museum.)

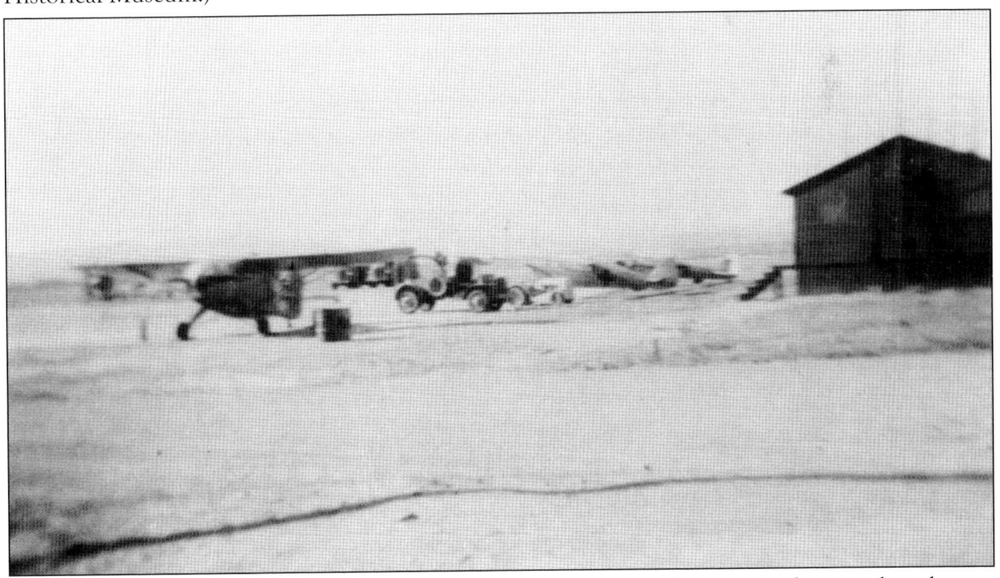

As construction began, the first building was a place for visiting pilots to rest that was directly next to the apron, so if needed, they could easily walk out to their aircraft. These aircraft are sitting on the apron with vehicles around them. The cross on the aircraft in the back could have signaled a German aircraft, but in this image, it is also the symbol for the American Red Cross. (Lakeview Historical Museum.)

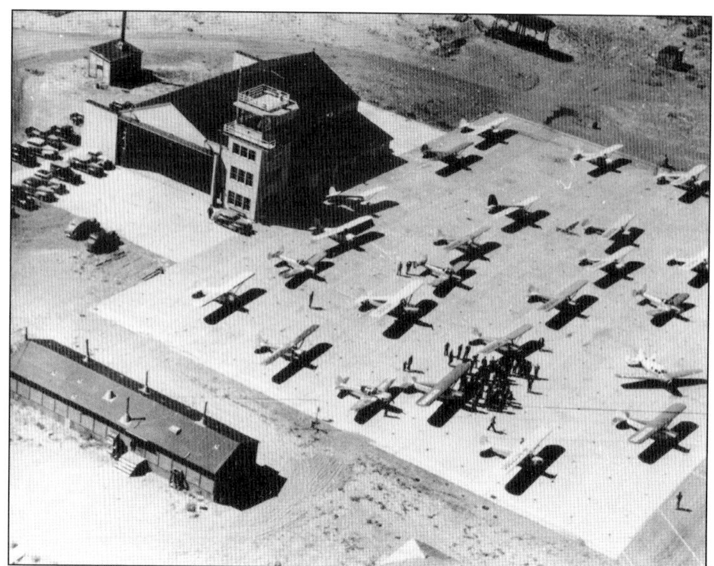

Compared to many of the other bases in Oregon, Lakeview NAAF was smaller, with only dedicated mechanics and administrative personnel stationed at the base. With Klamath Falls NAS being close, if Lakeview needed something or someone not stationed there, it was a short flight. This proximity also allowed for short trips from Klamath Falls to train at higher elevations. (Lakeview Historical Museum.)

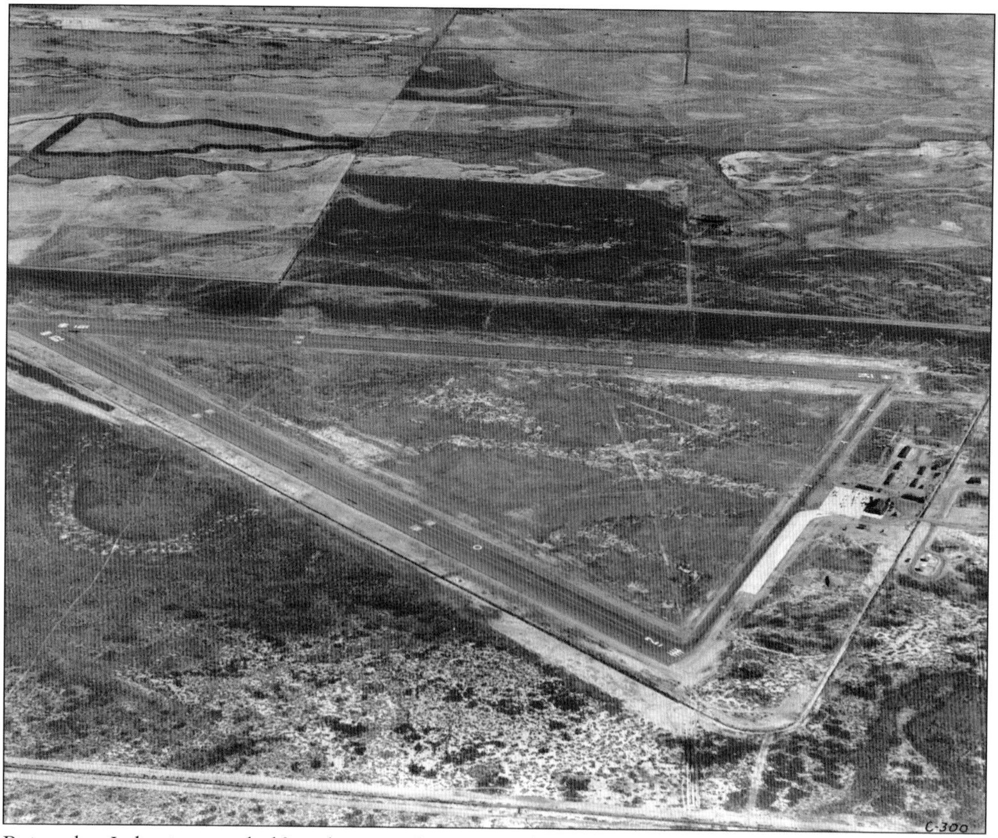

Being that Lakeview was halfway between bases in California and Pendleton, Navy officials believed that it would be a perfect location to have aircraft needing repair to set down. With large aircraft traveling frequently between the bases, the Navy wanted enough space for those big transport aircraft, so officials created two large runways, each 5,300 feet long. Few aircraft were stationed there permanently, but some were for training purposes. (Lakeview Historical Museum.)

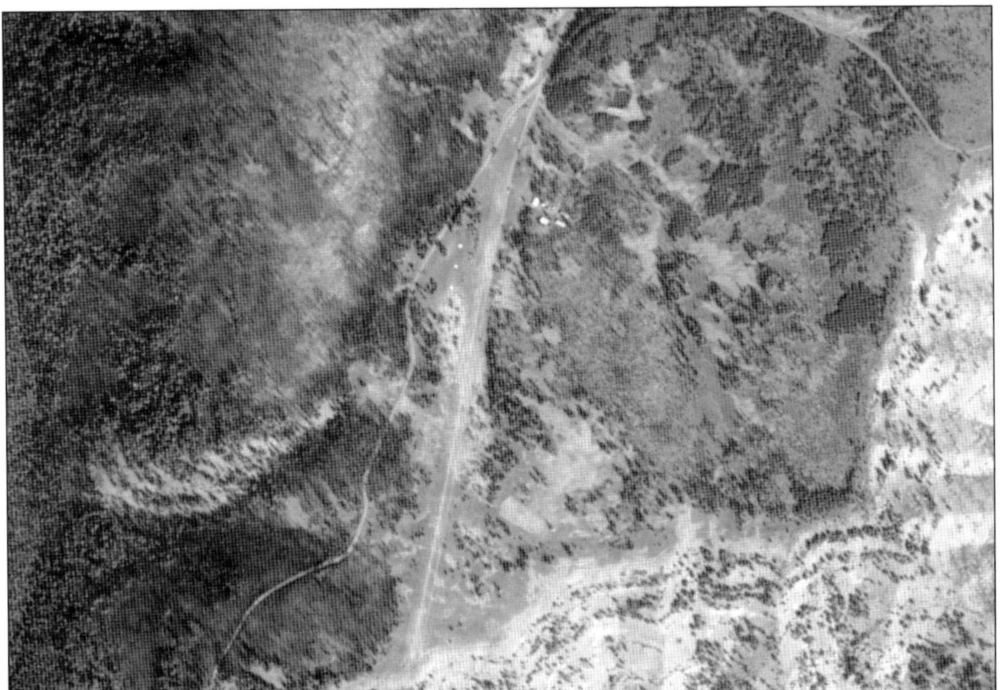

In 1943, when the US military was at its most active in Oregon, it decided to create a field strip near the Idaho border. This served multiple purposes in that it gave pilots a place to land if they passed one of the other bases, but it also allowed for aircraft to be stored out of sight if needed. It was returned to USFS control shortly after the war. (USFS.)

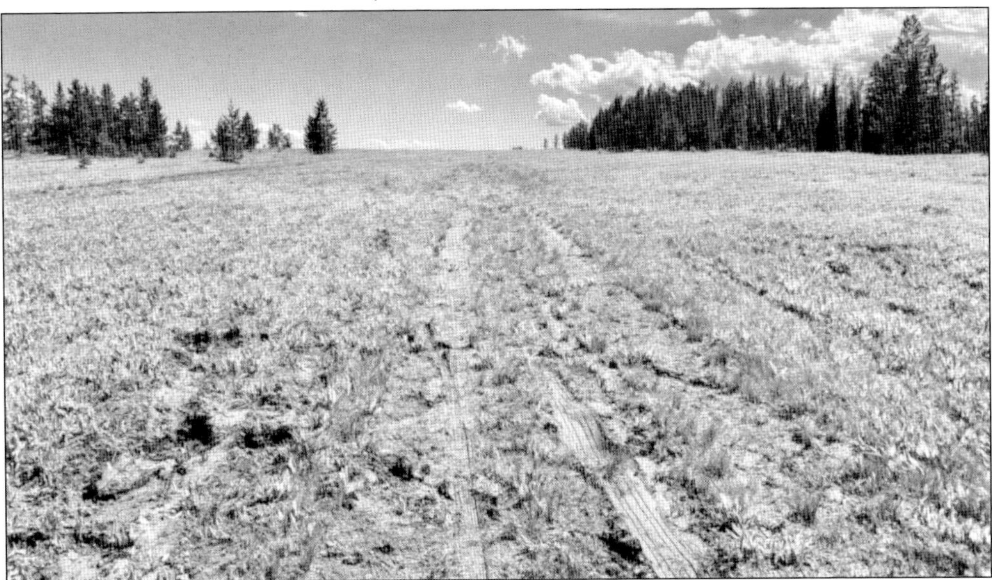

While once highly maintained and able to accommodate small military aircraft, Memaloose FS is now maintained by the US Forest Service and is used exclusively by backcountry pilots as a place to land to eat or take a break. If needed, however, small US Forest Service spotter aircraft can land. Due to environmental concerns, some aircraft are unable to land there at certain times of the year. (USFS.)

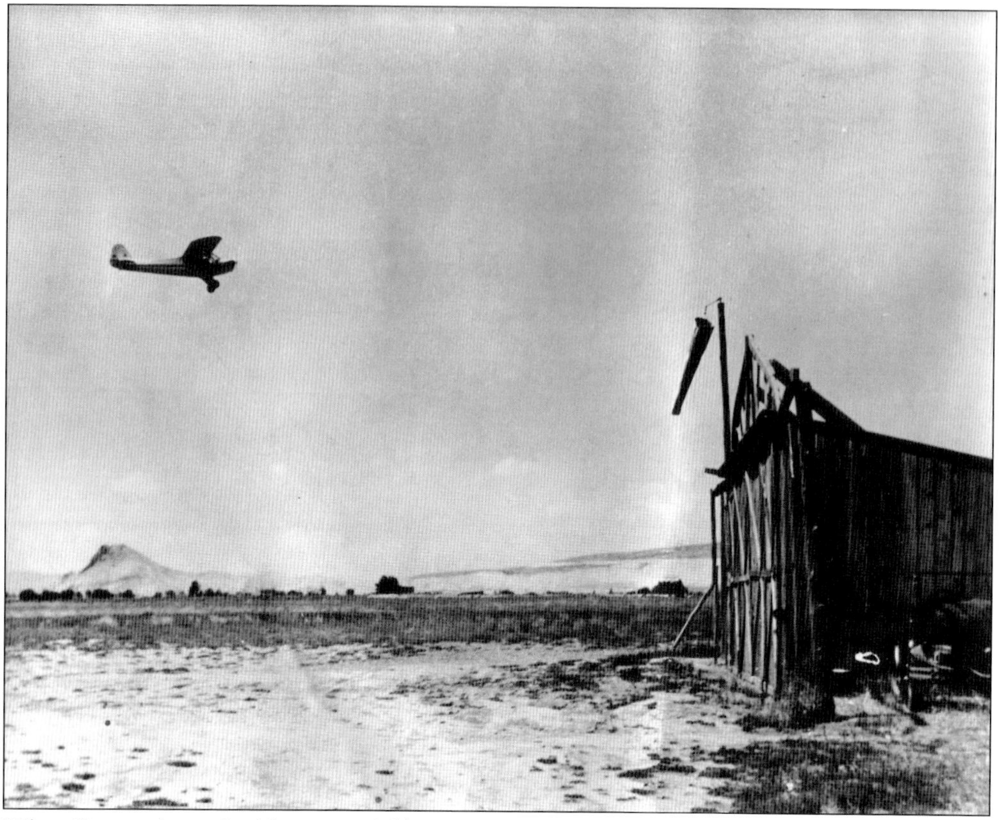

When Ontario began building an airfield, it was for crop dusters and other agricultural commercial aircraft, so the buildings were not required to be large. A small building, along with a dirt runway, was enough for the pilots who used the area. As more pilots began to frequent the airport, larger buildings and more accommodations were needed. This image from the early 1930s shows how rustic the airport was. (Ontario Airport.)

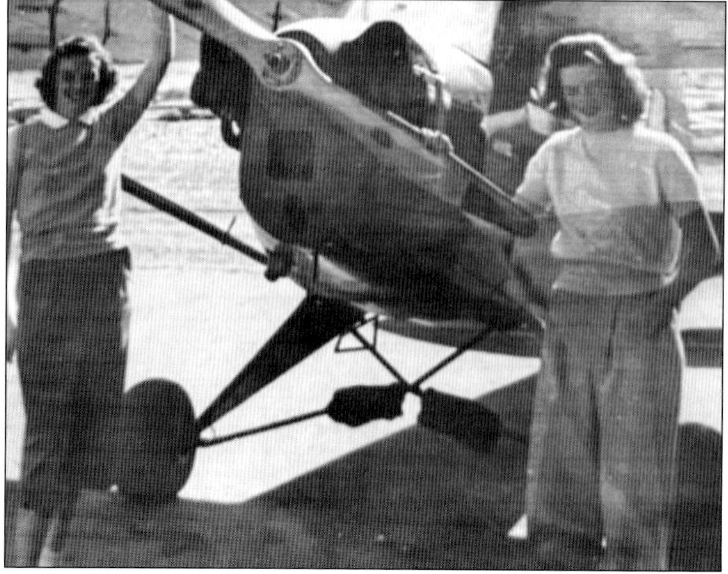

One woman who helped to pave the way for the Ontario Airport was Lourana Ellen Preston Echanis. She received her pilot's license in 1945 but had been participating in activities at the airfield before that. She was also the first to fly solo from Ontario to Caldwell, Emmett, and Boise, Idaho, and back. Even though life took her away from Ontario, she still supported the airport. (Ontario Airport.)

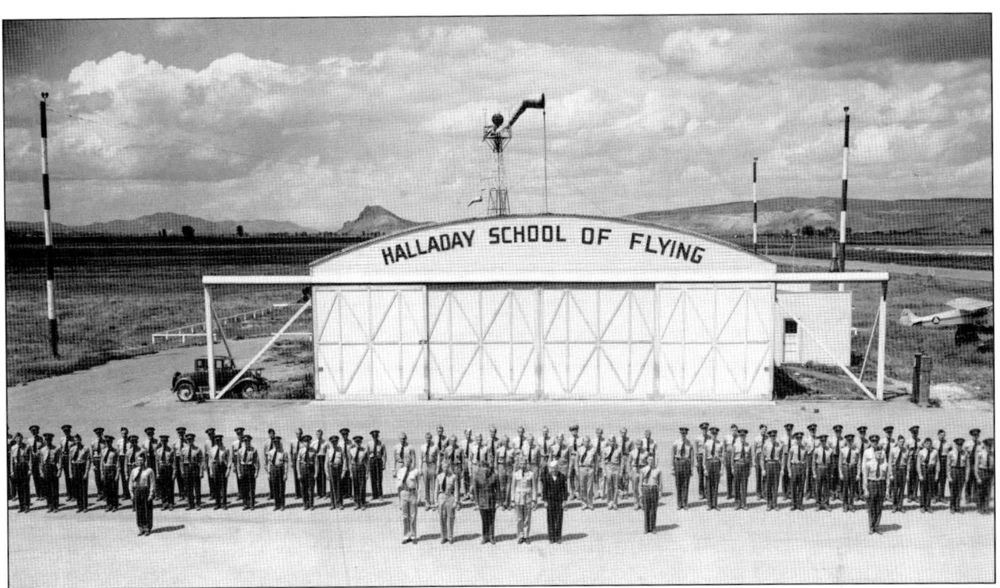

The land for the Ontario airfield was purchased by the city from Malheur County in 1929 with the understanding that if it was ever not to be an airport, rights would revert back. Initially, it was primarily an agriculture airport, but in 1942, it transitioned to a joint training and agriculture airport. Following Bessie Halladay's arrival in Ontario, over 500 naval aviation cadets were trained at the Halladay School of Flying. (OHS Research Library, 00269138.)

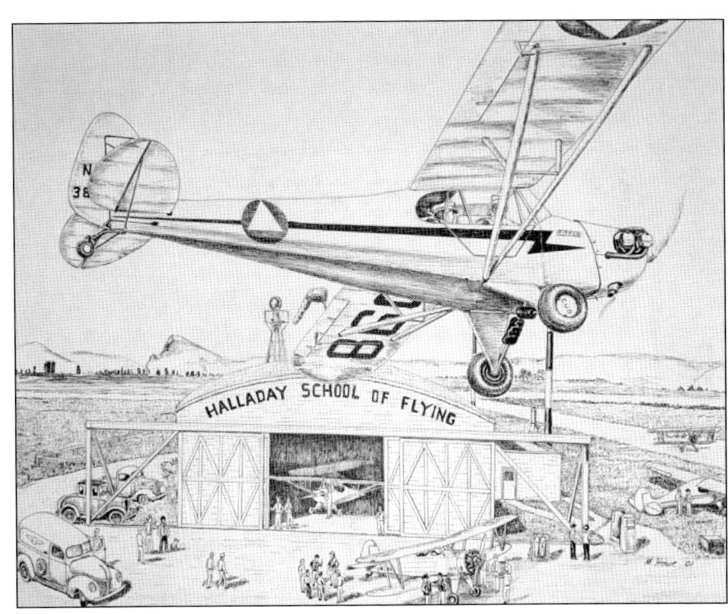

Bessie Halladay was one of the first women to receive her pilot instructor's license in Oregon. She initially trained students at Swan Island under the civilian pilot training program. However, due to war activities, civilians were not allowed on coastal waters starting in 1942. Halladay decided to move her training school to Ontario, far from the ocean. This is a drawn replica of a photograph taken of her school. (Ontario Airport.)

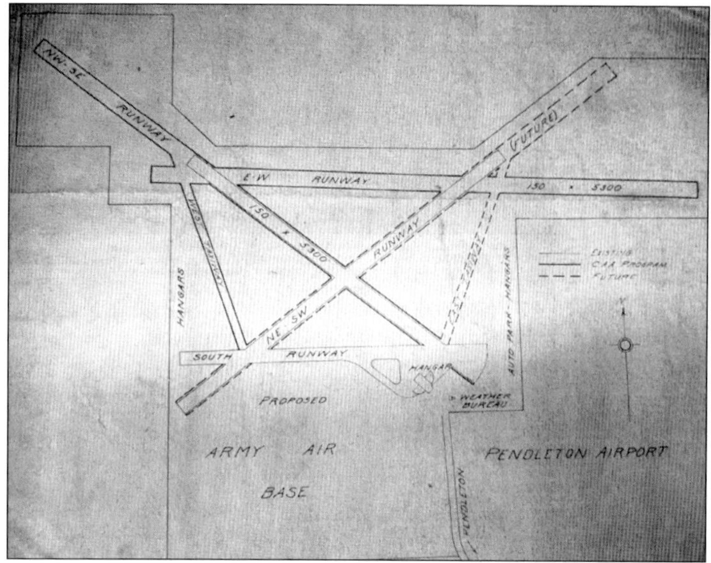

On December 18, 1940, plans for the Pendleton airport and air base were submitted for approval. Some of the land, highlighted with thin lines, already existed. The CAA had just announced that Pendleton was going to receive $282,000 to help extend the runways. With the Army moving in, it was imperative that the airport be enlarged to accommodate the additional aircraft, the needs of the Army, and staffing. (PAM.)

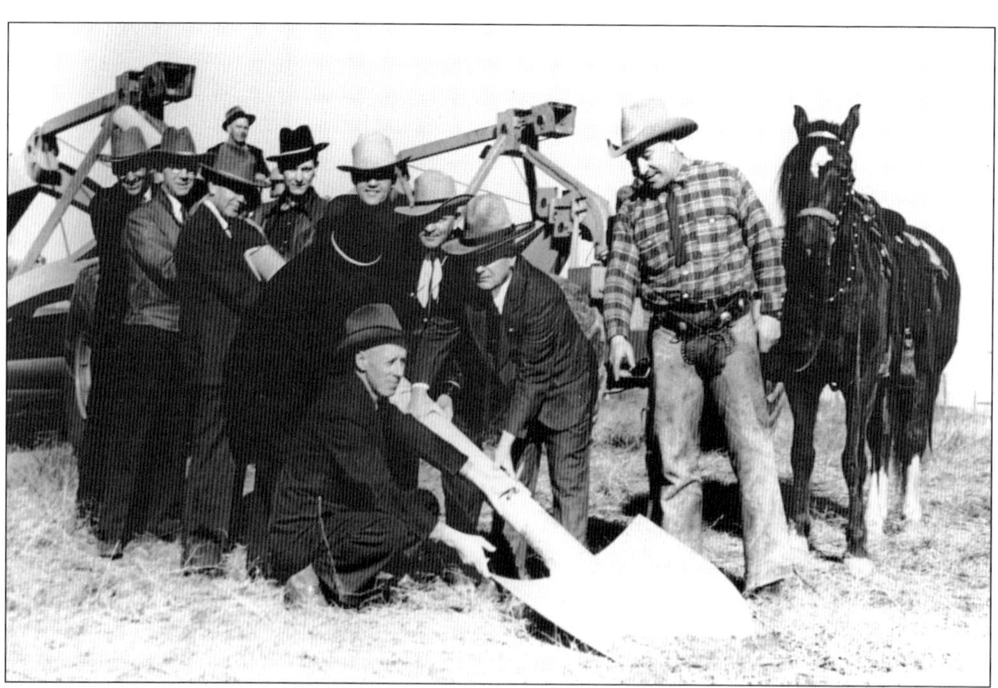

Initially, the property was called Pendleton Air Base, but it was quickly named Pendleton Field. This groundbreaking ceremony took place on February 16, 1941, in which Jack Allen, one of the men responsible for securing the rights and funding for the air base, is kneeling in front of the oversize shovel. Other men, including council members, local businessmen, and a rancher, were all in attendance. (Umatilla County Historical Society Collection, 2008.100.1950.)

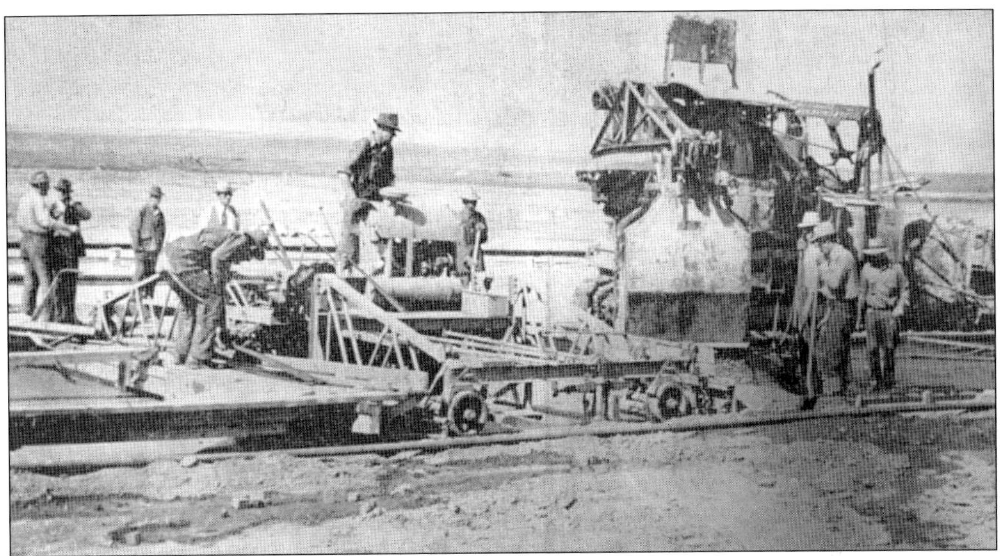

Construction for Pendleton Field began on May 16, 1941, with the concrete apron being laid down. In the first two days, a 25-foot side strip that was 1,000 feet long was accomplished. Jacob and Johnson received the contract to build the apron, and it took multiple men to run the machinery. After the machinery, men hand-finished the surface to make sure it was flat and without blemishes. (PAM.)

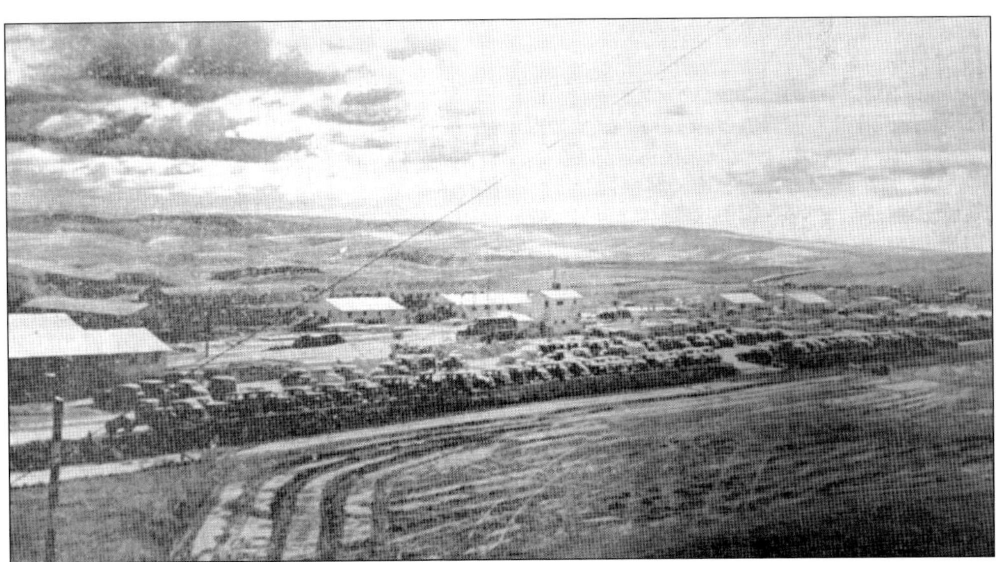

Slowly but surely, Pendleton Field began to look less like a collection of machines in the middle of a wheat field and more like the beginnings of an airfield. One of the first things constructed was the cantonment, or the residential section of the base. Until it was finished, workers had to drive back and forth every day, causing some disruptions and time delays. (PAM.)

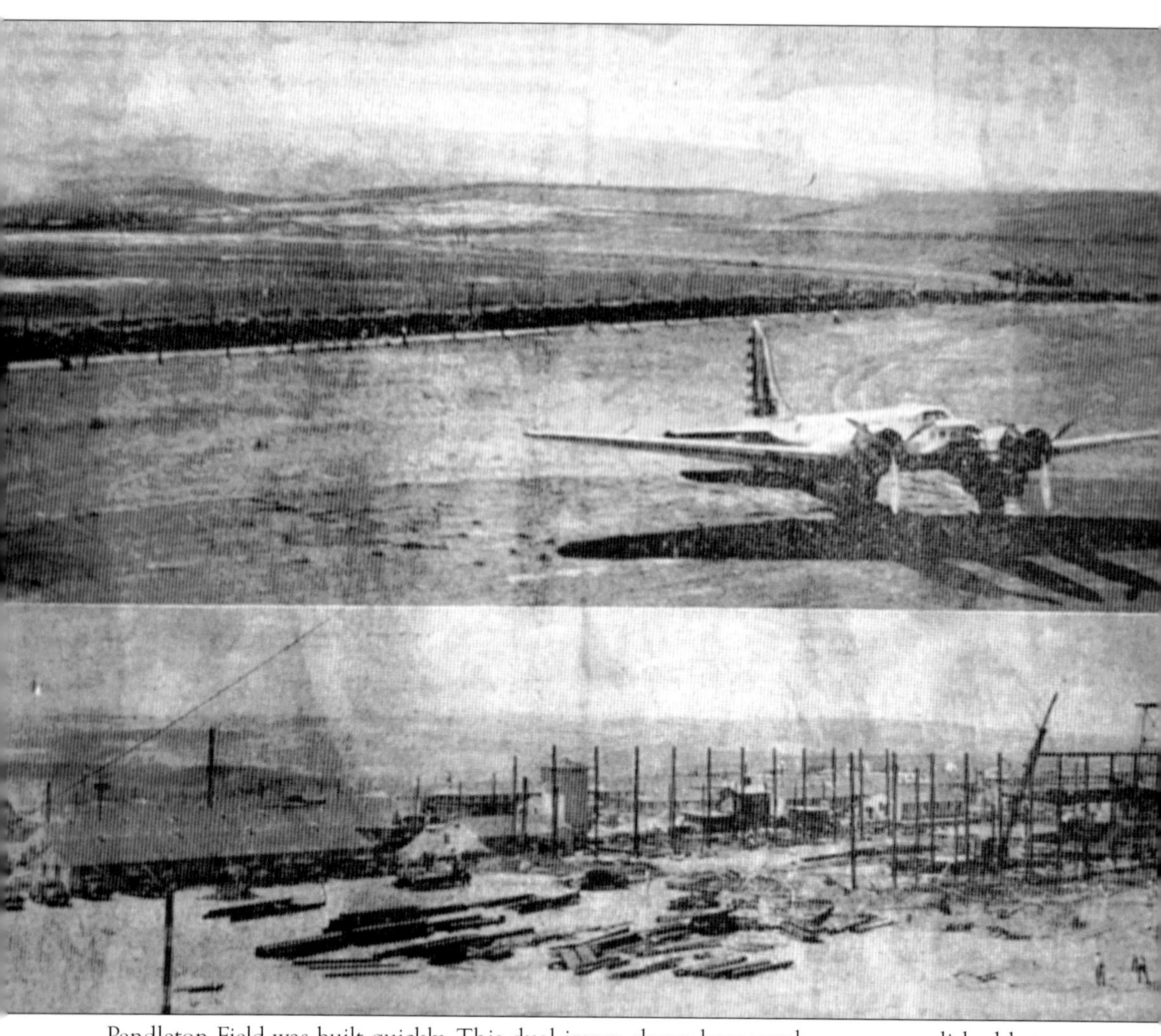

Pendleton Field was built quickly. This dual image shows how much was accomplished between January 1941 and July 1, 1941. The land that would become Pendleton Field was a farmer's wheat field. Near that field was already a small municipal airport that provided mail and short flights. When the US Army announced on November 29, 1940, that Pendleton had been selected, it was all hands on deck. The US Department of War allocated $1.6 million for the construction. This enabled the contractors to build quickly and efficiently. The upper image shows a US Army bomber landing on the flattened wheat field as it taxis toward the existing airport. The lower image is taken from the same viewpoint, less than seven months later. In that time, 122 buildings were completed, with only the large hangar and control tower left to be finished. In the next few months, secondary construction for paved roads and outbuildings would not only start but also be completed. (PAM.)

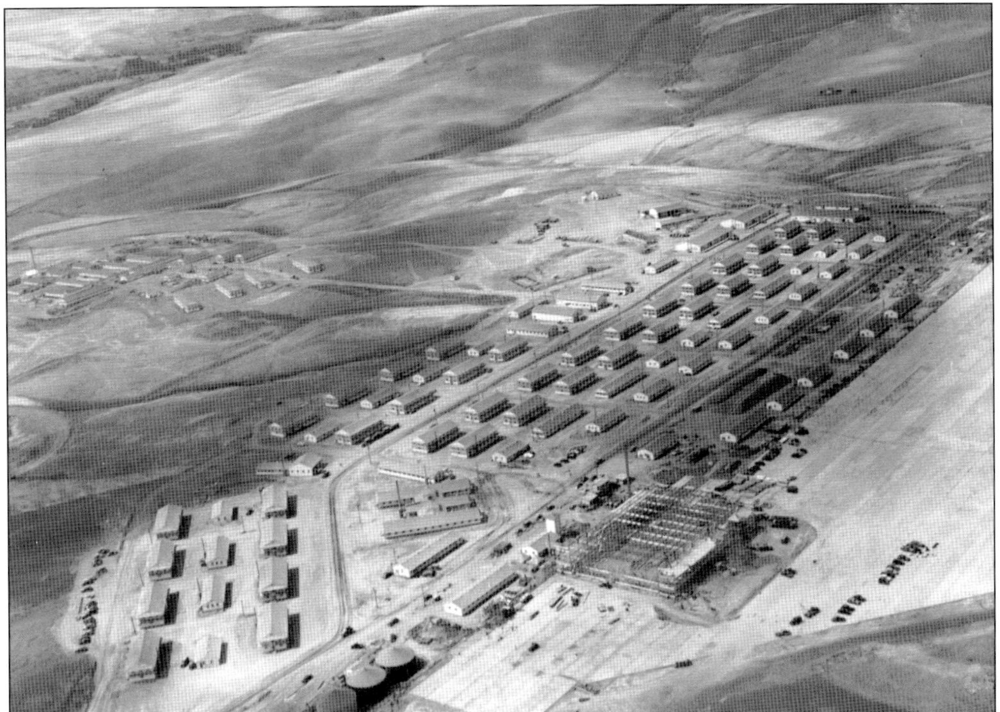

Pendleton Field was one of the largest airfields in Oregon. This was due to the number of staff that were stationed there as well as the aircraft the base worked with. With the number stationed there at the height, crew housing was important, which can be seen from the numerous buildings in the photograph. The concrete apron on the far right is near a hangar being built. (PAM.)

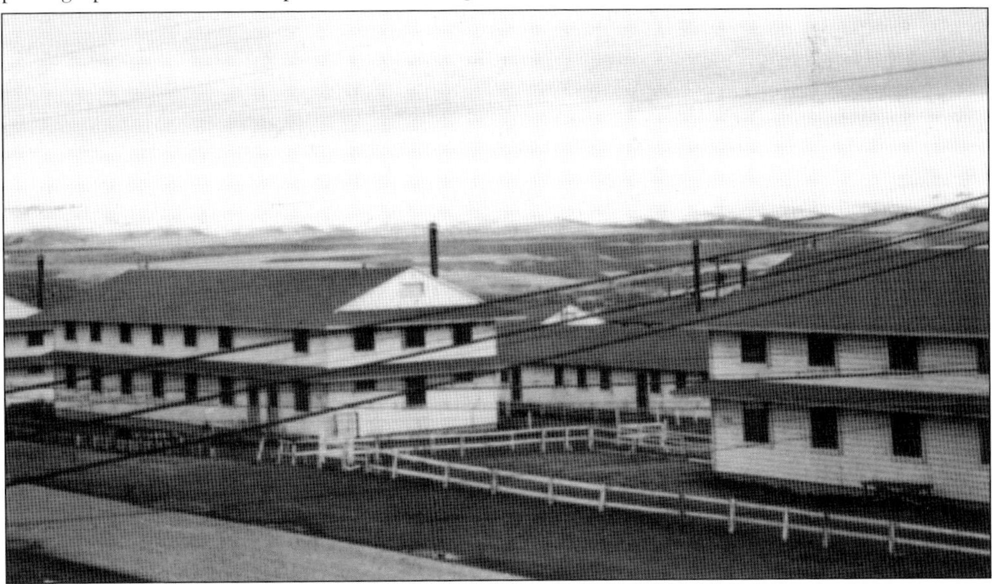

Housing for those permanently stationed on Pendleton Airfield was simple but adequate for the mostly single service members assigned. These housing units were less like barracks and more like apartment complexes, overlooking the mountains. Each building even came with a small yard. The base at the height of activity housed 303 officers and 2,218 enlisted men. (PAM.)

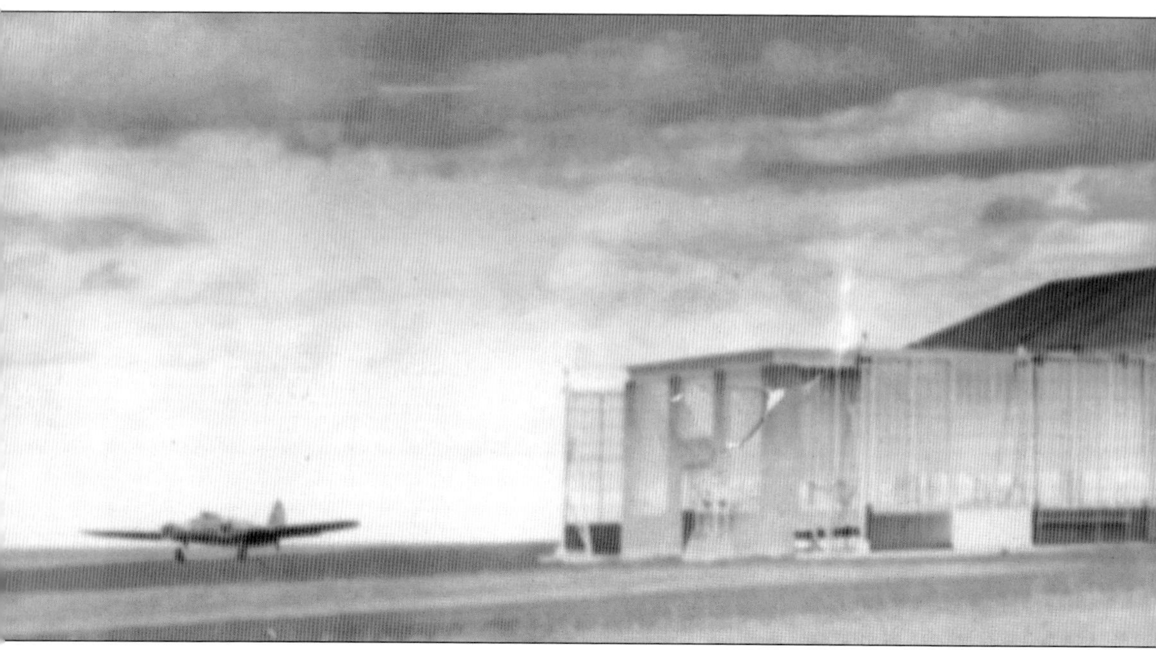

The main hangar at Pendleton Field is in the middle of construction, with smaller buildings in the background. This hangar would hold the flight ops, pilot ready room, and maintenance for aircraft that need repairs. When construction began, it happened very quickly, with over 800 mostly men working on the buildings and the ground surrounding them. The money from the CAA, along

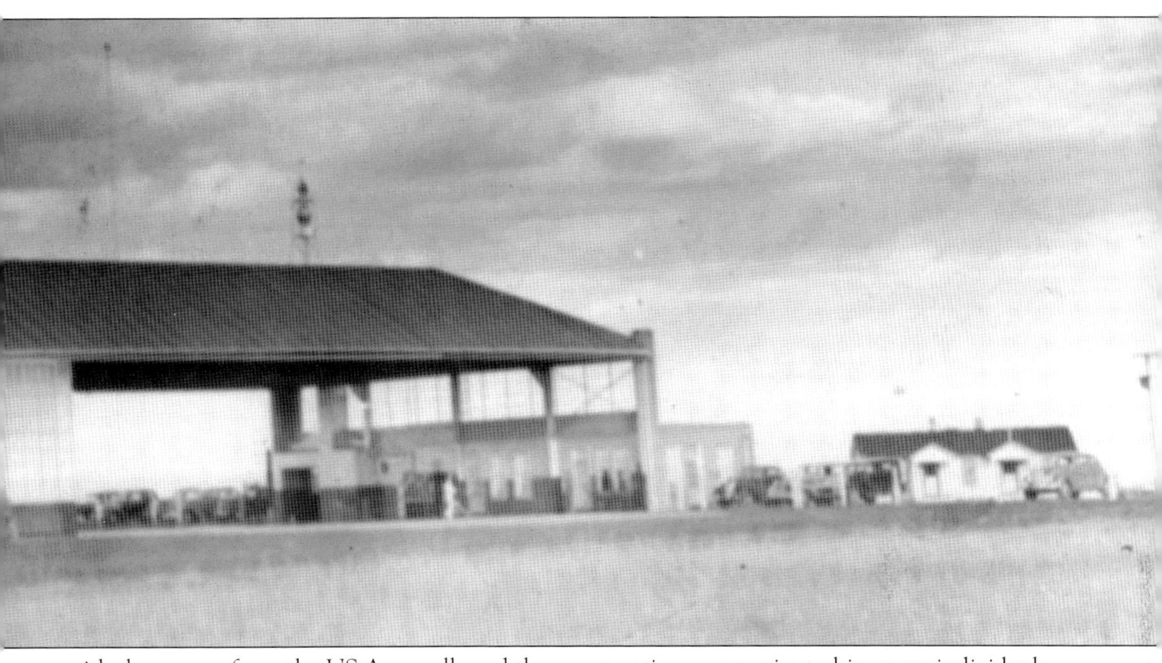

with the money from the US Army, allowed the construction companies to hire more individuals. The quick nature was needed because a unit of large bombers was en route and needed a place for maintenance and for the flight operations to set up. A large bomber sits to the left of the half-built hangar. (Umatilla County Historical Society Collection, 1981.001.2310.)

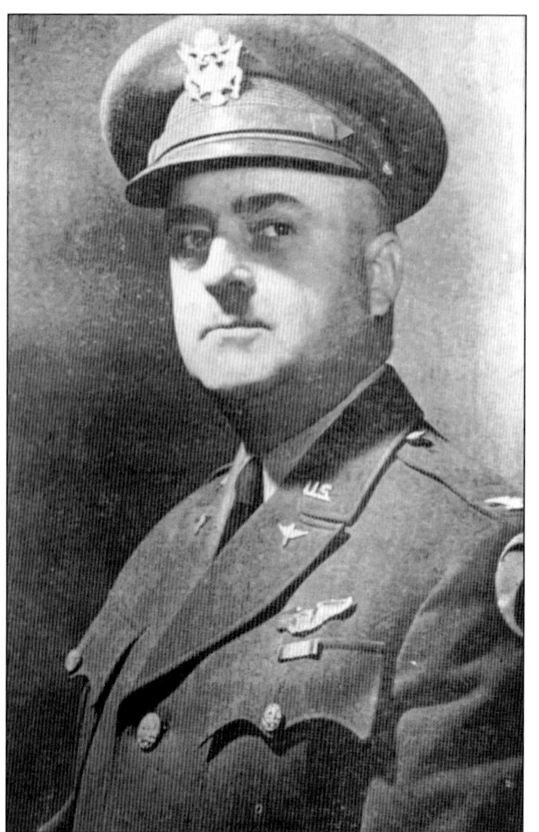

The first field commander for Pendleton Field was Col. Frank W. Wright. Wright was an Oregonian who served in the Oregon National Guard before World War I and became one of its first military pilots. Wright joined the Royal Air Force (RAF) 209 Squadron in 1918. Following the war, Wright continued his active-duty career, becoming the first commander for McCliord Field in Washington State in 1938. In 1941, he was again transferred, this time to become the base commander for Pendleton Field. (PAM.)

Many assistants and aides who worked at Pendleton AAF were from the local communities. Dorys Crow, a civilian, was born in Pendleton in 1921. When World War II started and the Pendleton AAF was built, Crow began work as an aide for the base adjutant. Soon after that, she was transferred to the advocate general's office, where she worked as an intelligence aide, writing secret orders sending the Doolittle Raiders on missions. (PAM.)

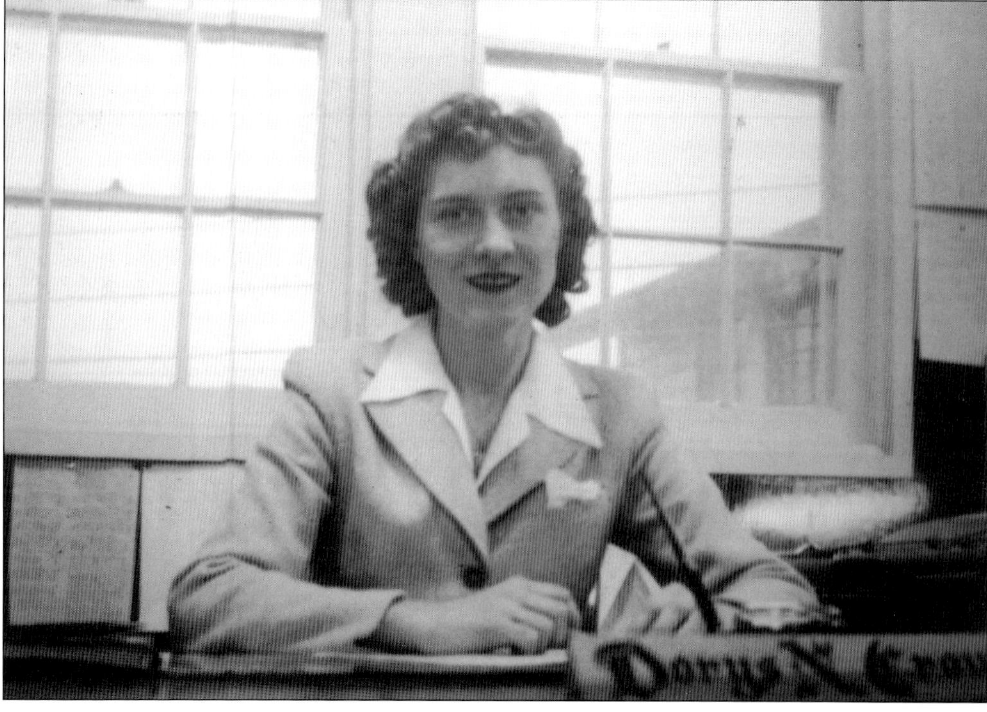

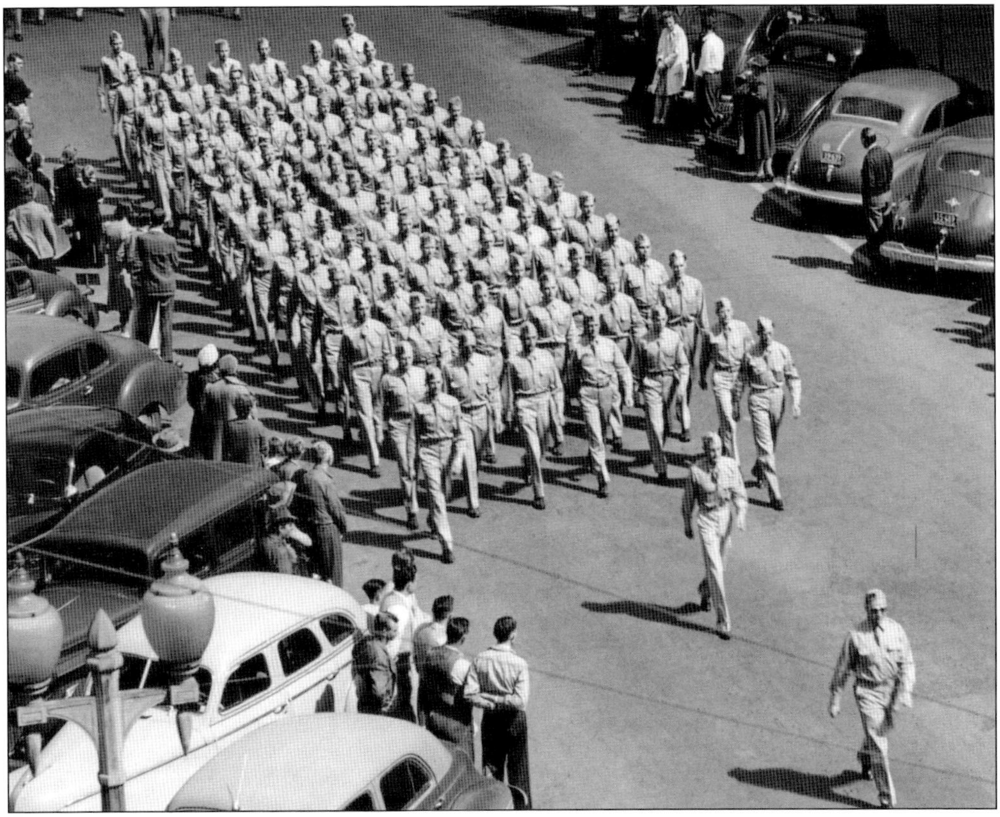

With how close the base was to the city of Pendleton, there were times when military units interacted with the public. This unit stationed at Pendleton Field was released from its normal duties to walk in a parade. Another unit is following them. This citizen outreach helped recruitment and reminded people that the air base and city were not two separate entities. (PAM.)

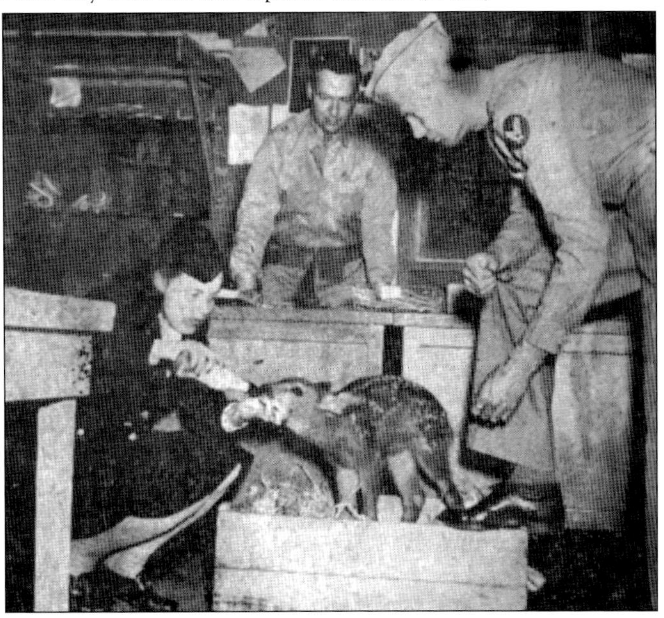

Military bases were not just work and training. There were downtimes like with any job. During one of these downtimes, the commander for the 20th Airbase squadron, Capt. William E. Borland, was looking for someone to care for the newest enlistee at Pendleton Airfield. Little "Jane Doe" was an instant favorite, finding a young civilian who would feed her and create a small bed for her. (PAM.)

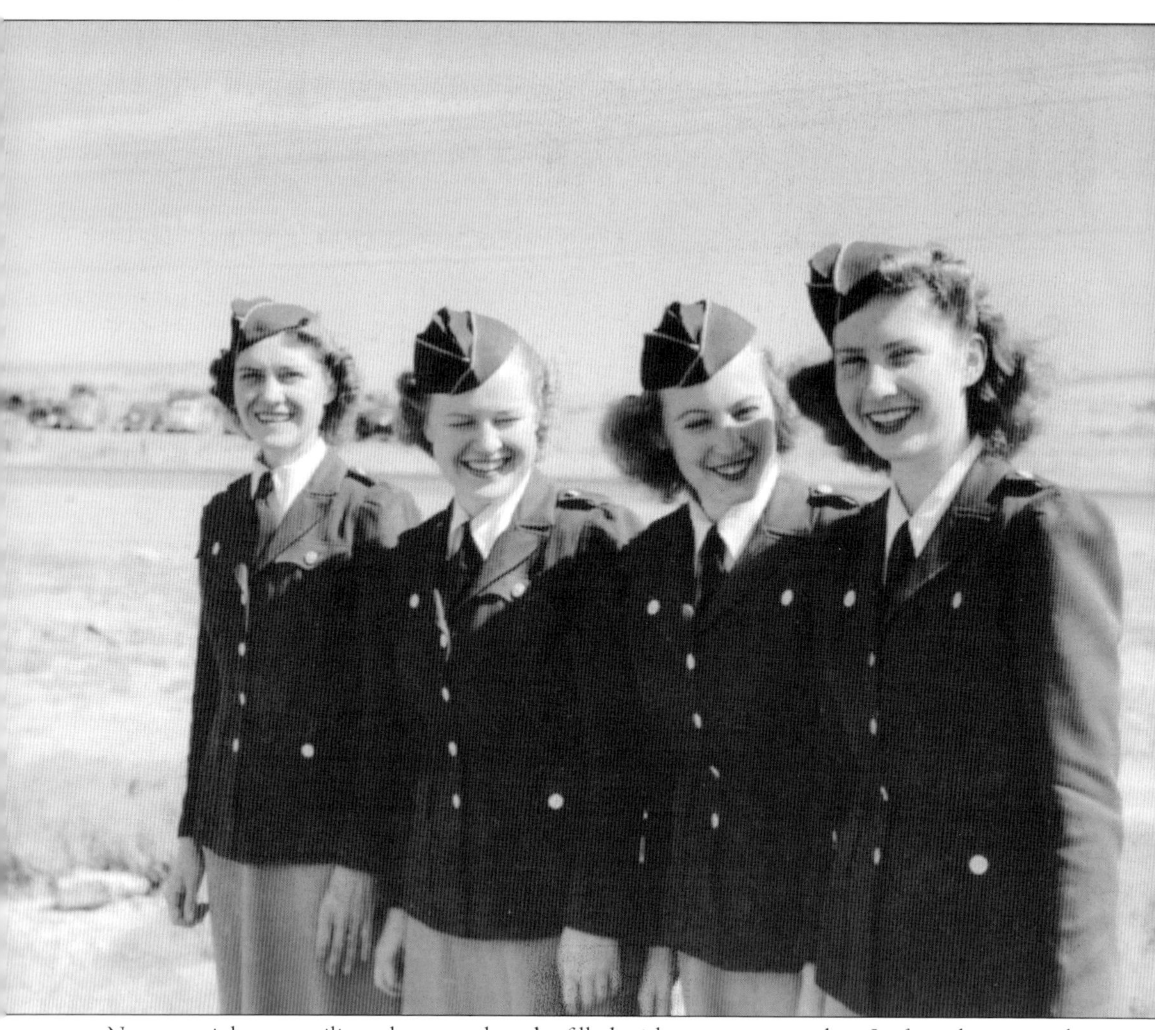

Not every job on a military base needs to be filled with a service member. In fact, there are a lot of jobs that civilians can do just as well as service members if not better. Service members were also trained and ready to deploy to war, so many positions that needed some form of continuity, they hired civilians for. Before women could actively serve as a WAC, there were the WAACs and women who volunteered on bases. These women occupied jobs in the canteen, mess hall, and administration. Some also worked in crucial positions such as Red Cross drivers and nurses. These four women—from left to right, Dorys Crow, Doris Nolan, Louise Kopp, and Florence DeYoung—had their picture taken in September 1942 while on duty at Pendleton Field. There is no record of these women being part of the military, so they were likely employed at Pendleton Field or were volunteers. (PAM.)

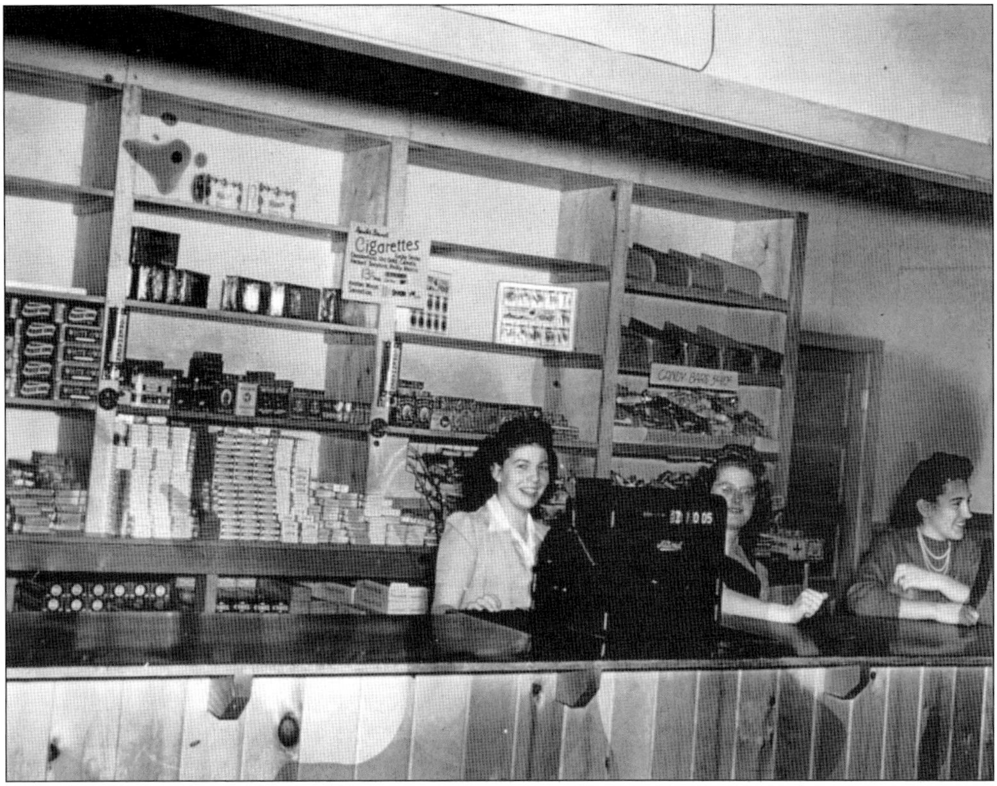

Every large base needed a canteen, a place where service members could relax. Another thing every base needed was a general store. Pendleton Field had both, operated by mostly women who lived in Pendleton. Some of these women would go on to marry service members, and Pendleton is home to almost 1,000 veterans and even more families of veterans who served during World War II. (PAM.)

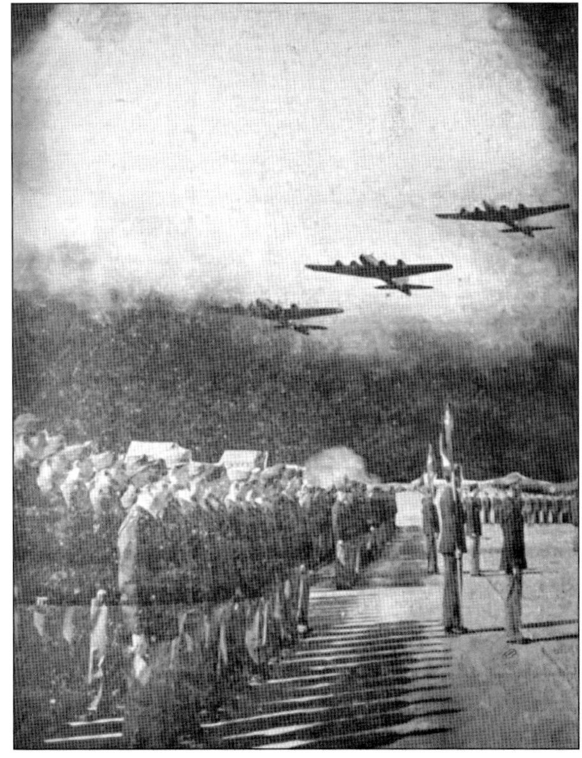

Pendleton was a large and important air base for the US Army. It was used for training, events, and, as in this image, a decoration ceremony. Any available service member that was at Pendleton on March 20, 1942, was standing at attention on the apron. Gen. Frederick L. Martin recognized Lt. Col. Curtis E. LeMay with the Distinguished Flying Cross as heavy bombers flew overhead. (PAM.)

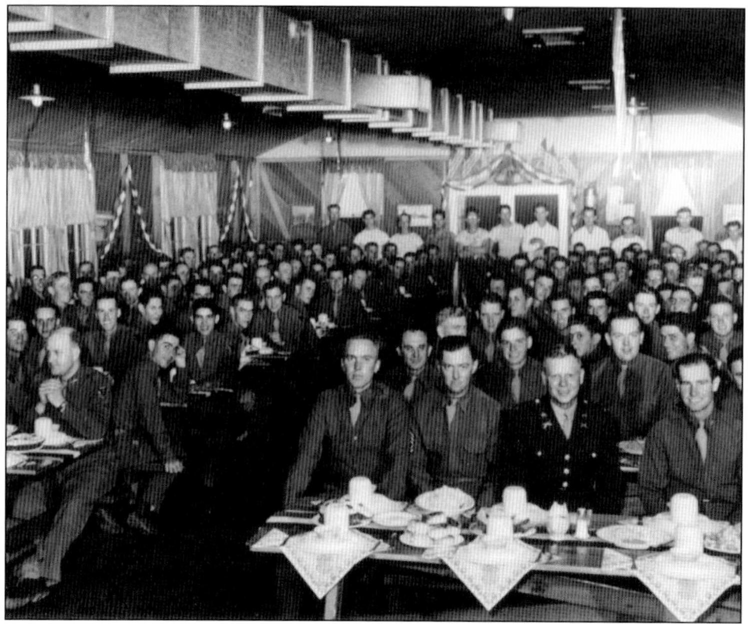

It was not always holidays when the men were treated to a good meal. Certain special days, such as a commander's birthday, or every Friday, as in some units, were days to celebrate. In this photograph, it was a meal for a specific shift following the presentation of the Distinguished Flying Cross. Due to the numerous shifts, the mess hall usually ran on close to a 24-hour schedule. (PAM.)

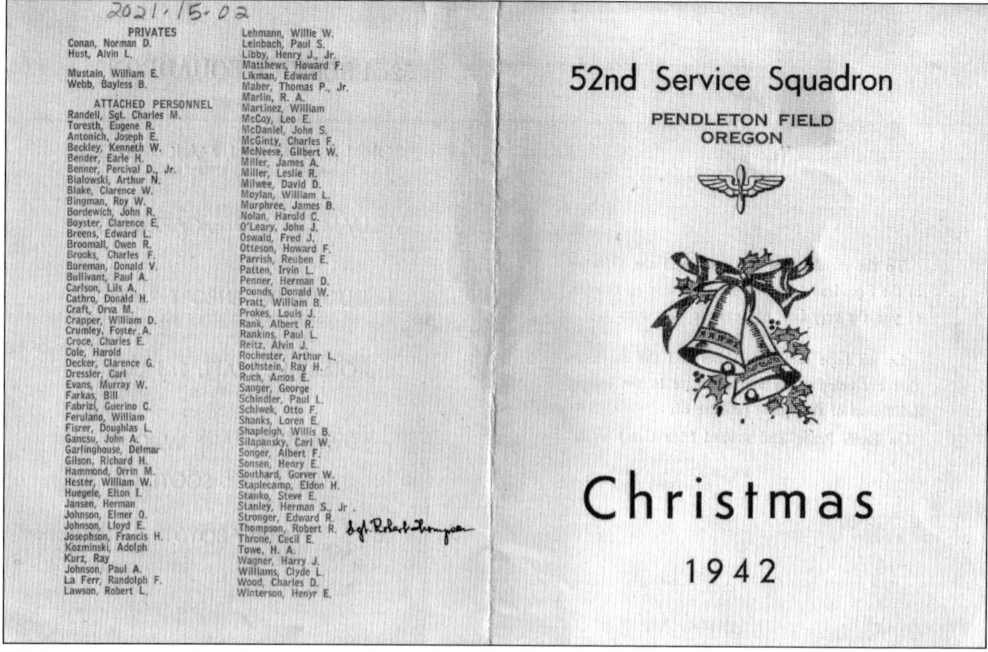

2021.15.02

PRIVATES
Conan, Norman D.
Hust, Alvin L.

Mustain, William E.
Webb, Bayless B.

ATTACHED PERSONNEL
Randell, Sgt. Charles M.
Toresth, Eugene R.
Antonich, Joseph E.
Beckley, Kenneth W.
Bender, Earle H.
Benner, Percival D., Jr.
Bialowski, Arthur N.
Blake, Clarence W.
Bingman, Roy W.
Bordewich, John R.
Boyster, Clarence E.
Breens, Edward L.
Broomall, Owen R.
Brooks, Charles F.
Bureman, Donald V.
Bullivant, Paul A.
Carlson, Lils A.
Cathro, Donald H.
Craft, Orva M.
Crapper, William D.
Crumley, Foster A.
Croce, Charles E.
Cole, Harold
Decker, Clarence G.
Dressler, Carl
Evans, Murray W.
Farkas, Bill
Fabrizi, Guerino C.
Ferulano, William
Fisrer, Doughlas L.
Gancsu, John A.
Garlinghouse, Delmar
Gilson, Richard H.
Hammond, Orrin M.
Hester, William W.
Huegele, Elton I.
Jansen, Herman
Johnson, Elmer O.
Johnson, Lloyd E.
Josephson, Francis H.
Kozminski, Adolph
Kurz, Ray
Johnson, Paul A.
La Ferr, Randolph F.
Lawson, Robert L.

Lehmann, Willie W.
Leinbach, Paul S.
Libby, Henry J., Jr.
Matthews, Howard F.
Likman, Edward
Maher, Thomas P., Jr.
Marlin, R. A.
Martinez, William
McCoy, Leo E.
McDaniel, John S.
McGinty, Charles F.
McNeese, Gilbert W.
Miller, James A.
Miller, Leslie R.
Milwee, David D.
Moylan, William L.
Murphree, James B.
Nolan, Harold C.
O'Leary, John J.
Oswald, Fred J.
Otteson, Howard F.
Parrish, Reuben E.
Patten, Irvin L.
Penner, Herman D.
Pounds, Donald W.
Pratt, William B.
Prokes, Louis J.
Rank, Albert R.
Rankins, Paul L.
Reitz, Alvin J.
Rochester, Arthur L.
Bothstein, Ray H.
Ruch, Amos E.
Sanger, George
Schindler, Paul L.
Schiwek, Otto F.
Shanks, Loren E.
Shapleigh, Willis B.
Silapansky, Carl W.
Songer, Albert F.
Sonsen, Henry E.
Southard, Gorver W.
Staplecamp, Eldon H.
Stanko, Steve E.
Stanley, Herman S., Jr.
Stronger, Edward R.
Thompson, Robert R. Sgt. Robert Thompson
Throne, Cecil E.
Towe, H. A.
Wagner, Harry J.
Williams, Clyde L.
Wood, Charles D.
Winterson, Henyr E.

52nd Service Squadron

PENDLETON FIELD
OREGON

Christmas

1942

With service members being away from their families for long periods of time, the command would attempt to make holidays something for them to remember. The 52nd Service Squadron, with the assistance of the mess hall crews, put on a Christmas dinner and event. These pamphlets listed everyone who was part of the unit and became a keepsake for many as they were transferred or deployed overseas. (PAM.)

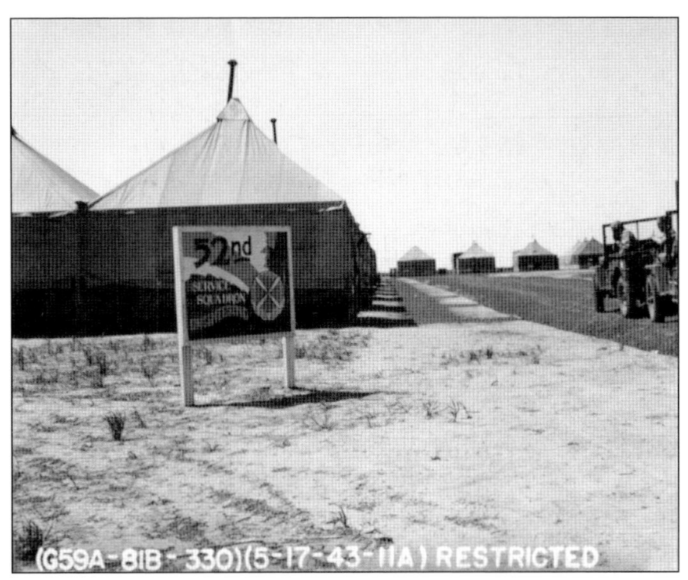

Not all service members lived in fully constructed buildings. The 52nd Service Squadron Engineering unit all lived in canvas tents. The tents were on wooden bases, which decreased moisture from seeping in, but it was still in the elements. These men deployed from numerous bases, including Pendleton Field, as support for heavy bomber units. With Pendleton having heavy bombers, this unit helped to prepare them for deployment. (Umatilla County Historical Society Collection, 1991.034.015.)

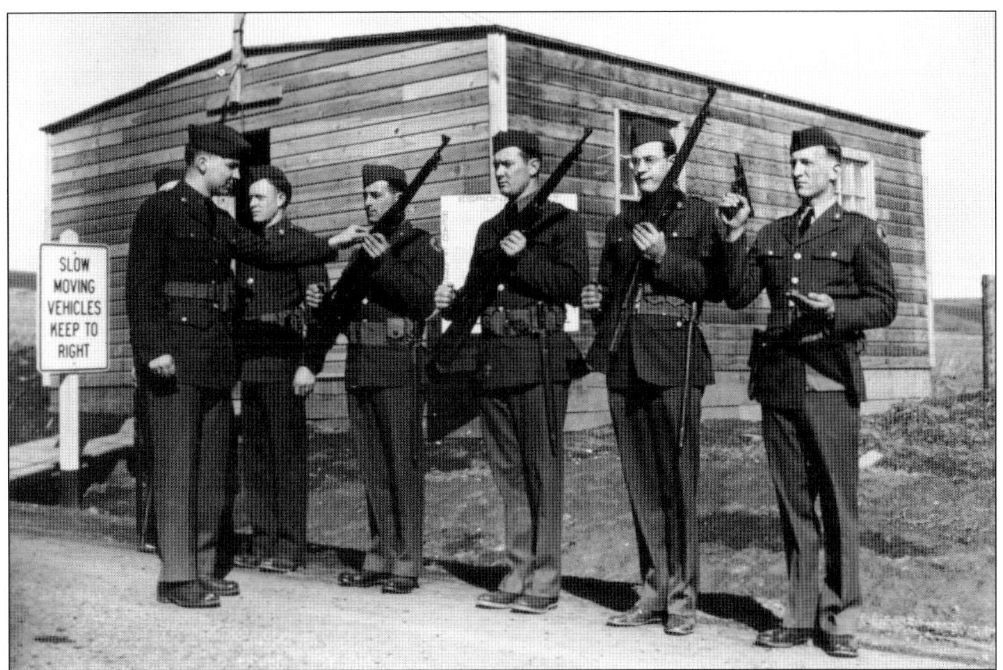

Even with some units sleeping in canvas tents, that did not stop the standard drill and ceremony practice. It was important that uniforms were correctly worn and weapons were cleaned and presentable. As a common part of inspection, the men with the rifles are holding their magazines in their right hand, while the man at the end is holding his pistol magazine in his upturned hand. (PAM.)

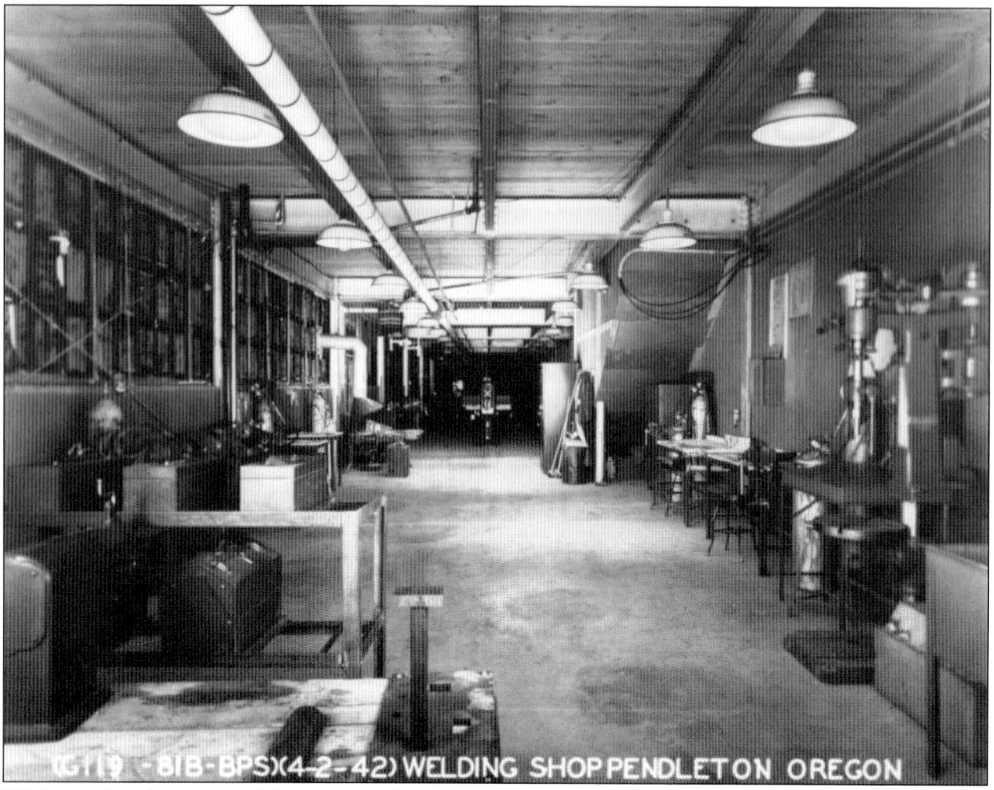

(G119 -81B-BPS)(4-2-42) WELDING SHOP PENDLETON OREGON

With much of the metal being transferred to create aircraft, every large base that performed maintenance and repair needed a welding shop. From small repairs to the skin damaged during training to larger repairs to engines and even the structural framework, good welding shops could do it. With Pendleton being a final training location for many, the welding shop was usually stocked with materials and with professionals working in it. (PAM.)

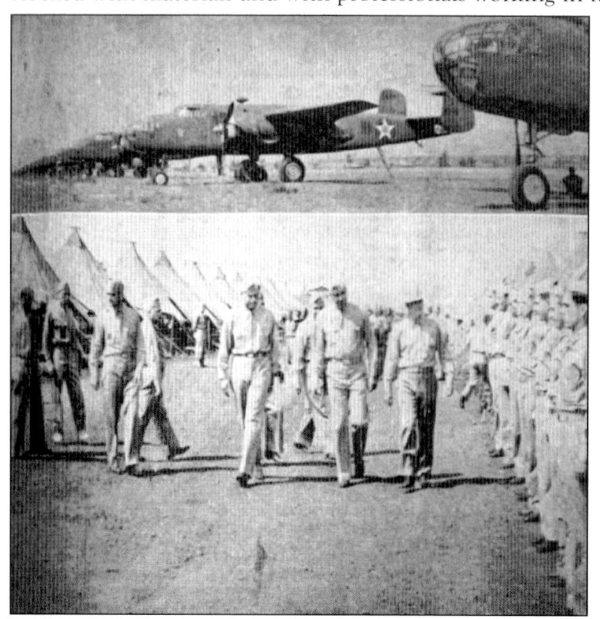

Maj. Gen. John Curry, the commander of the 2nd Air Force, paid Pendleton Field a visit shortly after the B-25s arrived. These B-25s and the men trained on them would later make up the Doolittle Raid. Except for the commanding officer, Lt. Col. James Doolittle, the entire unit trained at Pendleton Field. Curry witnessed field maneuvers by the 18th Bombing Group and the 89th Reconnaissance Squadron. (PAM.)

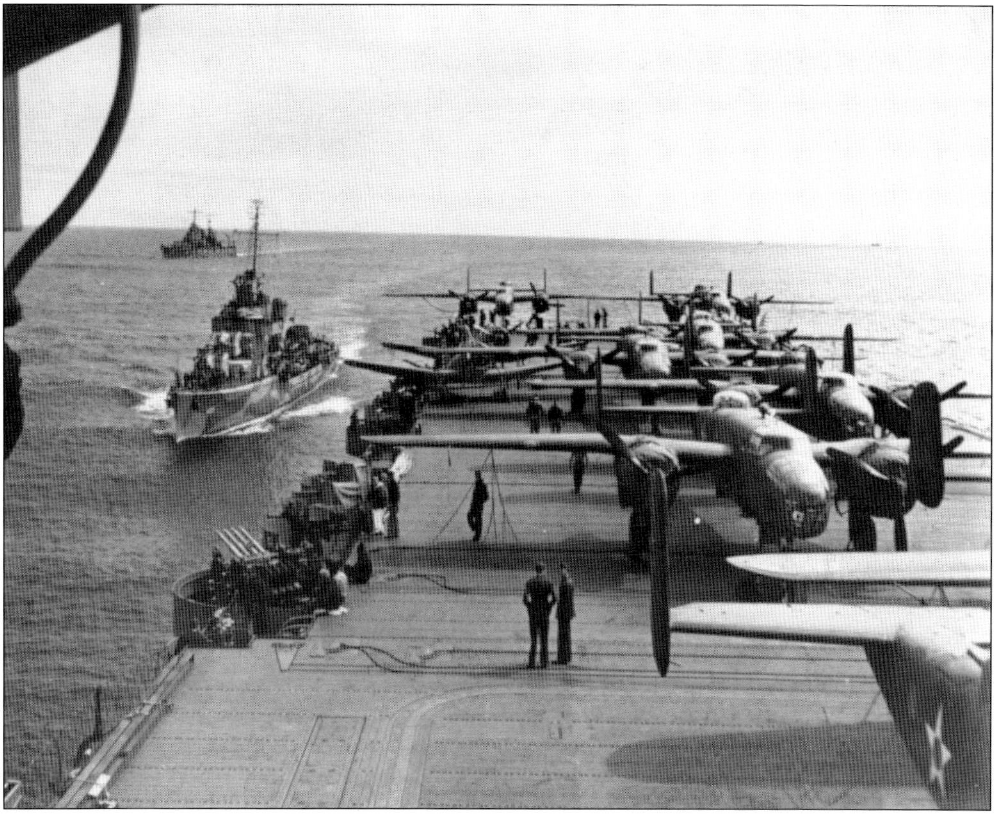

The Doolittle Raid, a joint Army-Navy air raid on April 18, 1942, was America's first attack on a Japanese island. The raid consisted of 16 B-25s that were transported by the aircraft carrier USS *Hornet*. When the men took off, they were alone, with no fighter escort. The goal was to attack military and industrial targets. The intended goal failed, but there was an increase in American morale. (USAF Museum.)

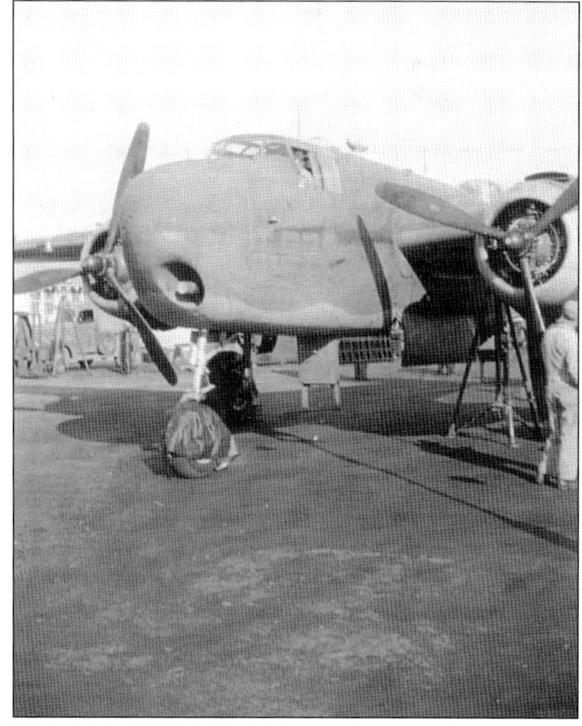

Pictured is the front of a medium bomber B-25 Mitchell as one of the wings is being looked at. This aircraft entered US military rotation in 1941. During the war, over 10,000 B-25s were built, serving in every theater and used by many Allied forces. This aircraft was a favorite among many for being safe and forgiving. With one engine out, the aircraft could still maneuver. (PAM.)

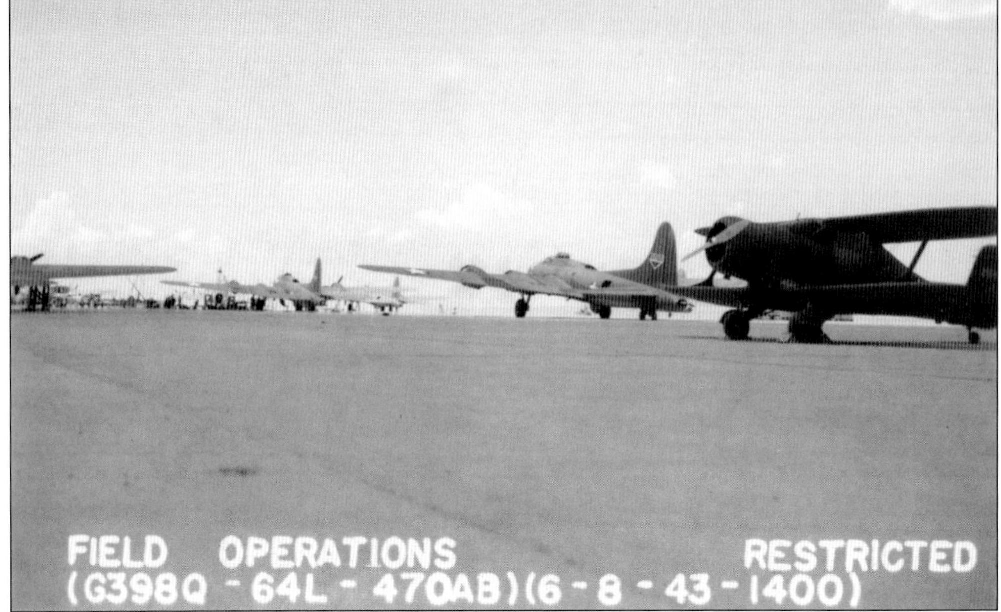

Pendleton Field was known for its heavy bombers, like the B-17 in the middle of the image, but there were also smaller aircraft used. The lesser-known UC-43 Traveler, shown in the foreground, was used by the Army, Navy, and the RAF. While the larger frames were used for transport and bombing, the smaller frames were exclusively for executive transport or courier from one base to another. (USAF Museum.)

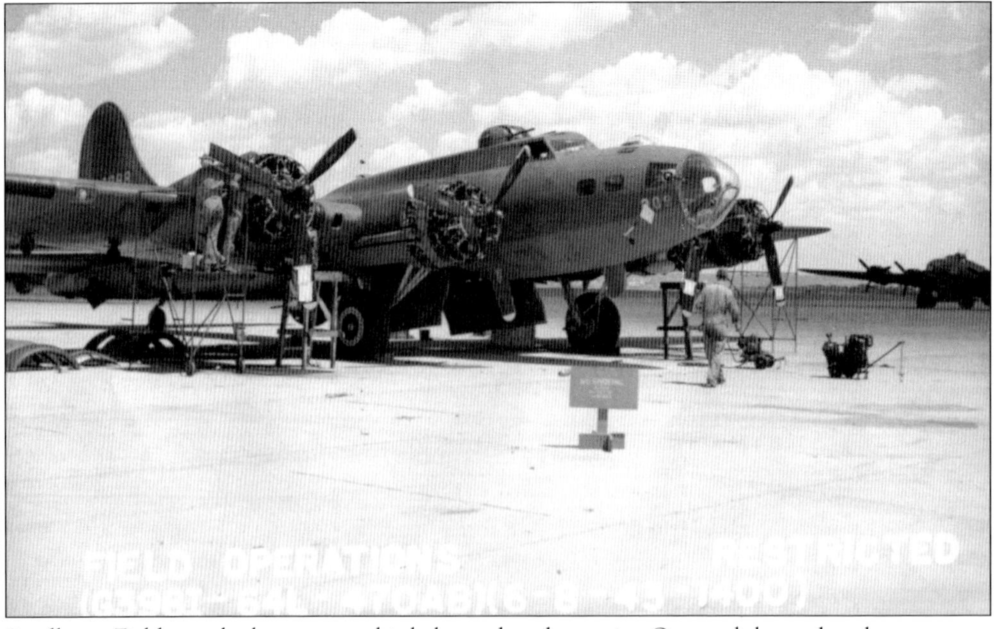

Pendleton Field was the home to multiple heavy bomber units. One such heavy bomber type was the B-17 Flying Fortress. This aircraft was equipped with four engines, which allowed for multiple engine failures to occur, and the aircraft still returned to base or at least landed safely. This specific aircraft is on the Pendleton Field apron, having at least one engine worked on. (Umatilla County Historical Society Collection, 1991.034.011.)

One of the many different aircraft that were stationed at Pendleton Field was the P-38 Lightning, which had the primary task of pursuit and interception. They could reach speeds up to 450 miles per hour when needed with their dual engines. In the European theater, they were used for aerial reconnaissance but really shone in the Pacific as a long-range fighter. (PAM.)

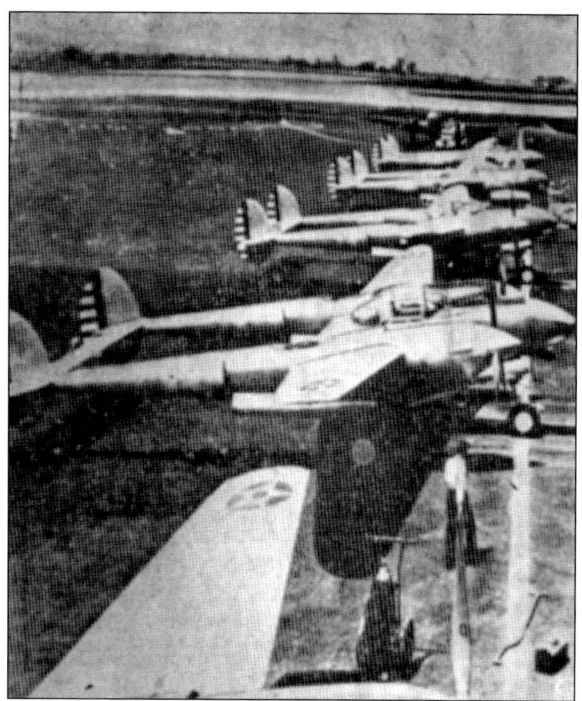

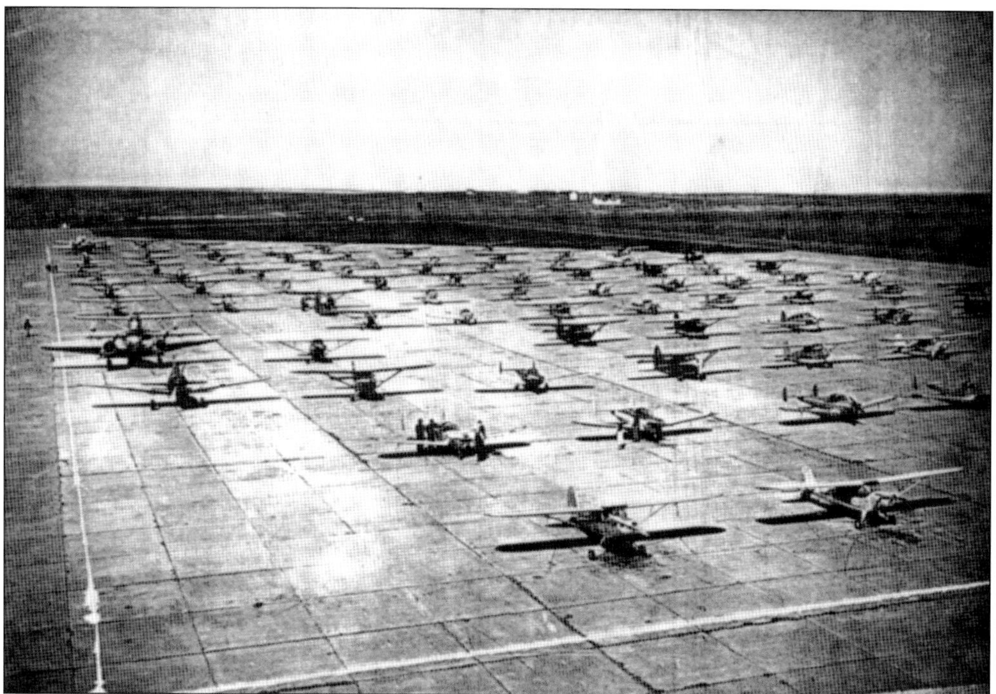

In November 1945, Pendleton Field was one of 11 airfields in Oregon considered surplus. This transfer of the air base to civilian control happened on July 13, 1948. The remaining buildings were maintained by the city, and the runways became part of Eastern Oregon Regional Airport. The airport is home to the Pendleton Army Aviation Support Facility and Chinook helicopters with the Oregon National Guard. (PAM.)

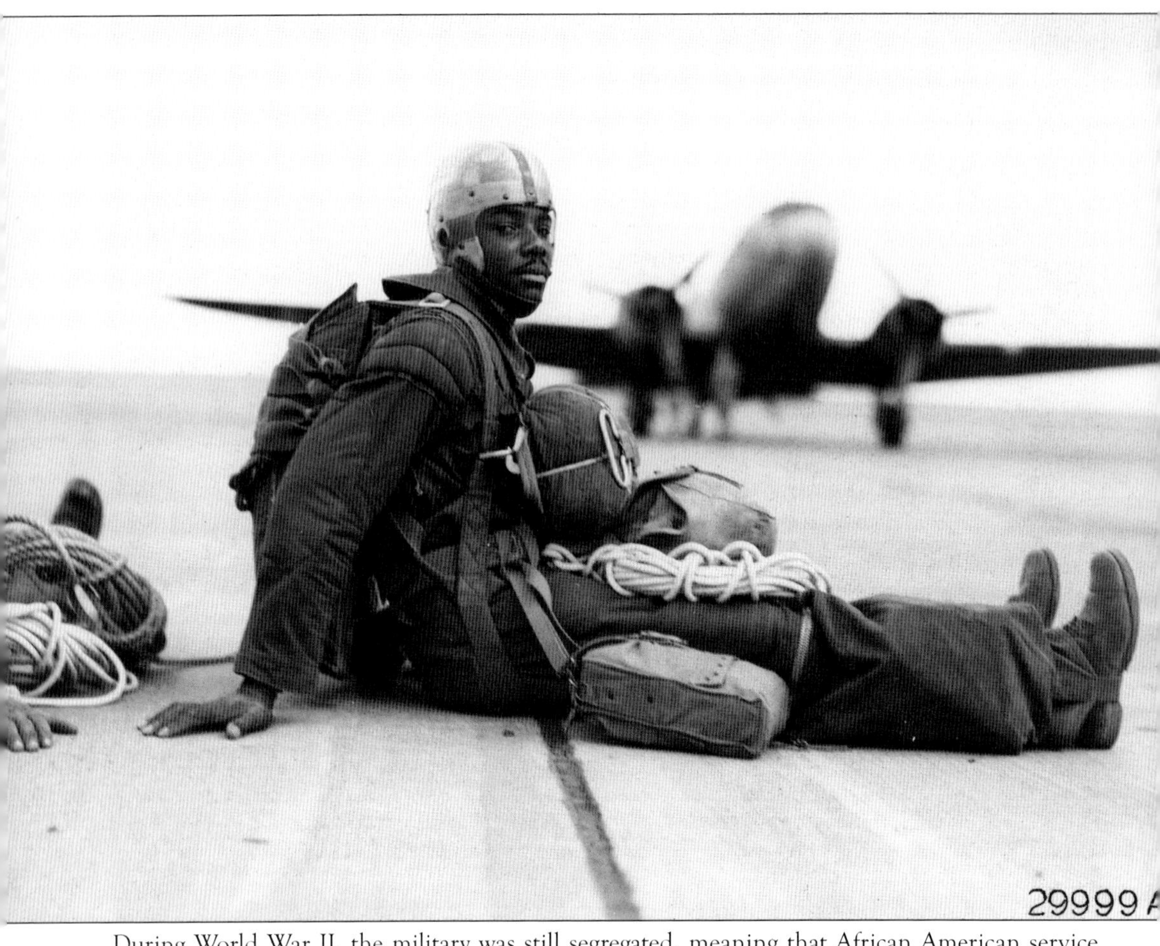

During World War II, the military was still segregated, meaning that African American service members could not be attached to the same units that Caucasian service members were. One of the methods that the Army used was to assign African Americans to units on the same base as Caucasian units but working different jobs. Being the only viable landing strip for large aircraft, Pendleton air base became an active base for forest fire suppression, and so the Army brought in an African American unit to fight fires. In 1944, the first group of African American infantry soldiers from the 92nd Infantry Division was selected to go through the rigorous airborne school. These men were known as "the Triple Nickles," the 555th Battalion of the 82nd Airborne. They were trained and ready to go to war, but instead, the Army, afraid of fires created by the Japanese balloon bombs, sent them to Oregon. (USAF Historical Research Agency.)

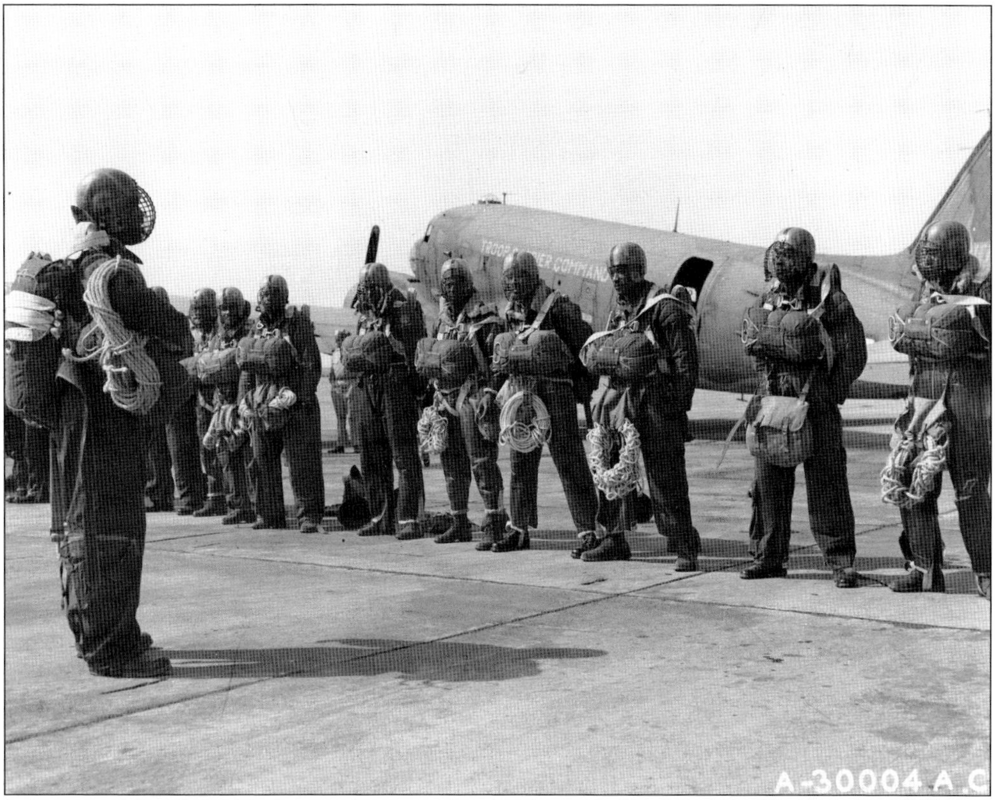

This unit of paratroopers trained alongside its Caucasian counterparts, but when the 82nd Airborne was initially set to deploy, the 555th Battalion was held back. That is when, in 1943, these highly trained men were sent not only to Pendleton Field but also along the West Coast, in hopes that with their knowledge of parachuting, they would be able to enter the area and assist with firefighting operations. (USAF Historical Research Agency.)

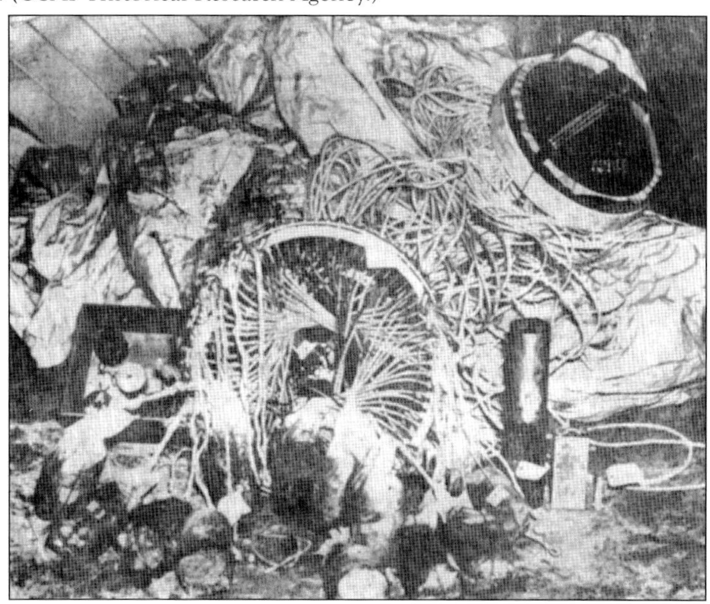

The 555th Triple Nickles were in search of this, the Japanese balloon bomb, also known as the Fu-Go Project. This specific balloon bomb was found near Echo in March 1945. The purpose of these balloons was to fly along the jet stream until all the ballast was dropped, at which point the larger bomb would land and hopefully start a forest fire. (PAM.)

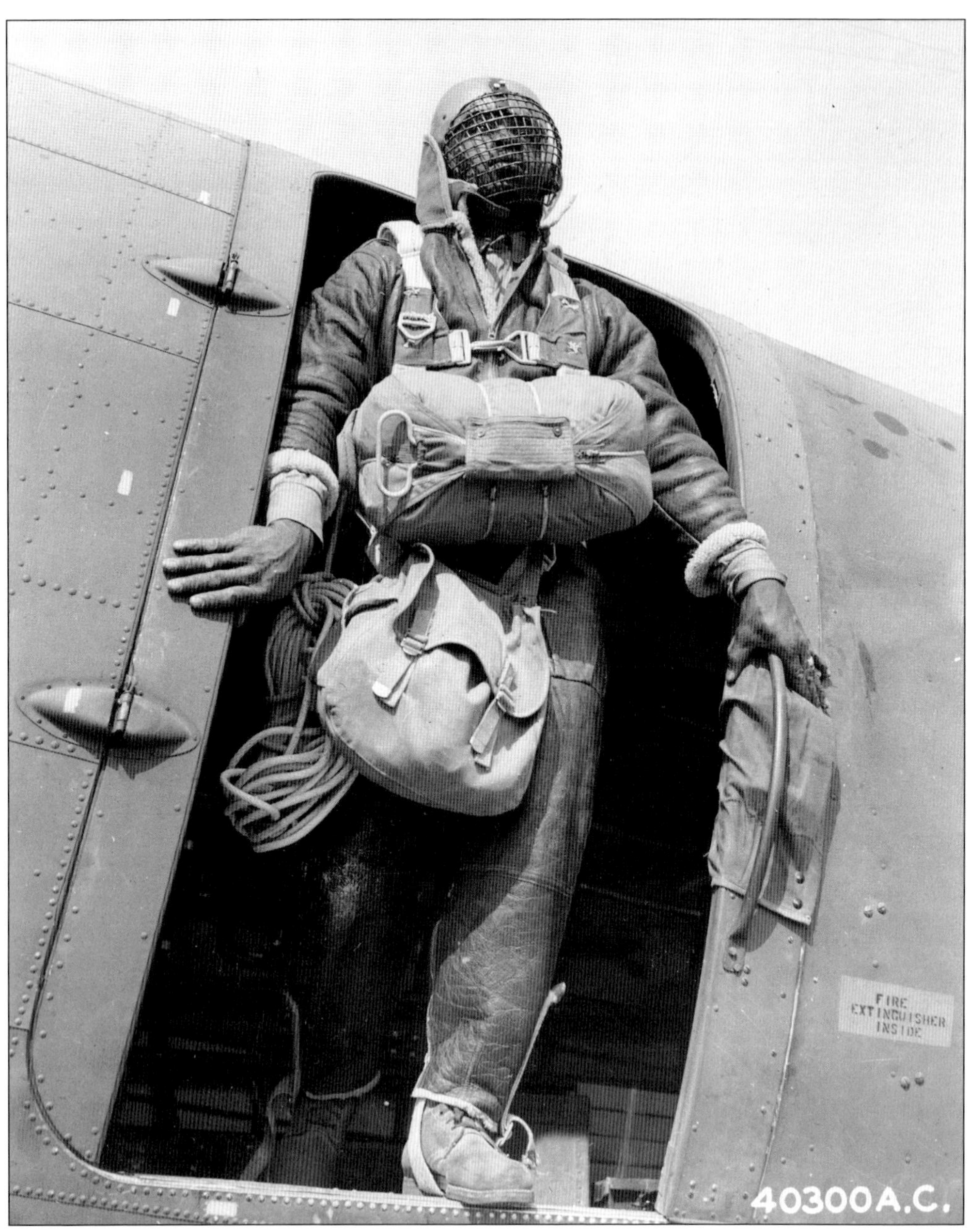

Known as Operation Firefly, the Triple Nickles were assigned to assist the US Forest Service in combating the flames. Their training allowed them to dismantle any munitions found along the way. The unit would fly out in a transport aircraft to where the smoke was and parachute in. Between July and October 1945, the 555th made over 1,200 jumps, fought 36 fires, and dismantled multiple balloon bombs. This soldier is training to jump with full gear on. There is a rope used for rappelling down mountains if needed as well as climbing up a steep cliff. He has two parachutes–one on his back and another on his front in the event the main one fails. The backpack hanging down consists of gloves, flares, and other necessary equipment. He is also wearing chaps, so likely he was one of the men in charge of using a chain saw if necessary. (USAF Historical Research Agency.)

Bibliography

Anderson, John D. *Inventing Flight: The Wright Brothers and Their Predecessors.* Johns Hopkins University Press, 2004.

Maurer, Maurer. *Air Force Combat Units Of World War II.* Office of Air Force History, 1983.

Oregon Department of Aviation, "Oregon Department of Aviation–Administrative Overview." October 2011: records.sos.state.or.us.

"Oregon Topo Map–Topographical Map," https://apps.nationalmap.gov/downloader/#/maps

Ravenstein, Charles A. *Air Force Combat Wings Lineage and Honors Histories 1947–1977.* Office of Air Force History, 1984.

Thole, Lou. *Forgotten Fields of America: World War II Bases and Training, Then and Now– Vol. 2.* Pictorial Histories Pub., 1999.

Watkins, John Elfreth. "Our Aero Amphibian Fleet." *Times-Picayune.* August 20, 1911: 1.

"Weather By Month, Average Temperature (Oregon, United States)–Weather Spark": weatherspark.com.